ML
3470
C56
1998

10

250-51

IT'S NOT ONLY ROCK & ROLL

POPULAR MUSIC IN THE LIVES OF ADOLESCENTS

THE HAMPTON PRESS COMMUNICATION SERIES

Mass Communications and Journalism
Lee Becker, supervisory editor

Magazine-Made America: The Cultural Transformation of the Postwar
Periodical
David Abrahamson

It's Not Only Rock & Roll: Popular Music in the Lives of Adolescents
Peter G. Christenson and Donald F. Roberts

American Heroes in the Media Age
Susan J. Drucker and Robert S. Cathcart (eds.)

Media, Sex and the Adolescent
Bradley S. Greenberg, Jane D. Brown, and Nancy Buerkel-Rothfuss

forthcoming

Journalism Education in Europe and North America
Christine Holtz-Bacha and Romy Frölich (eds.)

Newspapers and Social Change: Community Structure and Coverage of
Critical Events
John C. Pollock

IT'S NOT ONLY ROCK & ROLL

POPULAR MUSIC IN THE LIVES OF ADOLESCENTS

PETER G. CHRISTENSON
LEWIS & CLARK COLLEGE

DONALD F. ROBERTS
STANFORD UNIVERSITY

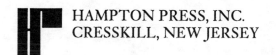
HAMPTON PRESS, INC.
CRESSKILL, NEW JERSEY

Printed in the United States of America

Library of Congress Cataloging-in-Publication Data

Christenson, Peter G.
    It's not only rock & roll : popular music in the lives of
adolescents / Peter G. Christenson, Donald F. Roberts.
       p. cm. -- (Hampton Press communication series)
    Includes bibliographic references and index.
    ISBN 1-57273-142-7. -- ISBN 1-57273-143-5
    1. Popular music--Social aspects. 2. Rock music--Social aspects.
3. Music and youth. 4. Popular culture. I. Roberts, Donald F.
II. Title. III. Series.
ML3470.C56 1998
306.4'84--dc21   97-43499
                                                        CIP

Hampton Press, Inc.
23 Broadway
Cresskill, NJ 07626

This book is dedicated to our children,
Nina, Jesse, Brett, Katy, David, and Rich,

our wives,
Lilia and Wendy,

and our teacher,
Nathan Maccoby

CONTENTS

PREFACE

Although many books have been written about popular music, we believe this is the first written about what social science research has to say about *adolescents* and popular music. The book reflects both our background as researchers and our interest in the welfare of youth, and our focus is probably more on the kids than the music. Nevertheless, since it underlies much of what we say here, we feel compelled to include a word or two about our relationship with music.

When we were first getting serious about this book, Peter spent some sabbatical time at Stanford University with Don gathering materials, outlining the project, discussing what should and should not be covered in the book, and drafting the early chapters. One balmy September evening, as Peter slaved away on the first chapter, the powerful sounds of a rock band burst forth from somewhere on the Stanford Quadrangle. The music was too loud, too close, and to be honest, too good to be ignored, so Peter made the choice that he so often makes—play before work. He left the office and strolled across to the quad to get a closer look and listen. There, amidst a throng of perhaps as many as 300 revelers, he ran straight into Don and his wife, Wendy, who had been drawn from some campus function to the same place by the same music. The band, as we recall, was named The Zazu Pitts Memorial Orchestra. We danced, the 3 of us and the other 297, until the campus police shut it all down in the early morning hours.

A delightful coincidence, but not just a coincidence, because we are both music lovers. Over the years, both of us have spent countless hours and countless dollars on our music habits. In fact, one of us (Peter) has even *earned* a bit of money playing music. In one of our chapters we discuss a study in which adolescents were asked to choose what mass medium they would take along if they were stranded on a desert isle. Most of the kids picked music over TV, newspapers, magazines, books, and so on. Chances are we'd make the same choice. It is doubtful, in fact, whether we could have sustained our interest in this project without a basic love of music (not *all* music, of course, but most) and a personal awareness of what music can do to make life livable. Our first acknowledgment, then, goes to all those people who have fostered our relationship with music—in particular, Peter's father, who forced him to practice trumpet an hour before school every day from the age of 8 to the end of high school, and Don's father, who taught him the words to "Mairzy Doats" when he was 4, introduced him to Count Basie at 10, and tolerated Bill Haley and the Comets just a few years later. And of course, we are indebted to all the musicians, from Bix Beiderbeck to Wynton Marsalis, from Bessie Smith to Yousou N-Dour, who have enriched our lives. Whether this attitude shows in this book or not (and whether or not it should), we'd like to state it plainly here.

We are, of course, parents and educators as well as music lovers, and we've had a lot of contact with kids along the way, most of it good, all of it interesting. So we are sympathetic to kids as much as to music. And we owe them a great deal in terms of this project. Our own children— Nina, Jesse, Brett, Katy, David, and Rich—are the ones we know best, obviously, but the hundreds of students who have sat in our classes and helped us with our research (most of whom are not really "kids," of course, except maybe in comparison to us) have also contributed immeasurably to our understanding of what really goes on when the headset meets the adolescent ear. For the reader who presses on with this book, it will become clear that most of what we say in the following pages is based on social science theory and quantitative research. What is less clear, perhaps, is the extent to which we have constructed our interpretation of the research around the qualitative input of the children, adolescents, undergraduates and graduate students we have known and worked with over the years. If what we wrote didn't make sense to them, we rethought it. Sometimes we even rewrote it.

Part of the credit for the fact that (albeit grudgingly) we ultimately did rewrite everything several times goes to Nathan Maccoby, the man who mentored each of us through our Ph.D. programs. Mac took a chance when he admitted each of us to Stanford. In equal parts and at appropriate times, he prodded, cajoled, led, pushed, and turned us free. He corrected our spelling, whipped us unmercifully on the tennis court, introduced us to untold brands of beer, and showed us that it is not the statistic but the interpretation of the statistic that is critical. And most important, he made us rewrite. Mac was a music lover, too.

Among the students (most of whom are no longer students) who deserve particular mention are: at Lewis and Clark; Betsy Begert, April Gunther, Eric Barth, Boreas van Nouhuys, and Eric Hare, and at Stanford; Helen Chen, Sheila Gosh, Lisa Henriksen, Dennis Kinsey, Peter Orton, and David Voelker. Their insights and ideas permeate these pages. We also need to mention the Communication Department staffs at both Lewis and Clark (Carol Wilson) and Stanford (Barbara Kataoka, Lola Romero, and Terese Weinlader). Without their willingness to take on many of the myriad little chores that no professor can completely avoid, and to find ways to help us find undisturbed time in which to read and write, this project might never have been completed.

We also owe thanks to Marcy Kelly, President of Mediascope, and Dr. Ruby Takanishi, former Director of the Carnegie Council on Adolescent Development, who now heads the Foundation for Child Development. When the Carnegie Council on Adolescent Development was looking for someone to review the research literature on adolescents and radio, Marcy Kelly recommended us. We had worked with Marcy on some seminars she arranged in order to link media professionals with academic researchers concerned with youth and media, and she was aware of our interest in adolescents and music. Ultimately, Dr. Takanishi asked us to review the empirical research literature and produce a technical report on adolescents and music media for the Carnegie Council on Adolescence, a report that formed the initial skeleton of this book. We are indebted to both of them for their confidence in the importance of our work and for providing us the support to begin writing.

And finally, we acknowledge our immeasurable debt to Lilia and Wendy, who have kept us sane through all the craziness, not just of writing a book but of day-to-day life. And who still deign to dance with us.

1

INTRODUCTION

Extraordinary how potent cheap music is.
—Noel Coward, *Private Lives* (1965)

A few years ago an 8-year-old boy we know developed, like many of his friends, a fascination with rap music. He was particularly intrigued by the controversial artist Snoop Doggy Dogg. The boy's father had listened to enough rap music and read enough about Snoop's scrapes with the law to become concerned with his son's infatuation. In an attempt to put his son off Snoop the father commented: "Jesse, Snoop's nothing more than a common hoodlum!" Jesse replied: "Don't worry, Dad, I can tell the difference between the man and the music."

Never mind that Jesse's father in his youth had listened to many artists with reputations for miscreant behavior; never mind that Jesse's last name is Christenson, that his father co-wrote this book! The boy made an interesting point. What he was saying, we think, was this: That music is just music, not the reputation of the artist, not what some people might say about the meaning of the lyrics or about the music's evil influences on kids. As far as Jesse was concerned he, the listener, was in control. To a great extent this book is about whether music is "just music," as many would have us believe, or whether it plays a much more central role in the lives of young people—indeed, has the potential to exert a significant influence on them.

1

Either way, two things are certain: one, we are embroiled in an increasingly bitter and divisive debate over the impact of popular media on youth; and two, the critical spotlight has now broadened to include popular music and music videos as well as television and motion pictures. In 1985, a group of concerned parents led by Tipper Gore, wife of then-Senator Al Gore, prevailed on the Senate Commerce Committee to look into the effects of "porn rock," in the process stirring up such negative publicity for the music industry that it reluctantly agreed to place warning labels on music with sexually explicit lyrics. Nearly a decade later a similar contingent of citizens outraged by the messages in "gangsta rap" forced a similar set of hearings before the Senate Juvenile Justice Committee. Even presidential politics has become infected with the issue. Senator Robert Dole kicked off his 1996 Presidential campaign with an all-out declaration of war against Hollywood's "nightmares of depravity," and rap music was just as high on his hit list as movies or television (Lacayo, 1995). President Clinton opened his campaign with a similar salvo in his 1996 State of the Union Address, admonishing the entertainment media—with specific reference to music companies—to assume some responsibility along with parents for raising America's children.

Never blind to a good story, the news media have given the pop music controversy its fair share of coverage. Items about the dangers of pop music, ranging in format and tone from straight news to the most unfettered commentary, fill the media agenda as never before. Every national news magazine has run at least one recent cover story focusing on the latest onslaught of racism, morbid violence, and graphic sex, with each article speculating on the powerful and dreadful effects these messages must surely be having. The obscenity trial of the rap group 2 Live Crew, the civil action for incitement of suicide brought against British rockers Judas Priest, the debate over explicit lyrics advisory labels, the abusive treatment of women in heavy metal music videos, accusations that rap music fueled the 1992 Los Angeles riots—these are only a few of the pop music controversies to hit the nightly TV news and the pages of newspapers and magazines.

Whether the messages in popular music have changed or not— and, as we'll see, they have—the volume of messages *about* the messages in music is unprecedented. To be sure, much of the political rhetoric is pure grandstanding and much of the media coverage superficial, overblown, and sensationalistic. Still, we believe the public debate reflects a widespread and genuine uneasiness about the impact of the "music media"— radio, popular recordings, and music video—on American youth. Clearly, the music media present an abundance of highly provocative imagery, and most kids pay at least some attention to it. It is only sensible to inquire what role the music media play in the lives of adolescents and what influence they exert on young people's attitudes, values, and behavior.

Some might be tempted to ask "What's new?" about this issue—after all, fears about popular music's insidious influence have a long history. Nobody now in their 50s can have forgotten the intense disapproval, even paranoia, with which middle-class parents reacted to the rough, primitive, "jungle" beat of 1950's rock and roll. Nobody now in their 40s can fail to recall the equally rabid diatribes heaped on the sex and drug music of the 1960s and 1970s. For that matter, even Plato admonished the citizens of Rome against the threat popular music posed to the moral education of youth. The essential critique, then, has been around in some form for a long time.

What *is* new, we believe, is the sense of urgency that surrounds it, an urgency arising not just from a feeling that music is on a rampage, but that it is rampaging at a time of particularly intense turmoil for American youth. Perhaps with good reason, today's young people are seen as an especially vulnerable cohort, cast adrift in a treacherous sea of AIDS, teen pregnancy, gang-banging, crack cocaine, failing schools, child abuse, soaring rates of suicide, violence . . . (fill in the ellipses yourself). Even if one rejects, as we do, the facile argument that popular music and MTV are somehow *to blame* for all these problems, the pop music culture is inextricably linked to the experiences, both bad and good, of today's adolescents.

WHAT IS AN ADOLESCENT?

Supreme Court Justice Potter Stewart wrote in the obscenity case *Jacobellis v. Ohio* (1964) that, although he could not satisfactorily define pornography: "I know it when I see it" (p.193). We suggest Stewart's pragmatic logic applies just as well to the task of defining *adolescence.* That is, although we all know an adolescent when we see one, the *concept* of adolescence is by no means easy to define. It is certainly not synonymous with *teenage*, notwithstanding the common tendency to use the terms interchangeably. True, by any definition most teenagers are adolescents and most adolescents teenagers, but in the United States today the median onset of adolescence occurs well before the 13th birthday. Child development experts employ a combination of biological (for instance, a spurt in growth and the development of secondary sexual characteristics) and social factors (increasing independence from parents, development of interest in the opposite sex) to mark the beginning of the period. By either set of criteria, the dawn of adolescence occurs considerably earlier than the 13th birthday. The Carnegie Council on Adolescent Development (1989), for instance, places the beginning of adolescence at *10* years, much earlier than popular wisdom holds, and earlier by at least two years than adolescence began 50 or 100 years ago. Whether we like it or not, our "children" are growing up sooner than they used to.

Because physiological characteristics remain in place once they are achieved (there is, obviously, no reversion to prepubescence), the *end* of adolescence is defined entirely by social indicators such as the establishment of one's own home, joining the permanent work force, and marriage. The timing of these events is often linked to the end of school, and so adolescence may end at a much different age for those who enter adult roles directly out of high school than for those who go on to college or graduate school. In any case, the boundaries of adolescence obviously cannot be defined merely in terms of age points. Perhaps the most consistent finding in research on child and adolescent development is the enormous *variation* in the ages at which youngsters reach developmental mileposts. Some children may exhibit secondary sex characteristics as early as 7 or 8 years old, others not until 13 or 14. Some may declare independence from adult authority the day they graduate from "Sesame Street," others not until they develop a taste for "Wall Street Week." Some quit school and go to work long before they finish high school, others manage to prolong their school years into their third or fourth decade. For our purposes, then, the appropriate definition of adolescence must be broad enough to encompass not just the 14-year-old heavy metal fan but the 10-year-old Jewel "wannabe" and the 30-year-old graduate student reggae devotee as well. Indeed, of all the social markers of adolescence, perhaps none is more diagnostic than a passion for popular music.

WHAT ARE THE "MUSIC MEDIA"?

We coin the term *music media* in acknowledgment that popular music, as a cultural form, extends beyond any particular mode of distribution or commercial structure. Music may be heard and learned about from a variety of sources. By "music media" we mean media that bring popular music to kids. Usually this means personally controlled recordings, commercial radio, and music videos, but these are not the only music media. Popular music is consumed at concerts and clubs as well, and these contexts play crucial roles in youth culture. Even the boggling assortment of teen and pop music magazines might be considered music media—they contain no music per se, but they play important interpretive and informational roles in the popular music experience.

Nor is the content of the music media limited just to music. Radio is not just music, but news, sports, talk, and above all commercials, and although adolescents turn to radio for the music, they are not unaware of or inattentive to this other content. Even the "purest" of the music media—that is, the stereo or Walkman playback of personally selected recordings—entails not just music but considerable print (liner notes, transcriptions of lyrics) and graphic information as well. The furor over the Beatles' *Yesterday and Today* album, after all, was not about the music but the cover art's depiction of the Beatles dressed in bloody butcher's aprons, clutching slabs of raw meat and decapitated baby dolls. Almost 30 years later, many African-American women protested just as vehemently the comic book-style sexual representations in the CD booklet for rapper Snoop Doggy Dogg's 1993 release, *Doggy Style*.

The importance of nonmusical content is most obvious in the case of music videos. Television has always presented popular music— "Your Hit Parade" in the 1950s, Elvis and later the Beatles on the "Ed Sullivan Show," music-oriented variety programs like "The Smothers Brothers" in the 1960s, and so on—and filmic visualizations of rock music existed long before the MTV network was launched in 1981. Still, the contemporary music video as marketed through MTV and other cable channels represents a powerful new force in contemporary adolescent culture. Whatever their real effects, music videos have raised the stakes of the game in many people's minds. It may be argued whether music videos are more music or more video, but as far as most parents and critics are concerned, it is the pictures that really count.

ASSUMPTIONS, POPULAR WISDOM, AND BROMIDES

To examine popular music in adolescence presents an especially daunting challenge because so many people are utterly convinced they already know the answers to all the important questions. They "know" what rap and heavy metal lyrics "really" mean. They "know" why kids are attracted to popular music. They "know" the impact music listening has on the audience. And they know these things with great certitude and fervor.

Whether one is talking about a 14-year-old "death metal" fan or his frantic and careworn 40-year-old mother, music evokes strong responses and opinions. Moreover, these opinions span a range as impressive as the conviction with which they are held. For every adult who is convinced pop music is responsible for the moral decay of our youth, there is an adolescent who believes music is the only positive force in contemporary society. For every critic who urges the censorship of rap and heavy metal lyrics, there is a free speech advocate who views these genres as a last bastion of meaningful social criticism. When it comes to pop music, rabid conviction and lack of consensus go together like Siamese twins.

Because they arouse such strong reactions, the music media provide fertile ground for the cultivation of lay theories, often arising from nothing more than the volatile ferment of sensational media coverage, unsystematic personal observation, and the secondhand ruminations of family and friends. Some of these theories on the meaning and effects of popular music get repeated so often that they evolve into simplistic, hackneyed "bromides." Consider, for example, the big question that is on so many minds, whether pop music consumption has any substantial influence on teenagers' values and behavior. One perspective on this question comes from the many parents, teachers, feminists, and Christians who (all for different reasons, obviously) find certain lyrics and music video images morally, politically, or socially offensive. From their point of view the answer is obvious. In bromide form, it goes something like this: "With images that powerful and explicit and all that listening going on, *of course* there are effects."

Missouri state Rep. Jean Dixon, a supporter of state-mandated labeling of violent and sexually explicit recordings, provided a good example of this bromide in action in her response to the suggestion that such legislation might await a bit more research: "Should we wait for a 10-year study and, after thousands and thousands of young people have either killed somebody or committed suicide, then say, 'Yes, we have a link here!' All we have to do is use a little common sense" (Harrington, 1990, p. 33).

Needless to say, Senator Dixon's common sense is utter *non*sense to the people in the music and entertainment industry who create and market the sounds, words, and visual imagery that galvanize the critics. They see the shocking music messages as nothing more than playful fantasy and music listeners as sophisticated, hard-nosed consumers. Their stock answer to the question whether music has any important effects usually takes this line of argument: "Kids know this stuff isn't meant to be taken seriously—after all, it's only music, it's only entertainment." Not surprisingly, perhaps, most adolescents adopt the same position. For example, in a special report on "What Entertainers are Doing to Our Kids" (1985), *U.S. News and World Report* quoted a 16-year-old Michigan girl: "Lyrics aren't all that important if you can dance to it. I don't think it's going to corrupt anybody. It's just music" (p. 48). In other words, many adolescents naturally resist the notion that something as trivial as music lyrics could influence them in any important way. Like adults, they see themselves as independent individuals capable of exercising free choice.

Not all bromides come in opposite pairs. With some issues, common wisdom stacks up mostly on one side. For instance, most people—ranging from Freudian psychologists to embattled parents on the front lines of childrearing—take as axiomatic what might be called a "storm and stress" model of adolescence. In this view, the predominant emotional state of adolescent youth is crisis and their primary motivational state one of rebellion against adult authority. Couple this with an important corollary to the axiom—that popular music is the crucial battlefront in the war between the generations—and one can derive a common conception that often takes this form: "Kids won't listen to any music that doesn't make their parents mad."

These are only a few of the many assumptions and popular theories concerning adolescence and popular music. Others include: "Rock music's always been that way," "Try to censor the stuff and the kids will only want it more," "Nobody pays attention to lyrics anyway," and so on. It is not that these notions are wrong, exactly. Rock music *has* always contained a strain of rebellion and naughtiness; attempts at censorship *may* backfire with some teens; lyrics often *are* incidental to the adolescent music listening experience. But the stock formulas are not particularly right either. At the very least, they mislead, overgeneralize, and brush aside the complexities of both adolescence and popular music.

On one side, the frightened adults who so readily rush to the conclusion that heavy metal music turns children into monsters not only forget that they survived their own youth, during which they were probably served at least a modicum of media violence and sex, but they also lose sight of the sad reality that many kids may be monsters already and simply seek out musical fare that resonates with their monstrous inclinations. On the other side, the music industry apologists who so fervently deny any possibility that their products might influence America's hip, sophisticated young consumers ignore the fact that most human learning is incidental in nature and takes place outside of designated educational settings. To say that music is "just" entertainment or that lyrics are not the primary draw in no way precludes the possibility of influence. After all, we don't drive down the highway in order to see billboards, but we see them nonetheless. Industry thinking also neglects that many kids are quite *un*hip and *un*sophisticated. For every bright, critical, actively two-parented 16-year-old watching MTV there is a gullible, enthralled, 8-year-old latch-key kid watching the same stuff.

Indeed, one may question even those cherished truisms about the fundamental nature of adolescence. As we will show, to characterize adolescence essentially in terms of crisis, rebellion, and conflict runs counter to a great amount of developmental research. For most kids, adolescence is a period of normal, gradual development in considerable harmony with parental values and cultural expectations. Bizarre as it may seem, this harmony is often reflected even in music taste.

BEYOND POPULAR WISDOM

On average, American adolescents spend somewhere between four and five hours a day listening to music and watching music videos—at least as much time as they spend watching standard television fare and more than they spend with their friends outside of school. Their involvement with music media and the music culture extends well beyond sheer time spent. Music alters and intensifies their moods, furnishes much of their slang, dominates their conversations, and provides the ambiance at their social gatherings. Music styles define the crowds and cliques they run in. Music personalities provide models for how they act and dress. Given the pivotal role of music in adolescent life, it seems obvious that oversimplified, formulaic thinking about it will not do. The decisions we make for and about our youth and their music should be grounded in something deeper and more reliable than casual observation and dramatic news reports.

Not that thoughtful firsthand observation is useless—indeed, in the rearing and education of the youth closest to us, our own children or students, it is essential. However, when it comes to establishing broad policy—whether at the family or governmental level—our thinking should also encompass the accumulating body of research on popular music and adolescence. Many studies have been conducted concerning the content, uses, and effects of the popular music media, and some have quite a bit to say, even despite their methodological flaws, inconsistencies, and omissions. Yet too often the public discussion proceeds as if there were no research at all. Astoundingly, people who would never consider purchasing a 5-year-old used car without consulting the frequency-of-repair data in *Consumer Reports* do not hesitate for a moment to make policy about 15-year-old human beings based on scary tales from the next-door neighbor. If nothing else, our aim in this book is to provide an antidote to those tales.

Even at its best, of course, research cannot answer every important question. Assuming a convincing case could be made on the basis of social scientific research that certain kids are influenced in negative ways by popular music and music videos, this finding alone would not tell us what to do about the problem. Other social values and cultural traditions—free expression, parental prerogative, even the right of the people in the industry to make a living—may outweigh any danger perceived. (After all, the used car buyer may still buy the unreliable gas guzzler because it "just feels right.") However, if in the end good parents, effective teachers, and wise policymakers choose to override or de-emphasize certain evidence in their deliberations on music and adolescence, their decisions should at least proceed with an awareness of what is there to be disregarded.

Perhaps it would be useful to illustrate with an example from our own work. As most readers probably know, a system exists today whereby record companies identify albums containing potentially offensive lyrics with a sticker or label saying, PARENTAL ADVISORY: EXPLICIT LYRICS. Assumptions about record labeling abound, but for the moment we consider just two. One comes from the system's proponents, who often argue that parents need the same sort of information about the content of music lyrics that they have about motion pictures. Record labeling thus becomes not a scheme of subtle censorship but a simple form of consumer information for parents, much akin to a "PG-13" or "R" movie rating. However, this argument for record labeling assumes that significant numbers of parents involve themselves in the monitoring and control of their children's popular music diet. In fact, our research suggests that the active monitoring and control premised by the advocates of record labeling is much more the exception than the rule. Relatively few youth report that their parents accompany them on trips to music stores, cull through their CD collections, or otherwise interfere with their freedom to select and listen to whatever music suits them. So "parental advisory" labels are really "kid advisories," and the real question becomes what effect this "advice" will have on adolescents themselves.

A common assumption operates here, too. Ask people to predict the effect of advisory labels on the typical teen music listener and they almost always say something like: "Well, since kids are rebellious and naturally seek out anything that's disapproved by parents, sticking an advisory label on an album *will only make them want it more.*" If true, this "forbidden fruit theory" would presumably be a pretty good argument against labeling. After all, few of us would want to do anything affirmative to increase kids' exposure to sexually explicit or violent lyrics.

Do labels really operate this way? Maybe not. We conducted an experiment in which junior high students judged how much they would like to own certain albums based only on hearing a short music sample and seeing the album cover (Christenson, 1992a). All the students heard the same music, but half saw album covers with a parental advisory label and half without. Our overall findings ran directly *counter* to most common wisdom; that is, rather than producing a forbidden fruit effect, the presence of a label actually *suppressed* the attractiveness of the albums.

Neither the rarity of parental monitoring nor the absence of a forbidden fruit effect in one sample of middle school students settles the question of whether record labeling is sound social policy. If most parents do not bother themselves with their children's music listening behavior, labeling might still be worthwhile just to assist those few who do. If labeling has the possibly healthy effect of diverting some kids from the hardest core stuff, this benefit still might not outweigh the concomitant overtones of censorship. In either case, although research evidence might be overridden, it surely ought to be considered.

By no means are all of the research findings as counterintuitive as the results of our record labeling experiment. Many studies tend to confirm common sense and casual observation. Few readers will be surprised by surveys linking adolescent delinquency with a preference for heavy metal music or findings that girls like romantic ballads more than boys do. Yet even when the effect of the evidence is to certify the suspected, the research usually adds some fine grain to our picture of how adolescents interact with the medium that is closest to their hearts.

Our basic goal here is simple: to summarize, synthesize, and, when possible, comment on what social scientific research has to say about popular music and adolescence. Our approach to this task, however, is neither exclusive nor exhaustive. At several points we have seen fit to include theoretical perspectives and points of view from outside the social science research perspective. Moreover, we make no claim that *all* the research finds its way into the book. We hope, however, that our coverage is broad enough to provide a reasonably clear and confident picture of what is known—and what is not known—about the various issues raised.

The book is organized into seven remaining chapters. In Chapter 2 we comment on the nature of adolescence generally, comparing traditional "storm and stress" conceptualizations with more contemporary theories which characterize the period in less turbulent terms. This chapter also outlines the key developmental tasks and trends of the adolescent period. Chapter 3 describes the research on music "uses and gratifications," that is, how and why the music media fit into the lives of young people, what sorts of pleasures they derive from listening, and so on. Music preferences form the focus of Chapter 4, in which we argue that "popular" or "rock" music is not just one type of music but many distinct and recognizable genres and types, each with its own sound, meaning, and reputation. Chapter 4 also discusses how the audiences for these various types differ according to the social background and personality of the listeners.

Chapters 5 and 6 can be seen as the groundwork for the final two. Chapter 5 describes and characterizes the content of the music media— their prevailing themes, portrayals, and imagery—according to systematic content analyses. The following chapter examines how this content is interpreted by young listeners. As we will see, quite often what adults think they hear or see in the music is not what kids get from it. Finally, Chapter 7 pulls together what is currently known about the impact of the music media on the attitudes, values, and behavior of young people, and Chapter 8—the concluding chapter—considers what, if anything, should be done about the music media in terms of governmental regulation, industry self-regulation, and parental policy.

Two major themes run through these various topics. First, we contend, as have many others, that popular music is not "just music," but a major force and presence in contemporary American adolescence. To crib from Kenneth Burke, music provides adolescents important "equipment for living." At the same time, we say there is less to worry about in terms of the music media's influence than many people think. However intense the relationship between music and adolescence, music listening remains fundamentally an active, voluntary process. Kids use the equipment more than it uses (or abuses) them. The sorts of effects parents and critics most fear—effects on sexual behavior, violence, rebelliousness, drug use, and so on—are probably not terribly broad or massive. For one thing, there is the comforting fact that most kids, including most fans of hardcore metal and "gangsta" rap, are basically all right. As for those who are not all right, one must look far deeper for an explanation of their problems than the music they consume. If we are outraged by certain lyrics or music video imagery, our real concern should be that there is such a hot market for such material. In the areas that cause the greatest public consternation, popular music and MTV probably reflect reality more than they create it.

This is not to say the music industry should be let off the hook. For one thing, the absence of general effects does not rule out more narrowly delimited ones. Many individuals, and even some fairly large segments of the adolescent population, are probably influenced in the ways feared. To ignore the negative effects of music media exposure because they impinge only on certain subgroups makes no more sense than to ignore the causes of homicide because only a tiny minority ever commits murder. Moreover, one must consider effects and influences other than the obvious ones: Music may, for instance, shape patterns of group interaction, alter study habits, define modes of personal appearance, damage eardrums. Such consequences may not spring as quickly to mind as sex and violence, but they may ultimately play just as crucial a role in adolescent development. Finally, whatever the effects of music media on adolescent attitudes, values, and behavior, there remains popular music's most important "consequence"—its capacity to involve youth. Adolescent listeners invest prodigious amounts of time, money, and ego in the pop music habit. Music matters to adolescents, and they cannot be understood without a serious consideration of how it fits into their lives.

2

THE NATURE OF ADOLESCENCE: MYTHS AND REALITIES

Adolescence is a time when one has to lose one's mind in order to come to one's senses.
—A high school teacher

Adolescents may well be the most maligned and misunderstood age group in our culture.
—Ruby Takanishi, Carnegie Council on Adolescent Development (1993)

What is adolescence? What distinguishes it from childhood? From adulthood? What is it that makes us think that popular music plays such an important role during this period that it deserves a book? To a large extent, the answers to such questions (indeed, whether they are even meaningful questions) depend on the social and historical context in which they are asked. In the United States and most other industrialized nations, contemporary definitions conceive of adolescence as beginning with entry into puberty—a biological definition—and ending with the adoption of adult roles—a social definition. Thus, adolescence begins at about 9 1/2 years for girls and 11 1/2 years for boys, the mean ages of the growth spurt before the emergence of secondary sexual characteristics. It is a bit more difficult to pin down when adolescence ends, but one is generally thought to have achieved adult status somewhere in the early 20s, depending on when he or she leaves school and assumes adult roles such as going to work or marriage and child rearing (Brooks-Gunn & Reiter, 1990; Elliott & Feldman, 1990).

This sort of definition stretches adolescence over a much longer period than in the past. Indeed, it extends over a much longer period than obtains even now in many cultures. Not too many years ago in the United States, a large majority of young men and women assumed adult roles immediately after high school. The move from adolescent to adult occurred during the late teen years, and "teenager" and "adolescent" were almost synonymous. Today, however, although many young people still take on jobs and family immediately after high school, a significant proportion delay entry into adult roles until after college or even graduate school, thus extending adolescence into the middle 20s and beyond. In many nonindustrialized societies this definition of adolescence is extremely problematic. In societies and cultures where youngsters begin working and raising families by their middle and even early teen years, and where at least among girls marriage and childbearing follow closely on the occurrence of menarche, the term *adolescence* may be almost meaningless.

ADOLESCENTS AND SOCIETY

In the United States and most other industrialized nations, however, adolescence is a recognized and important period. Indeed, it has become an accepted part of society's infrastructure. Our political and legal systems explicitly promote special treatment for individuals under the somewhat arbitrary ages of 16, 18, or 21 years. Our child labor laws regulate when and under what conditions adolescents can enter the workforce. In most instances, no one under the age of 21 can sign contracts. Adolescents are usually segregated when they break the law, placed in juvenile detention centers instead of regular prisons. In most states, they cannot drive until 16, enlist in the armed forces or cast a ballot until 18, or drink alcohol legally until 21. Perhaps most important, compulsory schooling through high school, in concert with strong normative pressures to obtain at least some postsecondary education, almost forces us to view adolescence as a distinct stage of life for the simple reason that "student culture" is generally accepted as a preadult way of life. In other words, various legal and social structures promote dependence on parents or other "adults" until well into the beginning of the third decade of life.

THE ADOLESCENT MARKETPLACE

To characterize adolescence as a period of dependence is not to deny its importance in contemporary society. Adolescents wield a tremendous amount of economic clout, and many would argue they are the engine that drives popular culture in America. The sheer number of dollars that adolescents directly control is large and growing. For example, *American Demographics* (Dortch, 1994) reports that in 1993, 13-to 15-year-old boys received $32 per week in earnings and allowance and girls over $37; by 16 to 19 years old the amounts were over $75 per week for boys and $82 for girls. And they spend it. Patricia Sellers (1989) found that although the U.S. teenage population actually declined between 1978 and 1988 (it is on the rise again now), spending by 12- to 19-year-olds during that same period increased from $32.2 billion to $55 billion per year. Horst Stipp (1993), Director of Social and Development Research for the National Broadcasting Company, reports that in 1990, 15- to 17-year-olds alone spent $23 billion of their own money, and that's just direct spending on personal purchases. Stipp also estimates that 15-, 16-, and 17-year-olds influenced an additional $90 billion of their *parents'* spending. When one includes direct purchases for the family (busy parents gave their adolescent offspring over $33 billion for household grocery shopping in 1990), influence on other family purchases, savings, and so forth, the overall impact of 12- to 19-year-olds on the economy in 1988 surpassed $248 billion (Sellers, 1989).

Large segments of our production and marketing systems recognize and cater to the existence of "adolescence." Many companies, even entire industries, appear to exist solely to create and satisfy adolescent demands. Consider what would happen to such retail chains as The Gap or The Limited or to the No Fear or Levi's lines of clothing if everyone under the age of 20 cut their spending by half. The sports and recreation industry would be in equally serious trouble if adolescents curtailed their purchases of athletic shoes, bicycles, roller blades, skateboards, or bathing suits.

Recent trends in advertising also underscore the importance of 10- to 24-year-old consumers. Appeals to and by adolescents, appeals of a type and style that were unknown 25 years ago, are now commonplace. Not only are the "Pepsi generation" and those who "Just do it!" for Nike predominantly young, but so too is a large portion of the intended audience for ads for a number of other products not so immediately—or appropriately—associated with adolescents. Critics often contend that many beer commercials aim at a 24-and-under market, with how far "under" being a major bone of contention. A similar debate surrounds cigarette advertising. Indeed, notwithstanding tobacco and advertising industry denials, it is difficult to imagine that the (now-abandoned) Joe Camel campaign was ever targeted to mature adults. At times the appeals are as controversial as the products, as with the uproar over Calvin Klein's use of adolescent, or even preadolescent, models in sexually suggestive poses.

ADOLESCENTS AND POPULAR CULTURE

Much of the content of our popular media is produced for, and often by, adolescents. This is probably nowhere more evident than in the film and music industries. It is quite clear that the core audience for motion pictures is young. The Motion Picture Association of America (MPAA) currently estimates that although teenagers, those between 12 and 20 years old, comprise only 15% of the U.S. population, they make up 30% of the movie audience. If we push adolescence into the mid-20s, 40% of the movie audience is 24 and under (see, e.g., Dominick, 1994).

The music industry's core audience is just as young. Figure 2.1 displays data released by the Recording Industry Association of America (1995), the trade association for most U.S. companies that create, manufacture, or distribute sound recordings. The figures show that in 1994 consumers under the age of 24 accounted for over 40% of all purchases in the rock, pop, black/urban, and country categories, the genres closest to the concept of "popular music." If we focus on rock and black/urban music, the two most dominant sales categories, the under-24 group accounts for over 50% of sales.

The adolescent influence on music videos is even more concentrated. Adolescents have been the primary target audience for music videos from their inception. In his popular text *Mass Media in America*, Don Pember (1992) notes that MTV was the most thoroughly researched cable TV channel in the U.S. Its founders conducted hundreds of interviews with potential viewers in the 14 to 34 age range before transmitting its first program. Currently, MTV has over 50 million subscribers, and even the most casual observer of MTV quickly realizes that this is a channel exclusively targeted to adolescents. The look and feel of music videos and MTV have clearly influenced other media. Music video techniques, both visual and aural, are increasingly common in motion pictures, TV commercials, and TV programming, a good recent example being NBC's MTV-style "featurettes" on athletes at the 1996 Olympics.

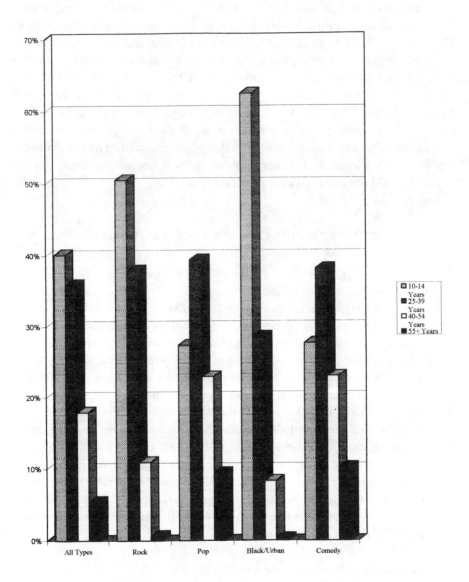

Figure 2.1. Type of music purchased by age in 1994

Note: Figure compiled from data released by the Recording Industry Association of America. Adapted by permission.

Kids look to music and music video stars for guidance on fashion and other cultural issues. When Sheryl Crow changes hair styles or Madonna changes clothes, so too do tens of thousands of adolescents. When Shaquille O'Neal or Coolio sport gold chains and earrings, jewelry begins to jingle in the gyms, the school hallways, and on the street corners. Even politics has been affected. During the 1992 and 1996 election campaigns, Bill Clinton consciously courted the youth vote on MTV, and the MTV network's "Rock the Vote" public service campaign played a significant role in encouraging young voters to go to the polls. In short, were it not for adolescence and adolescents, the popular music industry would not exist as we know it. Furthermore, as we will see, adolescence as we know it would not exist without popular music.

COMPETING VIEWS OF ADOLESCENCE

The dominant characteristic of adolescence is *change*—change in physical, emotional, intellectual, and social functioning. During adolescence, the "still-nearly-a-child" leaving grade school evolves into an "almost-adult." Over the course of a fleeting 6- to 12-year span, youth develop an image of themselves, of others, of society, and of the relationships among these concepts, and they come to grips with myriad social and cognitive issues that must be resolved before achieving fully functioning adulthood. Clearly, given so many critical tasks in such a compressed time span, adolescence is a period when kids—and the adults who interact with them—experience some stress and dislocation. Seriously at issue, however, are the degree of stress and the intensity of the dislocation. Should adolescence be viewed as a violent, decade-long storm alternating between heavy gusts and hurricanes? Or is adolescence more accurately conceived as a relatively temperate weather regime, characterized by alternating sunshine and showers, with the occasional cloudburst more the exception than the rule? Both views have their advocates.

THE PSYCHOANALYTIC VIEW OF ADOLESCENCE

Characterizations of adolescence in terms of constant storm and turbulence stem from two disparate but mutually reinforcing sources: psychoanalytic theory and mass media content. A long tradition of psychoanalytic theorizing envisions adolescence as a time of persistent turmoil, rebellion, and intrafamilial conflict (Steinberg, 1990). Scholars who approach adolescence from a psychodynamic perspective tend to portray the teenage years with such modifiers as "stormy," "unpredictable," "neurotic," and as in a "state of disarray" (e.g., Blos, 1970; Eissler, 1958; Freud, 1958). According to John C. Coleman (1978), this perspective on adolescent development emerged at least as early as Plato, continued through the 19th-century German philosopher-psychologists and such early U.S. psychoanalytic theorists as G. Stanley Hall (1904) and Anna Freud (1936, 1958), and is championed in the modern era by the disciples of Erikson (1968) and in such books as *The Crisis of Adjustment*, edited by Meyerson (1975).

Briefly, the psychoanalytic approach views the central task of adolescence as the establishment of autonomy from parents and assumes that conflict is a necessary condition for achieving such detachment. Indeed, it is fair to say that the psychoanalytic theorists see storm and stress as the norm. Departure from the norm—that is, an adolescence marked by relative calm and harmony—is seen as cause for concern. Anna Freud (1958), a leading proponent of this model, wrote that the failure of an adolescent to manifest signs of conflict and turmoil, although convenient to parents, actually "signifies a delay of normal development and is, as such, a sign to be taken seriously" (p. 265). Similarly, Geleerd (1957) wrote: "Personally I would feel greater concern for the adolescent who causes no trouble and feels no disturbance" (p. 267).

A remarkable array of clinically oriented "how to" parenting books perpetuates this view. A few years ago, Steinberg (1990) reported that a quick inspection of the child development section of a typical bookstore revealed that most titles referred to the teen years as tumultuous and stormy—something to be "survived." In the fall of 1995, we followed up on Steinberg's observation by visiting the Stanford University Bookstore's section on childrearing. The shelves contained 12 different books concerned with how parents should deal with adolescents. As Table 2.1 shows, fully three fourths of the titles characterized the period in essentially the same way, with many using such terms as *conflict, upheaval,* and even *terror.*

Mass Media Characterizations of Adolescence

Given the general principle that conflict lies at the heart of any good story (Orton, 1996), it is not surprising that both the entertainment and the news and information media reiterate and reinforce this tempestuous view of adolescence. Although there are a few contrary examples, enter-

Table 2.1. How Parenting Books View Adolescence.

Titles noted by Steinberg (1990)

Adolescence: A Survival Guide to the Teenage Years (Hayman, 1986)
How to Live with Your Teenager: A Survivor's Handbook for Parents
    (Buntman & Saris, 1982)
How to Survive Your Adolescent's Adolescence (Klodny et al, 1984)
Teenagers: When to Worry, What to Do (Powell, 1986)

Titles located in the Stanford University Bookstore (1995)

Adolescence: The Survival Guide for Parents and Teenagers (Smith, 1994)
Anticipating Adolescence: How to Cope with Your Child's Emotional
    Upheaval and Forge a New Relationship (Gabriel & Wood, 1995)
The Art of Talking with Your Teenager (Swets, 1995)
Lonely, Sad and Angry: A Parent's Guide to Depression in Children and
    Adolescence (Ingersoll & Goldstein, 1995)
Positive Discipline for Teenagers: Resolving Conflict with Your Teenage
    Son or Daughter (Nelson & Lott, 1991)
Surviving Your Adolescents: A Vital Parent's Guide (Phelan, 1993)
Teenage Girls: A Parent's Survival Manual (Ayers, 1994)
Teenage Survival Manual (Coombs, 1995)
Treasure: The Trials of a Teenage Terror and Her Mom (Davidson, 1993)
You and Your Adolescent: A Parent's Guide for Ages 10-20 (Steinberg &
    Levine, 1990)
Uncommon Sense for Parents with Teenagers (Riera, 1995)
What Parents Need to Know About Dating Violence (Levy & Giggens,
    1995)

tainment content is much more likely to portray adolescent crisis and
rebellion than calm and harmony. The entertainment industry presumes
(probably correctly) that rebels, with or without a cause, draw greater
audiences than do the well-adjusted kids next door, and so they tend to
present the teen years in terms of identity crises, rebellion, generation
gaps, and persistent family strife. Nowhere is this "*Sturm und Drang*" image
more prevalent than in music and music videos. Themes of rebellion and
alienation have long been a staple of popular music. Anyone who pays the
least bit of attention knows that music lyrics, video imagery, and, for that
matter, the on-stage behavior and off-stage antics of many current rock
and rap stars lend credence to the storm-and-stress model.

The news and information media are no less concerned with creating compelling stories, and their taste for conflict and "bad news" clearly perpetuates this image. Several recent studies have examined how major daily newspapers, national and local television news shows, television talk shows, and TV news magazines cover youth and youth-related issues (Frank, 1994; Kunkel, 1994). The studies find adolescents to be a frequent topic in the news and information media. In 1993, daily newspapers averaged over 4.5 youth-related stories per issue, and television network news delivered 1.3 youth-related stories per broadcast. These studies also find that when children and adolescents appear in the news and information media, they usually are portrayed as "problem people." For example, 40% of youth-related newspaper stories and 48% of national television youth-related news stories concern crime and violence (Kunkel, 1994); for local television news, the proportion grows to 74% (Frank, 1994). When magazine-format shows and talk shows are included in the news and information category (a practice resisted by many journalists but readily accepted by the viewing public), thus adding such topics as child neglect, teen pregnancy, sexually transmitted diseases, and child labor to the mix, the image of the deviant or problem youth becomes almost overwhelming. The following list of talk show program titles in 1993 reflects the typical portrayal: "The State of Teen Sex" ("Geraldo," July 7); "Killer Kids" ("Geraldo," August 13), "How to Tell if Your Child's a Serial Killer" ("Donohue," August 23), "My Daughter's Boyfriend is Ruining My Life" ("The Oprah Winfrey Show," September 8), "Girl Gang Members and Their Mothers" ("Donohue," November 1), and "Teen Dating Violence" ("Oprah," November 8).

Mass media coverage of popular music issues promotes much the same image. Adult society has always denigrated the emergence of new types of music with special appeal to the younger generation—including ragtime and jazz as well as early rock and roll (McDonald, 1988; Peterson, 1972; Rosenbaum & Prinsky, 1991). Since roughly the end of World War II, the media have consistently reported "adult" outcries about the rebellion, defiance, and immorality promoted in the lyrics (e.g., Denisoff & Levine, 1970; "Pop Songs 'Brainwash...'," 1970) and even the beat of popular songs (Bloom, 1987). Although the early targets for criticism seem tame by today's standards, we should remember that in the 1950s and 1960s, stories and opinion columns lamenting popular music's assault on decency and morality formed a staple in the news diet. The implicit argument was (and is) that the songs and performances were defiant, thus the audiences to which they appealed were defiant—and even if they were not, listening to the music would make them that way!

Clearly, the past decade has produced a similar phenomenon. Coverage of popular music and youth has focused on heavy metal and rap and their presumed influence on adolescents, almost to the exclusion of other pop forms. We note in Chapter 5 that many, perhaps most, popular songs celebrate relatively mainstream, conventional views of life and love. Yet one is much more likely to encounter in the news media stories about the violence, sexual experimentation, drug use, Satanism, or suicide advocated in heavy metal and rap, or reports of the miscreant behavior of the relatively few performers who seem to act out their songs in real life. Consider, for example, the following from a George Will (1990) column in *Newsweek*: "Fact: some members of a particular age and social cohort—the one making 2 Live Crew rich—stomped and raped [a] jogger to the razor edge of death, for the fun of it. Certainty: the coarsening of a community, the desensitizing of a society will have behavioral consequences" (p. 64). Our point, of course, is not that the media are wrong to cover such issues; rather, it is that the way in which they frame stories about popular music and adolescents tends to perpetuate a picture of adolescence and its preferred entertainment as primarily rebellious, conflictual, promiscuous—in a word, stormy. But is this really an accurate picture?

THE EMPIRICAL VIEW OF ADOLESCENCE

Most adolescents experience some conflict and turmoil as they face issues central to becoming successfully functioning adults, and a small but worrisome number of youngsters seem to encounter massive, even debilitating crises during their teen years. Nevertheless, once beyond clinical data and anecdotal reports in the popular press, we find scant evidence for grand theories of enduring generation gaps or persistent, massive crises among the large majority of teenagers.

If conflict and turmoil were the order of the adolescent day, then (a) adolescents should experience more stress, depression, and psychiatric disorder than the adult population; (b) they should hold beliefs and values quite divergent from their parents; and (c) they should be alienated or estranged from their parents. Empirical studies simply do not support these predictions. Consider first the research on the prevalence of psychological disorders. Epidemiological studies from around the world consistently find that approximately 20% of the adolescent population manifest significant emotional disturbances (e.g., Graham & Rutter, 1973; Kandel & Davies, 1982; Krupinski et al., 1967; Offer, Ostrov, Howard, & Atkinson, 1988). Although this is a substantial proportion, it is far from a majority.

More relevant to our concern, however, is whether this is a disproportionate rate relative to the rest of the population—that is, whether adolescence is a period of *unusual* turmoil. The answer seems to be "No." In general, epidemiological research on mental disturbances among adults also shows a rate consistently hovering around 20% (Freedman, 1984), the same rate for adolescents. In one of the few studies to make direct comparisons among age groups, Rutter and his colleagues (Rutter, Graham, Chadwick, & Yule, 1976) examined rates of psychiatric disorder among otherwise comparable samples of 10-year-olds, 14- and 15-year-olds, and adults from the Isle of Wight. They found no support whatsoever for the belief that psychiatric disorder is particularly common during the mid-teens. The rate of psychiatric disorder was about 10% in all three groups examined.

Obviously, many adolescents experience some degree of emotional distress, but the proportion varies depending on diagnostic method. When interview questions were posed and interpreted by a psychiatrist, about 45% of the adolescents in the Isle of Wight study (Rutter et al., 1976) were judged to feel "miserable and unhappy" to the point that they were "tearful or wanted to get away from it all." However, when the same youngsters gave written responses to a more objective "malaise inventory," the proportion indicating they "often feel miserable or depressed" dropped to 22%. Fewer than 8% of those interviewed admitted to ever having suicidal thoughts, and only about one in eight was judged by a psychiatrist as *looking* sad or miserable during the interview. The researchers concluded that although there can be no doubt that many 14- and 15-year-olds experience marked feelings of inner turmoil, this description never characterizes the majority, and only a relatively small minority suffer true clinical depression.

Consider next the issue of differences between parents and their adolescent offspring—discrepancies in basic values, parent–child conflict, generation gaps, and so on. First, studies that directly compare value positions espoused by both adolescents and their parents report remarkable agreement on fundamental values. On such issues as race, marriage and sex, morality, religion, and political orientation, study after study finds that most adolescents recapitulate the beliefs of their parents (Bengston, 1970; Jennings & Niemi, 1975; Offer, 1969; Offer & Offer, 1975; Steinberg, 1990). Second, little hard evidence exists of persistent, epidemic, intergenerational conflict. In fact, surveys asking both parents and children about how they get along reveal a great deal of amicable communication. Although parents are seen as authority figures and disagreements do occur, teenagers general-

ly describe their relations with parents in terms that indicate satisfaction
and mutual respect (Horatio Alger Foundation, 1996; Youniss, 1988; Youniss
& Smollar, 1985). Most teens express positive feelings toward their parents
(Offer, 1969; Offer, Ostrov, & Howard, 1981), indicate more concern with
parental disapproval than with disapproval from friends (Coleman, 1961;
Epperson, 1964), say they are satisfied and happy at home, and approve of
their parents' discipline (Horatio Alger Foundation, 1996; Meissner, 1965).
In the Isle of Wight study of middle adolescents described earlier (Rutter et
al., 1976), two thirds reported that they *never* disagreed with parents about
their activities, and in a recent national survey of 1,000 U.S. school kids,
94% of 13- through 17-year-olds claimed to be either "fairly happy" or
"very happy" with their relationship with their mother and 81% made the
same claim about their father (Horatio Alger Foundation, 1996).

Of course, anyone who has been around a household populated
by adolescents knows that disturbing conflicts between parents and their
teenagers occur. The empirical data suggest, however, that these altercations are much more likely to concern relatively mundane behavioral
issues such as dating, leisure activities, tidiness and punctuality, doing the
dishes—and, most interesting given the focus of this book, music—than
fundamental beliefs and values (see Bandura, 1964; Coleman, 1978;
Coleman, George, & Holt, 1977; Douvan & Adelson, 1966). For most adolescents and parents, these are seldom the types of conflict that put family
relationships at risk. James Youniss (1988), writing in *Youth and America's
Future*, summarizes the work on parent–child conflict quite succinctly:
"The popular literature, which encourages the image of the lone adolescent struggling to 'find an authentic identity,' is contradicted by empirical
evidence which shows that parents help in the process and that adolescents look to them for guidance and support" (p. 8).

MERGING THE CONCEPTIONS

As with so many other "either/or" positions discussed throughout this
book, caution should be exercised before fully accepting or rejecting
either of the two models of adolescence. In particular, the failure of
empirical research to establish a "disturbance model" (Olbrich, 1990) as a
general rule should not lead us to ignore those who do experience severe
turmoil and distress. Although only 5% to 10% of families experience
dramatic deterioration in the quality of parent–child relations during adolescence, as many as 25% experience less than happy relations (Steinberg,
1990). Obviously, this is not a trivial minority. Moreover, the sampling and

questionnaire procedures employed by empirical researchers may under-estimate the prevalence and intensity of adolescent stress (Coleman, 1978). It is reasonable, for instance, to postulate that many teenagers experience and/or deal with their problems and crises intrapsychically rather than interpersonally. This sort of inner turmoil might not be detected in research focused on interpersonal disruptions. Another possi-bility is that many adolescents experience intense stress in relation to one or another of the many changes inherent in adolescent development, but resolve the issue within a relatively short period of time and then move on. If they are not sampled or interviewed during this interval, they may fail to report the previous experience—it is, after all, behind them. In other words, to say an image of storm and stress does not accurately rep-resent typical adolescent development is not to argue that turmoil and disturbance are foreign to adolescent development. As we said at the beginning of this chapter, adolescence is a period of dramatic change, and one of the hallmarks of dramatic change is stress.

How, then, to reconcile the two competing views of adolescent development? A reasonable solution is to eschew "either/or" positions in favor of a combined approach. For example, John Coleman (1974, 1978, 1993) sees adolescent development in terms of how adolescents confront and resolve changes in social relationships—changes in, for example, such areas as self image and being alone, sexual interactions, parent–child rela-tionships, friendships, large group situations, and the connections between the individual and society. Coleman speculates that most teenagers expe-rience significant concern and some level of stress over each of these. He also notes, however, that empirical research shows different issues to be of concern to different teenagers at different times. For example, he found that among a sample of British working-class boys conflict with parents was highest among 17-year-olds, fears of rejection from the peer group peaked at around 15 years, and anxiety over heterosexual relationships was most intense among 11-year-olds (Coleman, 1974).

Such findings underlie Coleman's (1978) "focal model" of adoles-cent development, which suggests that adolescents can adjust to stressful change and maintain relative stability simultaneously because, for the most part, they focus on a single issue at a time:

> [Adolescents] spread the process of adaptation over a span of years, attempting to resolve first one issue and then the next. Different problems, different relationship issues, come into focus and are tack-led at different stages, so that the stresses resulting from the need to

adapt to new models of behavior are rarely concentrated all at one time. It follows from this hypothesis that those who, for whatever reason, have more than one issue to cope with at a time are most likely to have problems. (p. 9)

Coleman (1993) argues further that different issues will surface at different ages and in different orders, depending on social class, gender, personality, culture, and so on. Regardless of such variation, the important point is that typically for any one kid at any one time, just one issue is the most important. Problems may occur when circumstances require two or more issues to be confronted simultaneously, but usually adolescents can adapt to the strains inherent in dealing with a single salient issue. In short, then, although it is proper to conceive of adolescence as a time of rapid change—hence, some psychological, social, and behavioral disruption—most normal adolescents deal with the disruption in relatively functional ways, separating their developmental issues and spreading them over time in order to avoid major crises.

THE DEVELOPMENTAL TASKS OF ADOLESCENCE

Most theories of adolescence frame the period in terms of a number of developmental issues or tasks central to the transition from childhood to adulthood. The developmental tasks mentioned most often include forming an identity; developing a positive body image; acquiring and refining formal problem-solving capabilities and moral reasoning; defining sex roles and establishing opposite-sex (or other sexual) relationships; achieving independence from family; establishing workable and satisfactory peer relations; and preparing for future occupational, family, and civic roles (cf. Adams & Gullotta, 1989; Avery, 1979; Conger & Peterson, 1984; Faber, Brown, & McLeod, 1979; Feldman & Elliott, 1990; Kirchler, Palmonari, & Pombeni, 1993; Violato & Holden, 1987).

These adolescent issues are rendered even more complex because satisfactory relationships must be achieved at each of four levels of social organization. That is, an adolescent must gather and assimilate information about each specific issue that will lead to the development of functional relationships with (a) the self, (b) peers, (c) the family, and (d) the larger social environment—including such institutions as the school, the community, the mass media, the polity, and so forth. For example, establishment of satisfactory sex roles implicates not just relationships with the opposite sex but also relationships with family members, same-sex peers, and teachers, as well as with one's own self-image. Moreover, each level of social organization imposes different constraints. Obviously, given this complexity, kids devote a great deal of energy gathering and processing information that will help them resolve various adolescent issues.

The process is further complicated because a significant amount of the needed information about these social relations comes from the social relationships themselves and because the levels of relationship are simultaneously interdependent and reflexive. That is, the information adolescents need to resolve issues concerning social relationships at any given level comes simultaneously from sources at all levels (interdependent), including the very social relationships that are at issue (reflexive). For example, we learn about social institutions—education, for instance— not only from parents, peers, and personal observation but also from the institutions themselves. At the same time that schools teach us about such things as governments, they also teach us about schools. Similarly, the development of a positive body image depends on one's view of oneself, but it also depends on messages from peers and family, as well as interactions with such social institutions as the mass media. The larger social environment shapes the standards by which people judge the self as well as the standards by which they judge the larger social environment. This process, of course, underlies much of the concern about media influences on adolescent development and results in, for example, warnings that the super-slim bodies portrayed in television commercials or music videos set unattainable and unhealthy standards for what constitutes an "acceptable" body image (Myers & Biocca, 1992) or fears that sexual imagery in music videos may lead to sexual activity in peer groups (Goodman, 1986).

These observations have several important implications for how teenagers use and respond to mass communicated messages in general and to music—which they regard as their special medium—in particular. First, periods of change are periods of uncertainty, and uncertainty leads to information seeking. This principle holds regardless of whether the "change" is an earthquake altering the topography of a city, a society changing governments, or a 13-year-old renegotiating her relationship with her parents. No matter what its origins, change stimulates increased information gathering and information processing to reduce uncertainty (cf. Berlyne, 1965; Roberts, 1971, 1973; Schramm, 1965). Because it is characterized by change, adolescence is inherently unstable. Not surprisingly, then, it is a time of intense information seeking. Kids at this age continually gather and process information as they wrestle with the tasks of adolescence and attempt to prepare for anticipated future life changes.

Second, even as adolescence accompanies increased information seeking, it also brings increased personal control over how information needs are satisfied. Indeed, we might go so far as to add "the development of information independence" to the standard list of critical adolescent tasks. About the time kids leave elementary school, their menu of information sources expands dramatically. The powerful gatekeeping role that parents tend to play in early childhood erodes rapidly during the middle school years (Comstock, Chaffee, Katzman, McCombs, & Roberts, 1978; Faber et al., 1979; Jones & Gerard, 1967), and alternative information sources gain prominence, particularly friends and the mass media.

The use of peers as sounding boards and sources of advice and information increases dramatically in the early teen years. James Youniss and Jacqueline Smollar (1985), for example, describe eight different studies in which largely middle-class, White samples of 12- through 20-year-olds from the Northeast answered questions about relationships with family and friends. As noted in our earlier discussion of the "generation gap," these adolescents reported high satisfaction with communication with parents on many topics. However, on many other topics, Youniss and Smollar found that friends played the most central role both as listeners and sources of advice—especially on the "hot-button" issues most likely to require openness and self-disclosure and hence spark embarrassment or reproach from parents. For example, 85% of the teenagers questioned said they discussed feelings about the opposite sex with their friends; only 11% indicated they did so with their parents. Although just 13% indicated they talked about their doubts and fears with parents, 73% discussed these concerns with friends. Finally, 70% of the teenagers responded "True" to the statement: "I feel I learn more from my close friends than from my parents." Clearly, parents are no longer the only, or even the dominant, source of information for their adolescent children.

Adolescence is also the period when kids largely take control of their media consumption. The great majority of adolescents say they get much of their information from the media (Comstock et al., 1978; Comstock & Paik, 1991; Newspaper Advertising Bureau, 1980). Moreover, by the time they reach their early teens, relatively few families impose rules designed to control the amount of kids' media use. With the exception of a brief increase when children are about 10 to 12 years old—just when they are likely to begin to ask embarrassing questions—relatively few parents make any effort to control the content of adolescents' media fare. The proportion of parents who report the existence of family rules governing either children's access to specific kinds of television content or to particular programs seldom exceeds 50% and more typically hovers at around a third (Comstock et al., 1978; Comstock & Paik, 1991; Greenberg, Ku, & Li, 1989; Lyle & Hoffman, 1972; Newspaper Advertising Bureau, 1980). Moreover, when such controls are reported, they typically apply to children below the age of 12, and they tend to drop off as the child grows older. Perhaps more telling, when the same questions about media rules are posed to *kids*, parental controls are reported even less frequently. We know of only one study reporting data on parental controls over popular music per se. Christenson (1996) asked a sample of middle-class, 3rd through 12th graders from the Portland, Oregon area whether their parents had ever forbidden them to have a certain music album because it had a "Parental Advisory" sticker. Thirty-seven percent of the third through fifth graders answered "yes" to this question, compared to 30% of the sixth through eighth graders and only 23% of the high school students.

Our main points, of course, are that entry into adolescence brings a dramatic increase in both information seeking and information independence, and that mass media in general and music media in particular are extremely well suited to provide information relevant to many of the questions adolescents face. We have already noted that one of the central tasks of adolescence is to establish relationships with peers; indeed, some maintain it is *the* central task. As we discuss in our next chapter, of all the media, music fits best with peer group activities. Print use is a solitary activity, and television, at least relative to other media, is a family activity. Music, however, is a primary currency of adolescence (Larson & Kubey, 1983; Larson, Kubey, & Colletti, 1989); it provides both background and foreground to adolescent peer interactions and grist for the teenage conversation mill. Moreover, the tasks and issues most central to kids at this time are also central to music media. Love, sex, loyalty, friendship, beauty, relationships with parents, authority, and the larger society—these are the issues adolescents grapple with. So too are they the stuff of popular song lyrics, music videos, record jacket pictures and notes, fan magazine articles, and public service announcements on radio and MTV.

This does not mean "objective" adult observers would characterize the information that kids find in music media as correct, adequate, or appropriate; often they do not. Nor would we contend that the interpretation a 15-year-old might make of a particular song or video would be the same as that of the artist, a music critic, or a parent; often it is not. As we shall see in Chapter 6, the meaning of a particular song or video is often not the same even for kids of the same age. Meaning is not so much discovered or assigned as it is constructed, and what any message "means" depends at least as much on what the individual brings to the message as on what the message provides the individual (Leming, 1987; Roberts, 1971, 1973, 1993).

One other point deserves mention here. Recall our earlier discussion of Coleman's (1978, 1993) "focal" model in which kids typically deal with one issue at a time. We would add that whatever the issue may be for any given adolescent, it is virtually all-consuming at the time it is confronted. That is, for most adolescents, the issue of the moment simultaneously creates a deep thirst for information and influences how events and messages are interpreted in relation to that issue (Roberts, 1993). Consider, for example, three different 14-year-old girls, each confronting different issues: One has just discovered boys, one is involved in establishing independence from parental authority, and one has just been told she is pregnant. Each will seek information from any and all available sources relevant to "her" issue, and each is likely to interpret the "same" message quite differently. To the first girl, Madonna's video production of "Papa Don't Preach" might concern true love; to the second, parent–child authority; and to the third, adult roles.

Given the developmental differences considered in this chapter and the widespread individual differences in the construction of meaning, then, we argue for what might be called an "individual differences" approach (Fine, Mortimer, & Roberts, 1990). That is, we take an approach that recognizes the power of social, personality, and structural differences to create important variations in how adolescents deal with their "tasks" and how they deal with the music media. As anyone who knows even a few adolescents can readily attest, for all their shared developmental processes and their attempts to "follow the crowd," they are nonetheless highly unique and variable, and this fact should be kept constantly in mind. Variations aside, however, as the following pages demonstrate, music media play a major role in the emotional, social, and informational life of the typical teenager.

3

EQUIPMENT FOR LIVING:
ADOLESCENT USES OF POPULAR MUSIC

Kids, of course, need music to call their own;
they need music that speaks to them while it
cruises over the heads of their elders, or even
better, turns them right off.
　—Jay Cocks, *Time* (1989)

When one considers the role of popular music in socialization, it must be acknowledged that socialization can be viewed from two distinct perspectives (Johnsson-Smaragdi, 1983). From the perspective of society—that is, of the adult world looking in on the world of the developing adolescent—popular music is seen as one of several distinct and often competing agents of socialization. The important questions relate to popular music's influences during the developmental process: the values music imbues, the behaviors it promotes, its impact on parent–child relationships, the effects of music subcultures within the culture of the school, and so on. These sorts of issues are dealt with later in Chapter 7. The process of socialization and the functions of the various "agents of socialization" look much different from an adolescent's perspective. Like all of us, adolescents can be seen not as the pawns of other agents but as agents themselves, actively choosing and using what parents, friends, school, and the media have to offer in their pursuit of full and successful membership in society. Applied to popular music, the question from this perspective becomes "How do kids use music in their lives?" This is the question that guides this chapter on music uses and gratifications.

We argued in the previous chapter that the appropriate way to view adolescent development is in terms of healthy, normal, and functional development. If this is true, then it makes sense as well to start with the assumption that most of what goes on with popular music is probably normal and healthy as well. In a sense we would ask adults to accord adolescents what they would accord themselves, that is, the benefit of the assumption that they are not usually under control or out of control but *in* control of an active process in which they seek experiences and make decisions that improve the quality of their lives and allow them to become more human. We agree with Gantz and his colleagues that for most adolescents, at most times, listening to popular music is a functional, gratifying experience (Gantz, Gartenberg, Pearson, & Schiller, 1978) and does not represent or cause any problem in their development and adjustment.

This is not to say that music is *never* a problem. As we discuss later, popular music probably does have some negative as well as positive consequences. For troubled, emotionally disturbed, depressed, or otherwise "at risk" kids, an obsessive absorption in certain types of music and music subcultures may well exacerbate their problems. Even for normal, well-adjusted kids, it is likely that the common practice of listening to music while studying interferes somewhat with the learning process. Still, it should be kept in mind that, despite the disproportionate concentration in the research and commentary on pop music on deviant adolescents and styles (Kotarba & Wells, 1987), music listening is a natural and largely benign part of growing up in contemporary Western society. In his 1962 essay, "Popular Songs and the Facts of Life," S.I. Hayakawa wrote these words about the role of blues music in the African-American community of the time:

> I am often reminded by the words of blues songs of Kenneth Burke's famous description of poetry as "equipment for living." In the form in which they developed in Negro communities, the blues are equipment for living humble, laborious, and precarious lives of low social status or no social status at all—nevertheless, they are valid equipment. (p. 161)

Contemporary popular music provides no less valid equipment for living the life of an American adolescent.

TIME SPENT WITH MUSIC MEDIA

Adolescents do not hesitate to state quite directly that they like music and that it is important to them. Some years ago, the Newspaper Advertising Bureau (1980) asked a national sample of more than 1,150 6- through 17-year-olds to rate on 5-point scales how much they enjoyed different media, including television, newspapers, radio and others. Radio, which is almost exclusively a music medium for kids, was "moderately liked" by most grade schoolers, but "most liked" by a large majority of 15- to 17-year-olds. Similarly, when James Leming (1987) asked a sample of 11- to 15-year-olds just how important music was to them, 46% percent replied "very important," and only 7% claimed that it was "not important at all." In a 1996 survey of U.S. 13- through 17-year-olds, 87% reported listening to music after school, and two-thirds named music as a hobby. Overall, music was the students' number one nonschool activity (Horatio Alger Foundation, 1996).

Recently we approached the issue of adolescent music media involvement from a somewhat different perspective. Junior and senior high school students from Northern California (Roberts & Henriksen, 1990) were asked which medium they would choose to take with them if they were stranded on a desert isle. They selected their first, second, and third choices from the following list: TV set, books, video games, a radio, computer, newspapers, VCR and videotapes, magazines, and music recordings and the means to play them. For analysis, radio and recordings were combined into a single "music" category. As Table 3.1 illustrates, at all grade levels music media were much preferred to the closest competitor, television, and the preference for music increased with age. Over 80% of the students in all three grades elected music media as one of their first three choices. More than half of the 11th graders listed music media as their first choice, and 90% included them in their first three choices. Clearly, by the time kids have reached their midteens, they make no bones about their commitment to popular music.

Given such data, it is somewhat surprising how many scholars view *television* as being at center stage during adolescence. We argue that music deserves that position, both in terms of time spent and intensity of involvement. To be sure, the research on time expenditure offers conflicting evidence, some counter to our argument. The first large-scale U.S. study of children's television (Schramm, Lyle & Parker, 1961) found 6th graders listening to 1.2 hours of radio per day and 12th graders listening to 1.9 hours. Daily TV viewing was higher, 2.9 and 2.3 hours per day,

Table 3.1. Which Media Would Adolescents Take to a Desert Isle?

	7th Grade		9th Grade		11th Grade	
	TV	Music	TV	Music	TV	Music
First choice	26%	40%	29%	44%	26%	52%
First two choices	43%	66%	49%	73%	43%	80%
First three choices	57%	82%	65%	86%	61%	90%

Note: Figures are rounded to the nearest %.

respectively, for the two age groups. Lyle and Hoffman (1972) found a similar relationship between radio and TV consumption: The 500 10th graders in their sample spent an average of 2 hours per day with radio and records and over 3 1/2 hours per day watching television. More recently, the Radio Advertising Bureau (1990) reported 2.5 hours of average weekday radio listening among 12- to 17-year-olds, whereas Nielsen Media Research (1989) estimated average daily television viewing in 1988 at just over 2.8 hours for roughly the same age group.

Other recent work reports greater overall amounts of both listening and viewing among adolescents, but continues to give television a slight edge. A sample of Southeastern junior high school students spent an average of three hours per day listening to music and over four hours watching television (Brown, Campbell, & Fischer, 1986). A larger study of randomly selected African-American and White 12- to 14-year-olds from metropolitan areas throughout the southeast United States reported radio listening in excess of 5 hours per day, but over 6 1/4 hours of daily TV viewing (Brown, Childers, Bauman, & Koch, 1990). Very similar amounts of both listening and viewing emerged from a study of over 1,100 9th- and 10th-grade students from three Michigan cities (Greenberg et al., 1986). A national study of students between the ages of 13 and 17 reported 3.6 and 4.3 hours of weekday and weekend radio listening, respectively, and 4.0 and 4.8 hours of comparable TV viewing (Horatio Alger Foundation, 1996).

Using a different method, Larson and Kubey (1983; see also Kubey & Csikszentmihalyi, 1990) also found that adolescents spent more time viewing than listening. They equipped high school students with electronic pagers programmed to "beep" at random times throughout the day for a one-week period. When a beep sounded, the students wrote down what they were doing at that moment—driving, studying, talking with parents, eating dinner, watching television, listening to music, and so forth—as well as who they were with and how they felt. Students reported watching television 10.2% of the times they were beeped and listening to music 6.4% of the time.

The studies reported so far, then, point to television, not music, as the dominant medium in terms of time spent. In our view, however, even the most casual observation of teenage behavior suggests these studies may underestimate how much adolescents listen to popular music. "Boomboxes," Walkmans, and personal CD players are now standard adolescent gear. Few teenagers drive even a minute in a car without the car stereo playing, and even fewer lack music playback equipment in their bedrooms. For most kids, music is as natural a part of the environment as the air they breath or the walls that surround them. Indeed, therein may lie part of the difficulty of measuring music listening time. Music is often a secondary, background activity rather than a primary, foreground one. It serves as a backdrop to other activities—reading, studying, talking, housework, driving—and it often appears in the adolescent's environment without any conscious decision to introduce it. For example, a teenager may be driving to school while chatting with a friend, all the while "listening" to music emanating from a car radio left on by a sibling who used the car the previous evening.

Obviously, music's tendency to slip between the foreground and background raises questions about what kind of "listening" should be counted as true *exposure* and how that exposure should be measured. We argue that background listening ought to count, and for those who might disagree we offer this challenge: Simply turn off the "background" music when adolescents are studying, chatting, or doing chores and observe their responses. They will respond in the clearest of terms that they are "listening." Of course, detecting this sort of exposure is tricky, but we believe most measures of listening time probably produce a bias toward occasions involving conscious use and higher levels of involvement. More often than not, adolescents will fail to report listening associated with other, more central activities. To put it in concrete terms, an adolescent who has spent an hour doing dishes with the radio blaring in the background is far more likely to define the time as "doing chores" than listening to music, even though both things were going on.

Estimates of music listening are also compromised by the frequent practice of equating music listening with *radio* use. Most studies prior to 1980, and even some since, inquire about radio use while ignoring other sources of popular music (e.g., Brown et al., 1986, 1990; Greenberg et al., 1986; Lyle & Hoffman, 1972). Although it is true that virtually all radio time is music time (Horatio Alger Foundation, 1996), not all music time is radio time. Many adolescents hear much or even most of their music from tape and CD playback and from viewing music video cable channels. In today's media environment, measures of radio listening are a poor indicator of total music exposure.

Recent studies measuring *all* music listening or that alert respondents to include background listening in their estimates find higher levels of adolescent exposure to music media than to any other media, television included. For example, Bradley Greenberg of Michigan State University and several of his colleagues interviewed 6th- and 10th-grade students from five different schools in Flint, Michigan (Greenberg et al., 1989). The students were asked how much time they had spent the previous day watching television, reading newspapers, listening to radio, and listening to audio recordings. Sixth graders reported 4.1 hours of television viewing and 3.8 hours of music listening (radio and audio recordings combined). Tenth graders, however, reported a full hour more of music: 4.9 hours versus 3.9 hours of TV viewing.

Roberts and Henriksen (1990) also included all music media in their study of more than 650 9th and 11th graders from several San Francisco Bay area high schools. Students made separate estimates of the amount of time they spent on school days listening to radio, recordings, and watching music videos. In addition, after these initial time estimates were obtained, participants were asked a question designed to sensitize them to *background* music listening:

> Now that you have thought some about your music listening, give us another estimate of how much time you spend on a school day listening to music. Include the time you do nothing but listen, and the time that music is on in the background when you work, do homework, visit, are in a car, and so forth. And be sure to include time with radio, records, tapes, and even MTV. (p. 16)

As Table 3.2 shows, television consumed anywhere from 2 to 2 1/2 hours of time each day (depending on age and gender). Based on the estimate including background time, however, music occupied from 3 to almost 4 hours per day. Music time exceeded television time by amounts ranging from half an hour (for 9th-grade boys) to almost 2 hours (for 11th-grade girls).

Table 3.2. Daily Minutes of School Day TV and Music.

	7th Grade		9th Grade	
	Boys	Girls	Boys	Girls
Television	154	139	137	115
Radio	79	134	87	107
Recordings	77	82	95	91
MTV	40	33	23	22
"All Music"[a]	179	230	200	227

[a]"All Music" data are from a separate question worded to include background listening—not simply the sum of radio, recordings, and MTV.

Adapted by permission from *Music listening vs. television viewing among older adolescents,* by D.F. Roberts & L. Henriksen, 1990, paper presented at the annual meeting of the International Communication Association, Dublin, Ireland.

Thus, when all sources of music are included and background as well as foreground listening is counted, adolescents—especially older ones—spend substantially more time listening to music than watching television. The precise amount of music listening time remains at issue. As we have noted, estimates range from as low as 2 hours per day in earlier research and radio-only studies (e.g., Lyle & Hoffman, 1972; Radio Advertising Bureau, 1990) to over 5 hours in more recent work (Brown et al., 1990; Greenberg et al., 1986, 1989). We have argued there is good reason to think the low-end studies underestimate current levels of music listening. At the same time, however, because the three studies on the high end also report higher levels of TV viewing than most research (including the Nielsen ratings), they may *over*estimate music listening time. We suspect that the middle-range figures obtained in the California study (Roberts & Henriksen, 1990) are probably the most realistic. That is, it seems reasonable to say that by the time they are in high school, kids spend somewhere between 3 and 4 hours a day listening to popular music, compared to 2 to 3 hours per day watching television. In essence we agree with Keith Roe (1987) that "it is becoming increasingly difficult to escape the conclusion, in terms of both the sheer amount of time devoted to it and the meanings it assumes, that it is music, not television, that is the most important medium for adolescents" (pp. 215-216).

Amount of listening is not uniform across all groups of adolescents. First, age makes a big difference: the older the adolescent, the greater the amount of time devoted to music. Although many children begin listening to popular music early in the grade-school years (Christenson, DeBenedittis, & Lindlof, 1985), music does not consume nearly the same amount of time for younger children as television does. At about the beginning of junior high school, however, things change. The early teen years mark a sharp increase in the amount of time kids devote to popular music, and the trend toward higher levels of music consumption continues through the end of high school.

It is also safe to say that girls listen more than boys, at least once adolescence is reached. Although research on grade schoolers finds no significant gender differences in amount of listening (Christenson & DeBenedittis, 1986; Lyle & Hoffman, 1972), the picture changes about the time kids enter middle school. Lyle and Hoffman (1972) found that girls reported more time spent listening than boys by the sixth grade, and substantially more by tenth grade, and Greenberg (1973) found a similar pattern among a sample of British adolescents. In the Michigan study cited earlier, the 6th- and 10th-grade girls reported significantly more radio listening time than boys (Greenberg et al., 1989), as did the girls surveyed by Roberts and Henricksen (1990; see Table 3.2). Brown and her colleagues' study of Southeastern students (Brown et al., 1990) reported gender differences both for different ages and different races. Twelve- and 13-year-old White girls listened about three quarters of an hour more per day than White boys; by 14 years the difference had grown to almost 2 hours a day. Gender differences were pronounced at all three ages among African-American students. In short, there is little question that while both boys and girls are drawn to popular music, girls devote significantly more time to it.

Several explanations can be suggested for age and gender differences in music use. We noted in the previous chapter that adolescence brings a shift in orientation toward peers and away from parents and family. As Larson and Kubey (1983) argue, it makes sense for a variety of reasons that this reorientation should be accompanied by a corresponding migration away from television, which they see as a family medium, toward the more adolescent-oriented popular music media. Concerning the relationship between listening and gender, Brown and her colleagues (1990) argue that because girls mature earlier and begin to establish peer relationships earlier than boys, it is reasonable that girls should move toward music media earlier as well.

Some of the patterns also probably stem from age and gender differences in opportunity and available time. Older adolescents are more likely than their younger counterparts to be outside of the home, where the television typically resides, and more likely to engage in activities that preclude television but allow music listening, such as parties, driving, homework, and household chores. (Indeed, kids say they can even "listen" while they read.) Finally, girls are more likely than boys to find themselves in some of these settings. Whether one approves of the pattern or not, girls still spend more time in the home and do more household chores than boys. With more time spent in their bedroom and on routine tasks, girls would seem more likely to fill their hours with music. Boys are more involved in sports and other sorts of organized out-of-home and afterschool activities that tend not to be associated with music listening.

Very few studies have examined racial or ethnic differences in music listening, but those that do explore such differences find higher levels among minority youth than Whites. For instance, Lyle and Hoffman (1972) found that Mexican-American 10th graders engaged in significantly more radio listening than their Anglo counterparts, and Brown and her colleagues (1990) found substantially more music listening, regardless of age or gender, among African-American youth than Whites. Surprisingly, little attention has been given to the effects of socioeconomic status or family structure on music listening time, although Brown and her colleagues (1990) present some data suggesting a negative relationship between parental education and music use. They also found higher levels of use among kids from families in which the father is absent.

MUSIC VIDEO VIEWING

MTV, the network that has become synonymous with the music video form, was launched in 1981. A decade and a half later it has been joined by a host of other music video channels, and music videos are an increasingly hot item for sale and rental at home video outlets. The vast majority of adolescents and preadolescents watch music videos at least occasionally. Brown et al. (1986) found that over 80% of a sample of 12- to 14-year-olds reported at least some viewing. Christenson (1992a) noted similar levels of exposure (75%) among 9- to 12-year-olds, and even higher estimates have been published (Stipp, 1985).

Still, music video viewing is considerably less frequent and regular than music listening. Some studies indicate that the proportion of adolescents exposed to videos on a daily basis is in the range of 35% to 40%

(Brown et al., 1986; Sun & Lull, 1986). Table 3.3 compares the frequency of music and music video consumption both generally (whether they ever watch) and at specific times of the day for young adolescents enrolled in public schools in Portland, Oregon. As the table shows, music listening was more frequent in all categories. The difference was especially striking during the evening and before school. For example, over 60% said they had listened to music the previous night. The corresponding frequency for music videos was 15%.

Estimates of actual time spent with music videos vary considerably due to variations in study methodology, age and ethnicity of respondents, geographical region, and the availability of cable television. Most published reports set the average amount of viewing time at between 15 and 30 minutes a day (Christenson, 1992a; Kubey & Larson, 1989; Leming, 1987; Wartella, Heintz, Aidman, & Mazarella, 1990). Our study of California youth found daily averages of 40 minutes for 7th graders, 30 minutes for 9th graders, and 20 minutes for 11th graders. These figures also suggest that interest in music videos peaks early in adolescence, then

Table 3.3. Early Adolescents' Use of Music and Music Videos.

	Music (%)	Videos (%)
Do you ever listen to music/watch music videos?	98	75
How much do you like listening/watching? (% either "pretty much" or "a lot")	97	60
Do you ever listen/watch in the afternoon?	84	62
How often do you listen/watch in the afternoon? (% either "most days" or "every day")	72	62
Did you listen/watch last night?	62	15
Did you listen/watch today before school?	51	7

Note: Figures are based on responses of 100 10- to 13-year-old public middle school students. All music versus video comparisons are significant at $p < .001$.

Adapted by permission from "Preadolescent perceptions and interpretations of music videos," by P. Christenson, 1992b, *Popular Music and Society, 16*(3), p. 67. © 1992.

drops off in the high school years. The highest estimate we have found comes from Sun and Lull (1986), who reported a daily average among 14- to 17-year-old California youth in excess of 2 hours. The discrepancy between their findings and most other studies is difficult to explain, although it likely reflects the very high level of cable penetration in the survey location as well as the heavy representation of Latinos in their sample. The Latino students reported an hour more daily viewing than the other ethnic groups represented in the study. In any case, because most studies converge on figures in the 15- to 30-minute range, we are inclined to accept these lower amounts as the best estimates of overall daily consumption. Gender differences are usually small, but when they are reported females have watched more. Studies also report higher viewing time among ethnic and racial minorities than among Whites (Brown et al., 1986; Sun & Lull, 1986). Whatever the individual and group differences in music and music video consumption, however, listening to popular music, rather than watching television, is the dominant leisure activity for most adolescents.

THE MANY USES OF POPULAR MUSIC

Some tools have more uses than others, and as we will discuss, popular music qualifies as a most versatile piece of equipment indeed. Still, at the simplest, most global level, children, adolescents, and adults—all of us, in other words—listen to music because, above all, it gives us pleasure. The pleasure of music can take many forms, of course, and it can be segmented, divided, and categorized. However, no matter how much of it we may attribute to specific "gratifications," there is a residuum that defies identification: in the end we "just like it." Often, of course, it is a much more intense matter than just "liking." For many adolescents and adults music either creates directly or contributes significantly to the most intense, "peak" experiences of life. As Lull (1992) put it: "Music promotes experiences of the extreme for its makers and listeners, turning the perilous emotional edges, vulnerabilities, triumphs, celebrations, and antagonisms of life into hypnotic, reflective tempos that can be experienced privately or shared with others" (p. 1).

As Table 3.4 shows, it is easy to identify many specific ways in which listeners, young and old alike, find music rewarding and useful in their lives. Music can make a good mood better and allow us to escape or "work through" a bad one. It can relieve tension, provide escape or distrac-

Table 3.4. A Partial Inventory of Popular Music Uses and Gratifications.

Pleasure, fun
Improve or intensify a certain mood
Ruminate on a bad mood
Get energized, "pumped up"
Relieve tension
Relax
Pass the time when there's nothing else to do
Distraction from troubles
Evoke past experiences and memories
Form impressions of others and establish new friendships
Acquire status in the peer culture
Stay current with popular culture
Reduce drudgery of homework, work, chores
Ambiance for parties, social gatherings, ceremonies
Something to talk about with friends
Dancing
Singing (or other participation)
Rhythm for exercises (aerobics, weight lifting, etc.)
Provide company when lonely
Fill gaps in conversation
Social lubricant—make conversations flow more smoothly
Learn how to sing or play a musical instrument
Stimulate interest in sex
Offend or irritate others
Establish private, personal space
Block out or mask unwanted sounds
Relate to the meaning of lyrics
Learn new language, slang
Learn about the world, other cultures, alternative points of view
Identify with one's "crowd" or subculture
Claim public space for one's group
Express resistance to authority
Identify with favorite artists
Articulate social or political attitudes

tion from life's problems and complications, keep us company when we are alone, fill the time when there is nothing much to do, and ease the drudgery of repetitive, menial tasks and chores, including, to the chagrin of many parents, studying, and homework. Music also fills a variety of functions in social situations: It fills uncomfortable gaps in conversations, provides topics of conversation, and makes parties or social gatherings more lively, comfortable, smoother. Indeed, for most adolescents and college students, a good party is unthinkable without a good sound system. Music also allows, indeed at times compels, dancing, singing, clapping, and other forms of direct participation. Listeners identify with the romantic themes in song lyrics, respond to the embedded political and social messages, even learn new vocabulary. Music preferences and tastes are used to form and solidify friendships, express resistance against adult authority, identify subcultures, and demarcate psychological and physical boundaries both within youth culture and between the youth and adult culture.

However, many of the specific uses and gratifications typically mentioned by listeners can be fit into broader categories, and so the lengthy inventory in Table 3.4 can probably be boiled down somewhat without losing much real information. Different scholars have suggested different typologies of media uses, but most recognize a division somewhat similar to that suggested by Dominick (1996) in his overview of media uses and gratifications. Dominick distills four main categories from the uses and gratifications literature, and we suggest a fifth.

1. *Cognition.* This category refers to the use of media for information. Obviously, newspapers and TV news come to mind first here, but entertainment content (soap operas, talk shows, situation comedies, etc.) carries a lot of information as well. In terms of music, when listeners say they use music lyrics or music videos to stay abreast of political and economic issues, learn about other cultures, or reflect on the meaning of social and romantic relationships, they refer to cognitive uses.

2. *Diversion.* This category is close to what others have called entertainment. In the context of music, it includes the emotional or affective rewards of listening. Several of the entries in Table 3.4 fit here, such as relaxation, relief from boredom and tedium, release of tension, getting energized, distraction from troubles, mood intensification, and enhancing the atmosphere at social gatherings. These are the most important uses of popular music, and they are discussed at length in the following section.

3. *Social utility.* Media are often used in ways that help to establish and facilitate relationships with family, friends, and groups. Among the entries on our list that fall into this group are the

use of music to provide something to talk about with friends (Dominick refers to this "conversational currency"), as social lubricant, to identify with one's crowd, to facilitate parties, and to enhance sexual encounters. Social uses may also include instances of what researchers refer to as "parasocial interaction," in which individuals establish vicarious social relationships with the media and the people in the media, often to compensate for social isolation or loneliness. When adolescents listen to music to keep them company or when they fantasize about romantic relationships with artists, they engage in this sort of behavior. Thus music listening can be, perhaps paradoxically, both solitary (that is, experienced alone) and social at the same time. One may even include behavior that is consciously aggressive or territorial as a "social use," at least in the sense that social relationships are at issue.

4. *Withdrawal.* Finally, Dominick pays homage to a category of media use motivated primarily by the need to be left alone, to avoid social contact, to establish barriers between the self and others. The archetypal example of this is the adult buried behind the newspaper at the breakfast table: The news may be important, but so is the message to be left alone. Music listening behavior, too, provides clear examples of the use of media for withdrawal. The invention of the Walkman personal stereo provided much more than a new way of listening to music; it gave listeners a powerful tool for establishing personal space and privacy. Personal stereos also make it possible to avoid interpersonal conflict in situations in which individuals are forced into contact with one another. We have no data on this, but our observation (and personal experience) suggests that the Walkman has promoted a sea change in the U.S. automobile vacation. Today few families will embark on an extended car trip unless all children are equipped with their own Walkmans and fresh double-A batteries. This phenomenon bears testimony as well to the power of music preferences: One may hardly overestimate the discomfort and conflict that may ensue when a 14-year-old alternative rock fan's Walkman runs out of power and he is forced to listen to the parents' classic rock station or, even worse, the 9-year-old girl's pop rock tape.

5. *Personal identity.* Dominick's four-part scheme is not the only way to classify media uses and gratifications, nor does it exhaust

the range of important categories (Roberts & Bachen, 1981). Most critically, it is difficult to locate a comfortable home in his four categories for the sorts of music uses and gratifications referred to by others as "personal integration" (Katz, Gurevitch, & Haas, 1973) or "personal identity" (McQuail, Blumler, & Brown, 1972), including formation of a clear sense of self, establishing self-confidence, and seeking moral guidance and social status. It might be argued that this fifth category could be parceled out to the other four—for instance, the learning and guidance aspect could be assigned to "cognitive" uses, status seeking to social uses and so forth. However, given its clear relevance to the developmental tasks of adolescence and the frequency and forcefulness with which the literature speaks of the link between popular music and personal identity, we argue for keeping it distinct and separate.

The preceding categories provide a reasonable summary and consensus of the major types of media uses and gratifications (Murray & Kippax, 1979) and a reasonable entree to some other key points about media and music uses. First, even granting that the five broad categories of uses and gratifications may apply at some time for some people to virtually all media, it is clear that different media, depending on their essential characteristics, exhibit varying profiles of use. For example, unlike television (and leaving aside for the moment the issue of music videos), music has no "pictures," except perhaps the ones listeners may paint in their own minds. Because music offers fewer opportunities to observe and acquire the sorts of information about human behavior and relationships that can be gleaned from watching a television show, presumably music listeners will be less likely than TV viewers to report that they use music to learn these sorts of things. Popular music is not only poor in verbal information compared to other media, but its words are usually secondary in importance to the "sound." Given these various differences between music and other media, we should not be surprised to find that "cognitive" uses for music are considerably less central to the music listening experience than they are to television viewing or newspaper reading.

On the other hand, these two characteristics of popular music— the absence of visual information and the primacy of sound over words— also dictate some ways in which music is *more* useful than television. Television may provide visual information, but it also enslaves the eyes. It is no coincidence that automobiles are equipped with audio systems rather than video. The fact that sound is always there no matter where you look enables music to perform its functions of establishing atmosphere at social occasions and ameliorating the tedium of routine or repetitive tasks.

Music differs from other media in other obvious and important ways. Notwithstanding the advent of "personal TV's," music playback equipment is generally much more portable than video playback equipment. It is the boombox or the Walkman, not the TV set, that goes to the beach or on car trips. The economics of popular music also figure in. We have mentioned Larson and Kubey's (1983) argument that popular music fits especially well with adolescence because (not forgetting that some very large corporations are involved here, too) it is not just consumed but is also produced by youth. With the exception of magazines, no other major mass medium can profitably cater to a population whose tastes are as fragmented and segmented as the popular music public. As Lull (1992) notes, one of the major uses of popular music in adolescent culture is to establish and maintain subcultures around different genres or styles. Thus it tends to be music preferences, not television preferences, that provide a focus for the identification of adolescent subcultures and "crowds."

These are only a few examples of how differences between popular music and other media influence the way they are used in daily life. The major difference between popular music and other media, though, lies in music's unique ability to influence mood and emotion—to produce an "affective effect." Other media can move us deeply: TV shows, movies, books, even newspaper articles, may provoke powerful emotional reactions. As we will see, though, when adolescents talk about what music does for them, they almost invariably make some reference to the way it makes them feel.

THE AFFECTIVE USES OF POPULAR MUSIC

As we have noted, most popular music uses and gratifications can be accommodated within the general categories identified in the research literature on uses and gratifications research—cognitive, entertainment or diversion, social uses, and so on. However, because these general categories have been derived primarily from studies of adult TV use (Rubin, 1994), it makes sense to expect somewhat different patterns when the attention shifts to a different medium and a different age group. We turn now to research specifically on adolescent motivations for and gratifications from listening to popular music.

Gantz and his colleagues (1978) asked junior high school and college students how often several different uses or motivations applied to their radio listening. The focus was on radio, not music per se, but because adolescents listen to radio primarily for its music content, the results speak reasonably well to the issue of what motivates music listening. The following list identifies the various radio gratifications the students considered, followed by the percentage who said they listened either "very frequently" or "somewhat frequently" for that particular reason:

- helps me pass the time or relieves boredom when I am doing other things (such as homework, cleaning, driving)—91%
- relieves tension or takes my mind off troubles—83%
- gets or keeps me in a certain mood—79%
- relieves loneliness when I'm by myself—67%
- sets a mood when with others—62%
- think about the meaning of lyrics—58%
- fills silence in social settings when nobody is talking—51%.

Although the levels of agreement to the statements were all reasonably high, these findings clearly suggest the primacy of two functions: (a) simply to pass the time or relieve boredom, and (b) to control mood states. Social uses (such as setting a mood when with others and filling in uncomfortable gaps in conversation) and cognitive uses (attention to lyrics) were acknowledged, but not nearly as frequently as personal diversion and affective uses.

Rosenbaum and Prinsky (1987) presented a different task with a somewhat different list of gratifications to a sample of 12- to 18-year-olds, asking them to reflect on their favorite songs and why they were attractive. The authors report, again in descending order of importance, these reasons for liking the songs: relaxation and "stop thinking about things," getting into the "right mood," usefulness as dance music; the extent to which "the words express how I feel," creating an atmosphere when with others, simply passing the time, and "I want to listen to the words." Although these two studies framed the issue somewhat differently—Gantz and his colleagues targeted radio listening generally, whereas Rosenbaum and Prinsky focused on a favorite song—both point to mood control and relaxation as primary motivations for music listening, with social uses and orientation to lyrics lagging behind. The difference between the two studies in the salience of the "time-filling" motivation probably arises from the fact that radio listening is less involving than listening to a favorite piece of music, which would more likely be a fore-ground activity than a simple time-killing mechanism.

Perhaps the best information on adolescent music (as opposed to radio or one's favorite song) uses and gratifications comes from Roe's (1985) work with Swedish adolescents. He presented 12 possible gratifications for listening to music—through radio or recordings—and asked students to indicate how often each applied to their listening. Using factor analysis, a statistical technique designed to convert the information in a large number of variables into a smaller, more manageable set of underlying concepts, Roe was able to reduce the original 12 into three general groups: (a) atmosphere creation and mood control (relax and stop thinking about things, getting in the right mood, setting a social atmosphere, and dancing), (b) silence-filling and passing the time when there's nothing else to do, and (c) attention to lyrics (they express how I feel, I want to listen to the words). Of the three classes, atmosphere creation and mood control emerged as the most important, with time-filling second and attention to lyrics a distant third.

Roe's results suggest that when "music" is the focus, the mood management aspect of the more global diversion or entertainment function takes precedence over routine time-filling and boredom relief. A recent U.S. study reveals a similar pattern of music gratifications among middle to late grade-school students. Christenson (1994) used an open-ended format in which children explained in their own words why they liked listening to music. Although many of the students answered with a generic "I just like it," those who provided a more specific answer most often mentioned atmosphere and mood control. Next in frequency were "background and passing time," followed by lyrics. By 6th grade the relative strength of the three categories was remarkably close to that reported by Roe: About 40% mentioned atmosphere and mood control, 20% passing time, and just under 10% the meaning in the lyrics.

This research suggests a principle that might be labeled "the primacy of affect." That is, for most adolescents, music use is governed above all by a desire to control mood and enhance emotional states. Music's ability to influence mood and emotion has been widely noted. When teens want to be in a certain mood, when they feel lonely, when they seek distraction from their troubles, music tends to be the medium they choose to accomplish the task (Brown, 1976; Christenson et al., 1985; Larson et al., 1989; Lyle & Hoffman, 1972). Nearly all youth use music for mood management at some time. In one study of college students, 80% agreed that they had used music to change their mood; presumably the proportion would have been even higher if the question had included the notion of reinforcing or reflecting an existing mood (Wells, 1990).

One of the interesting contradictions relating to popular music use is that although numerous studies document a strong positive correlation between peer (versus parent) orientation and involvement in popular music—that is, the more a kid prefers the company of friends over parents the more involved in music he or she will be—the same research shows that most listening is solitary and personal. The typical listening situation, in fact, is alone in the bedroom. This pattern of solitary listening begins as early as late grade school. One survey reports that about 40% of 3rd and 4th graders and 70% of 5th and 6th graders said they were usually alone when they listened to music (Christenson, 1994). Only 1 in 10 said they were usually with friends. Listening with parents present was rare at both ages. By the end of grade school, none of the respondents said they usually listened to music with one or both parents. When music listening did occur in the presence of others, it was most likely to be with siblings. The predominance of solitary listening continues into middle and late adolescence, even as teens become increasingly oriented to their peers and more independent from the family. In a survey of 9th through 12th graders, Larson and Kubey (1983) found over two thirds of music listening occasions to be solitary. The difference between their results and Christenson's data on preadolescents was that co-listening among the high school students was usually with friends rather than siblings.

To note that most listening is solitary, however, is far from saying popular music use is independent from the peer group. As we have mentioned, higher levels of involvement in popular music tend to go with higher levels of peer orientation. Most likely, the predominance of solitary listening reflects the common social and environmental constraints on adolescents. Even though they would often rather be with friends, parental rules, homework, and other commitments force them to be alone (Czikszentmihalyi & Larson, 1984). In these circumstances music probably helps to make a bad situation more tolerable. Indeed, as we mentioned earlier, solitary listening may incorporate a social dimension, putting youth psychologically in touch with their physically absent peers, or fulfill a parasocial function, acting as what Dominick (1974) called a "portable friend." Still, notwithstanding these quasi-social aspects of solitary listening, most music listening is a personal behavior rather than a group phenomenon, and it is in the context of listening alone that most mood management occurs.

The issue of mood management is complicated, though, in various ways. First, different kinds of music work in different ways and depend on different circumstances. Lull (1982) found that college students chose to listen to new wave music when they wanted to get "rowdy, crazy, or hyped up." The same music, however, was unsuited for various other contexts. Writing in more general terms on the same issue, Murdock and Phelps (1972) suggest that "teenagers may operate with a primitive sort of mind-body dualism where some records are classified primarily as 'head' music and others as 'body' music and both have their place depending on the circumstances" (p. 147).

Second, youth differ in their degree of reliance on music for mood control. Frith's (1981) interviews with British adolescents, for instance, showed a relationship between social class and music orientation. Middle-class, college-bound students were more likely than working-class youth to relate to popular music on an intellectual level by analyzing lyrics for their deep meaning. Working-class kids tended to look to music more for its beat and sound and especially for its ability to create the right atmosphere for dancing and socializing.

Music preferences relate to the salience of emotional uses as well. In Roe's (1984) research on Swedish teens, those who preferred progressive rock or new wave music reported using music to manage atmosphere and mood more often than those whose tastes ran to mainstream pop. More recent research on American teens suggests personality characteristics may also play a role in this area. Gordon and his colleagues report that students with higher levels of general trust in others and greater independence from peer group influence were not only more likely to report the use of music to manage their emotions, but also associated their preferred music with different and generally more positive emotional states (love and hope, for instance, versus anger and grief) than did students who were less trusting and more driven by a need to be accepted by others (Gordon, Hakanen, & Wells, 1992).

Finally, in addition to the complications introduced by different types of music and different listener characteristics, "mood management" is itself a complex process. Lull (1992) points out that music can put one in the "right mood" for everything from sex to funerals. In one study, a heavy metal devotee reported that he loved the music because it put him in a "good mood," by which he meant a mood conducive to smashing mailboxes with bricks. Another said hardcore metal put him in the mood to "go and beat the crap out of someone" (Arnett, 1991a, p. 84). In other words, mood management comes in various forms, and getting a good sense of the affective effects of music requires some specification.

When studies differentiate between different types of mood control, they tend to find high and approximately equal degrees of agreement with items suggesting tension relief, distraction from problems, strengthening a current mood, and getting into the "proper" or "right" mood for a given circumstance. Both Roe (1984) and Gantz and his colleagues (1978) reported that that 75% to 80% of adolescents surveyed said they listened to "get into the right mood" or to "relax and stop thinking about things." The use of music to relieve feelings of loneliness, although frequent (above 60% in both studies), was somewhat less prominent than the other two categories. Evidence also suggests that music is more likely to perform an energizing than a de-energizing or "mellowing out" function. Gordon and his colleagues asked 1,500 11- to 19-year-olds to rate the extent to which they used music to manage various emotional states. The highest scores were obtained for "lift my spirits," "get me pumped up," and "strengthen my mood," which averaged about 7 on a 9-point scale. "Calm me down" and "mellow me out" averaged about 5.5 (Gordon et al., 1992). Wells (1990) reported similar results on similar measures for college students.

As it does in so many areas related to popular music use, gender makes a difference in the nature of emotion management. Consistently, males are more likely than females to use music as a tool to increase their energy level and seek stimulation—that is, to get "pumped up" or "psyched up." Females are more likely to listen in order to lift their spirits when they are down or lonely or even to ruminate on or "work through" a somber mood (Arnett, 1991a; Larson et al., 1989; Roe, 1985; Wells, 1990). Larson and his colleagues (Larson et al., 1989) provided an interesting illustration of this phenomenon using the electronic paging method mentioned previously. At the prompting of the pager, students from 5th to 9th grade recorded what they were doing and how they felt emotionally—whether they were happy or sad, cheerful or irritable, friendly or angry, and so on. These different "feeling" scales were combined into a measure of "average affect," which was then related to the kids' various activities, including music listening. For boys, average affect during music listening rose steadily with age and was on the positive or "feel good" side of the scale from 7th through 9th grades. For girls, average affect went down with age, and by 9th grade it was solidly on the negative side of the scale; for them, music listening went with a "down" rather than an "up" feeling. This trend in mood coincided with a sharp increase in the frequency of music listening—older girls were both listening to more music and indicating more negative emotional states while they did so. Larson and his colleagues (1989) wrote:

> For girls, whose listening tastes are more often directed toward ballads and love songs, music is not elevating, but rather is associated with sadness, depression and sometimes anger. While boys appear to use music to pump themselves up, young adolescent girls' use of music may be driven more by a need to both explore and cope with new concerns and worries that accompany this age period, perhaps especially those surrounding intimate relations that are so often the themes of these songs. (p. 596)

Although it is less common overall, the practice of matching music with negative moods applies to many boys as well. Male heavy metal fans, for example, often choose music that deepens rather than counteracts their negative emotional states. Arnett (1991a) asked a sample of male heavy metal fans whether they were more likely to listen to heavy metal when they were in a "particular mood." About a quarter said they listened to it without regard to their mood, but almost half said they were more likely to listen when they were angry. Fewer than 10% said they tended to listen when in a positive mood. Thus, in the same way girls often listen to sad songs when they are sad, many male heavy metal fans apparently listen to angry music when they are angry. As one respondent said, he sought out "full-blown thrashing metal" when he was "mad at the world" (Arnett, 1991a).

At first glance this seems like a rather dysfunctional process. In his theory of mood management, Zillmann (1988) argues, logically enough, that people generally are motivated to seek media experiences that produce more positive moods and avoid those that promote aversive ones. Yet people routinely seek out troubling, unpleasant, even depressing media fare, including popular music. Zillmann's essentially hedonic principle would have little trouble with cases in which the immersion in depressing or angry music serves a purgative function, allowing teens to work through or out of negative emotions. In fact, many of the angry listeners in Arnett's study claimed such an effect. It is more difficult, however, to explain the rumination and dwelling on negative moods reported by Larson and his colleagues or the accentuation of anger and depression that often occurs during heavy metal listening.

In her explanation of the "problem of tragedy"—that is, why audiences enjoy dramatic presentations in which admired characters suffer misfortune—Mary Beth Oliver (1990) has suggested two processes that provide a clue to what motivates adolescents to immerse themselves in music that seems to make bad moods worse. The first process, "downward social comparison," posits that although we are normally disturbed by media content in which bad things happen to good people, on occasion such material may have the positive effect of making our own plight seem less dreadful in comparison to others. As we will see later in our discussion of the content of popular music in Chapter 5, popular songs provide a wealth of opportunities for such downward social comparison. Adolescents snubbed by a boyfriend or girlfriend or experiencing conflict with their parents can almost invariably find a song that depicts an even more desperate situation than their own.

The second process described by Oliver entails a distinction between the negative mood itself (grief, anger, loneliness) and what she calls a "meta-mood," that is, one's feelings about the feelings. Oliver argues that meta-moods may be positive even though the feelings that generate them are negative. In other words, we may be sad yet feel good about it in some way or justified in it. Indeed, she says, people can even feel bad about a good mood—a teen, for instance, may be highly aroused sexually or feel deeply attracted to someone, yet feel out of control and afraid of the powerful emotions. It seems plausible, then, that under some circumstances the affective rewards of music listening lie in the meta-moods it produces. Sad, angry, or depressed popular songs, in other words, may make sad, angry, depressed moods seem normal or justified. Not only is it all right to feel this way, but this is the right way to feel.

This said, two caveats are in order. First, as far as we know, neither downward social comparison nor the action of meta-moods has been studied empirically in the context of popular music and adolescence. We suggest them only as plausible (and partial) explanations for the practice of matching negative feelings with negative music. Second, it is important to distinguish between the motivations for music listening and the actual effects of listening. Teens may find it somehow rewarding and validating to wallow in their misery through music, and they may feel the music has helped them "deal with" or make sense of their negative emotions. Nevertheless, the net emotional effects of the experience may remain negative. Few people, we suspect, would say it is a good thing to deepen an adolescent's anger or depression, even if the adolescent somehow feels good about feeling bad.

THE SOCIAL USES AND SIGNIFICANCE OF POPULAR MUSIC

We have referred to the social or subcultural meanings of music—its importance as an aid to peer group interactions, its use in establishing group identity, and so on. Some scholars contend that, important as certain personal affective gratifications are, these social aspects of popular music provide the real key to understanding its niche in the lives of youth (Frith, 1981; Lull, 1987; Roe, 1984, 1985). For instance, Roe (1985) refers to popular music as "essentially a group phenomenon" (p. 355). Indeed, even though most listening is solitary, many of music's functions are "social" in the broad sense that they relate to adolescents' relationships with each other and with the culture at large.

Of course, some uses are literally social in that they take place in the company of others. As our partial inventory of music uses indicates (see Table 3.4, p. 42), music is used to form friendships, to provide atmosphere for parties, to make conversations and interactions flow more smoothly, and to serve as grist for the conversation mill. Even these functions, though, may be served by solitary listening (as, for instance, when one listens alone to acquire music expertise to be trotted out in later conversations) and may deliver affective as well as social gratifications. The distinctions we have introduced, then, are far from airtight. Solitary listening may be partly or mostly social in some sense or degree, and listening with others may be at once a form of personal mood management as well as a mechanism for encouraging social interaction.

For this discussion, we suggest three divisions within the broad category of "social uses":

- "quasi-social" uses, by which we mean uses of music listening that usually do not occur in the company of others, but that nevertheless serve goals and needs that surround or influence social relationships
- "socializing" uses, which occur in dyadic or group contexts such as dates and parties
- "cultural" uses, which establish and maintain the cultural boundaries between youth and adult culture and between various adolescent crowds and subcultures.

Quasi-social uses. The best evidence of popular music's association with adolescent social relationships is the strong connection between interest in popular music and peer orientation. In a fundamental sense, those who are concerned with "the group" are also more oriented toward popular music. This connection between the self and others may be felt even during solitary listening. Perhaps the key manifestation of the social dimension of solitary listening occurs in the form of replacing or invoking the presence of absent peers. Teens frequently report listening to music in order to relieve feelings of loneliness. For instance, Gantz et al. (1978) reported that two thirds of their college respondents said they listened either "somewhat" or "very frequently" to "make me feel less alone when I'm by myself." This study and others also suggest that the use of music to relieve loneliness—that is, to provide the sense of company when one is alone—is significantly more common for girls than for boys (Larson et al., 1989; Roe, 1984).

As we have noted, at the extreme music may provide a basis for what media theorists often refer to as "parasocial" or imaginary personal relationships with music stars. This, too, appears to be more common among females, although it is hardly rare among males. Simon Frith (1981) has linked girls' greater interest in romantic lyrics with their greater tendency to idolize and fantasize about opposite-sex stars. For many of the British girls he interviewed, the phenomenon often assumed the form of a bittersweet, confidential romantic (and sexual) relationship with the "ideal boy next door." Boys are more likely to engage in another form of parasocial fantasy, imagining themselves on stage sharing the glory with their favorite rock groups (Arnett, 1991a). Solitary listening may evoke the presence of peers even when one is not feeling particularly lonely. Although we find no quantitative estimates of its frequency, anecdotal and qualitative references abound as to popular music's singular ability to stimulate reminiscences and evoke vivid memories of past loves, friendships and social occasions (Lull, 1992).

Solitary music listening may also perform a number of "delayed" social uses (Lull, 1987) by preparing adolescents for future peer interactions and relationships. Involvement and expertise in music are a crucial basis for relationships with peers. In many instances, those who know nothing about a group's favorite music or about the latest music trends are simply excluded from conversations. Often a shared interest in a certain type of music is both the spark that begins a friendship and the adhesive that binds it over time (Frith, 1981; Lull, 1992). Although most adolescents would find it ludicrous to judge a potential friend on the basis of his or her favorite TV show, agreement about music is widely considered to be a condition for friendship or clique membership. This connection between group membership and pop music orientation extends to seeking information about music. Those with more friends are more likely to report that they listen to radio in order to keep up with the latest music trends (Dominick, 1974), and the amount of time adolescents spend reading pop music magazines is strongly related to the number of friends they have who share their taste in music, suggesting that teens seek information about music as much to impress friends with their expertise as to satisfy their personal curiosity about favorite musicians (Clarke, 1973).

One of the earliest and most instructive examinations of the relationship between popular music and the teen social structure is Roger Brown and Michael O'Leary's (1971) study of British secondary school students. Brown and O'Leary found several interesting connections between involvement in popular music and aspects of the school experience. Their primary conclusion—and this should surprise nobody today—was that popular music occupied a central place in the adolescent social system. They found, for instance, that students with higher levels of integration into teen pop culture (defined as a combination of music knowledge, record buying, and radio listening time) had more friends than did those who were less involved in pop culture. In addition, students with reputations as pop music experts were judged by their peers as higher in both popularity and leadership.

The importance of music knowledge in peer acceptance was further emphasized by the considerable weight students gave music expertise relative to other sources of prestige. When asked what dimensions they found most crucial in judging their schoolmates' status, over half said music knowledge was an important factor. Only school performance and clothing were ranked higher: Knowledge of TV shows, number of friends, and the kind of house one lived in were all less important than music expertise. In general, then, the choice of popular music over other cultural forms correlated with higher social status in the school (see also Adoni, 1978, on this connection).

However, by a different criterion, pop music involvement seemed to indicate *lower* status. Brown and O'Leary (1971) reported that high levels of involvement in pop music were negatively correlated with standard measures of academic success. In both the middle and lower classes, students with higher reputations for pop music knowledge were lower achievers. Similarly, those who listened to more music and bought more records received lower teacher assessments. Because these patterns held without regard to social class, Brown and O'Leary concluded that "involvement in the teen culture is more a function of where youngsters are headed in the social structure than where they have come from in terms of parental status" (p. 411). Finally, they argued that pop music involvement and academic achievement seemed, to a certain extent at least, to be conflicting pursuits. Of all groups in the study, middle-class low academic achievers were the most involved with music, suggesting that for them music expertise served as a sort of "Plan B" in the search for social standing in school.

Socializing uses. When adolescents congregate on their own terms, popular music frequently functions as an integral part of the occasion. Moreover, given their general preference for the company of peers and the fact that music tends to elevate their mood when with peers (Larson et al., 1989), it is reasonable to say that most adolescents are happiest when pop music is part of the scene. Whether in dyads involving romance or sex, small groups gathered for a party, or the larger social gatherings at concerts or clubs, music makes three essential contributions to social occasions: (a) it sets the proper mood for the gathering; (b) it facilitates interpersonal interactions; and (c) it fills the silence when nobody is talking. Perhaps the best testimony to the importance of music in socializing is the impossibility of envisioning a party, of any size, without a sound system of some kind to provide the appropriate environmental backdrop. When teens or college students organize a party, the appropriate music is as crucial as the appropriate (or inappropriate) beverages.

James Lull (1987) points out that the "socializing" uses of popular music occur at several levels of interaction and in a variety of contexts. In male–female dyads, music is used to accompany dancing, courtship, and sexual behavior. In friendship dyads, music often provides a basis for the initial bond and often helps maintain the friendship. In larger gatherings, such as parties, dances, or clubs, music reduces inhibitions, attracts attention and approval, provides topics for conversation, and of course enables dancing. Popular music is even incorporated into situations in which adolescents gather to work or work out. Whenever teens mount a "free" fundraising car wash, the boombox is there doing its work along with the students. High-energy music propels participants through aerobics classes and weight-lifting sessions. When kids gather together to work on school projects or for "homework parties," music, for better or worse, is there in the background.

Of course, adolescents differ in the extent to which they incorporate popular music into social interactions. Obviously, teens who are not particularly interested in music or who affiliate more with parents and other adult figures rarely build their social occasions around pop music. Females exhibit socializing uses more frequently than males (Carroll et al., 1993; Gantz et al., 1978), and on average females report more interest in dancing, although males are just as likely to be true dance club zealots (Roe, 1985; Wells, 1990). Racial differences also exist. African-American youth, for example, are not only more involved with music generally than Whites, but they are more involved in dancing and more likely to view the ability to dance well as an important personal trait (Kuwahara, 1992; Lull, 1992).

The use of music in social contexts also varies according to music taste and subcultural membership. Two University of Houston researchers conducted an ethnographic study of audience behavior at a Houston area nightclub and found quite different styles of participation depending on the type of crowd drawn on different nights (Kotarba & Wells, 1987). The male-dominated heavy metal crowd tended not to socialize across genders as much as other groups of clientele did. Most of their communicative behavior was directed to other male fans—ritualized handshakes of solidarity, for example—or to nobody in particular, as in their unison salute to the stage with arms outstretched and pinkie and index finger extended from the fist. Very little "traditional" boy–girl dancing occurred. Rather, these "metalheads" tended to crush into a pulsating throng in front of the stage as their comrades engaged in "stage diving" (climbing on stage and then taking running swan dives into the audience) and "head-banging," that is, crashing their foreheads against the stage in time with the music. (Metal and punk crowds also "mosh" or "slam-dance" at clubs and concerts. In slam-dancing a group of individuals near the stage hurl themselves into one another at full running speed—not infrequently with at least minor injury.)

This style of club behavior contrasted sharply with groups that frequented the club on other nights. The crowd referred to as "yuppies" or "preppies" were not only attracted to a different type of music (Top 40) than the metal fans, but they dressed more traditionally (fewer tatoos, more Calvin Klein apparel) and exhibited different patterns of social behavior. They engaged in more verbal interpersonal communication in general and much more male–female communication than the heavy metal crowd. They were also more likely to laugh, hug, kiss, and smile. Dancing in this crowd invariably took the standard one-male-with-one-female form. For the preppies, in other words, socializing was the foreground activity and the music the background or context for it. The music played a much more pivotal role in the club experience of the heavy metal clientele.

Cultural uses. Music also works at a more diffuse level to define the important subgroups or "crowds" in adolescent culture and to identify who belongs to them. Although it is far from the only cue about group membership—academic achievement, extracurricular interests, social background, clothing, and other elements of personal style figure in too—an adolescent's music affiliation says much about his or her social affiliation. Popular music at once expresses, creates, and perpetuates the essential "us–them" distinctions that develop between groups, and not just symbolically. Whether played by groups in public places or by individual teens in upstairs bedrooms, music stakes a powerful territorial claim. Indeed, it may be the most highly charged "No Trespassing" sign in adolescent society.

The most basic us–them distinction is between youth and adults, and we have already remarked on the connection between involvement in popular music and the quest for independence from parental authority. Some scholars have argued that music's essential significance and usefulness to youth rests in its power to express opposition to the authority of parents and the adult mainstream culture. Lull wrote: "Generally, young people use music to resist authority at all levels, assert their personalities and learn about things that their parents and the schools aren't telling them" (p. 153). Lawrence Grossberg (1984, 1987) has made an even stronger assertion of this ideological function. He contends that the basic "work" of popular music is to provide a mechanism for the formation of what he calls "affective alliances," the fundamental one being the alliance of adolescents against the straight, boring, adult world. According to Grossberg, rock music embodies for many youth a deeply felt sense of rebellion against the discipline and expectations of parents, school and work. Music stands for the alternative: freedom from the restraints of authority and the right to seek pleasure in one's own way and in the moment.

Writers such as Grossberg and Lull also note music's importance in the formation and perpetuation of subcultures within the broader youth culture. Every U.S. or Canadian high school is divided into subgroups, and many are identified with a specific type of music. For those who are unsuccessful in school or alienated from the mainstream (e.g., racial and ethnic minorities), music allegiance is much more than one cultural marker among many—it is a primary means for expressing solidarity, pride, and defiance. Thus it makes sense to speak of alternative, punk, rap, heavy metal, or reggae subcultures because for these groups music may form the central pillar of group identity. The use of music to express subgroup resistance to the mainstream is not limited to the high school setting. Kuwahara (1992) finds that rap music provides Black students in predominantly White universities an important focus of resistance against the dominant authorities and cultural values of the university. To these students and others who either cannot or choose not to fit into the mainstream, music represents a sense of power and insurgence.

Despite these examples, however, there is reason to question the centrality of music's role in the teen-versus-parent power struggle and the pervasiveness of its oppositional uses outside certain music-centered sub-cultures. If, as suggested in Chapter 2, most kids are in fact not in a state of open warfare against their parents, not separated from adult culture by yawning generation gaps, and not on the fringe of adolescent culture—in other words, not rebelling—then it is obvious that popular music cannot be the crux of their rebellion. In other words, although it is certain that some 14-year-old boys crank up their favorite death metal album at least in part to infuriate their parents, we question whether popular music rep-resents for most adolescents *themselves* their alienation from parents, teachers, and other adult cultural authorities. When they are asked direct-ly why they listen to music or why they like a certain musician, song, or genre, relatively few suggest that it is because music cements their affilia-tions with crowds or subcultures or expresses their conflict with authority.

In fact, none of the "uses and gratifications" studies reviewed in this chapter—that is, studies in which a fairly large sample of students have responded to questions on why they listen to music and what they get from the experience—report explicit evidence of these subcultural or oppositional uses. It is possible, of course, that the methods used to elicit the information are too blunt to detect such uses. The self-report instru-ments employed in most uses and gratifications studies have been criti-cized for their insensitivity to any latent or unconscious motivations that may lurk below the surface. Any of us—adults, teens and children alike—may be unaware of certain of our motivations for music listening or unable to express them in words. Still, we would argue that if popular music's oppositional uses pervaded and defined adolescents' relationship with music, such uses should make more than just a cameo appearance in the research, whatever the methodological blind spots. That references to such uses appear as infrequently as they do suggests that most youth use music more for the affective and social ends described earlier in this sec-tion than to express cultural rifts.

Indeed, we believe many teens pursue adult-disapproved person-al styles and music preferences less to offend or distance themselves from adults than to cultivate a public image of rebelliousness and indepen-dence. Even if things at home are running smoothly enough, status is gained by making a show of conflict with parents and the adult world. Thus, for instance, one finds that adolescents report much "tougher," more rebellious music tastes in the presence of their peers than they report individually in private (Finnas, 1989). This tension between respect for parental authority and the need to project an independent public image is nicely illustrated by Kotarba and Wells' (1987) description of young adolescents' arrival at the Houston all-ages club described earlier. Too young to drive, many of these young patrons depended on their parents for transportation. Thus parents were aware of what their children were doing and had permitted it. The kids insisted, however, on being dropped off a full city block away and then walking to the club alone or with their friends. As one said: "It isn't cool to have everyone see your mother driving you to Roma's" (pp. 402-403).

We do not mean to say that popular music lacks a political dimension or that it never performs a consciously oppositional function. These elements are undeniably important for certain groups of youth (e.g., African-Americans), certain types of youth (e.g., those who are in some way "at risk," operating on the social margins, doing poorly in school), and during certain times. The Depression-era protest folk songs of Woody Guthrie, the protest rock of the late 1960s and early 1970s and the rap music of the late 1980s and 1990s represent high water marks in this ebb and flow. Nor do we deny that music can symbolize, publicize, and exacerbate group and individual differences. From Memorial Day picnics in city parks to college dorm rooms on Friday afternoon, popular music is often broadcast by insiders as an anthem and taken by outsiders as a challenge, often leading to serious conflict (Margolis, 1992). For most adolescents, at most times, however, music use is motivated more by personal and social pleasure than by any purposeful attempt to articulate hostility or difference.

THE USES OF POPULAR MUSIC LYRICS

When adolescents talk about why they like to listen to music or why they are attracted to their favorite songs or musicians, lyrics seldom rise to the top of the list of reasons. Typically, it is something about the sound, not the words, that attracts them. Yet lyrics are far from irrelevant. The lyrics and what they seem to say about and to young people are what draw the attention of adults concerned about the social impact of contemporary popular music. When music is attacked or threatened with censorship, it is usually because of the lyrics, not the sound. It could be argued, of course, that the critics are worrying about the wrong thing, that the sound has a greater impact and perhaps poses a greater threat to adult authority than anything in the words (Bloom, 1987). Yet the sound cannot be transcribed, printed, and published in *Time* and *Newsweek*, and perhaps that alone accounts for the seemingly disproportionate share of attention given to lyrics in the public discourse on the impact of popular music. Writing during the heyday of protest rock, Denisoff and Levine (1970) pointed out that although most of the lyrics of the 1960s were apolitical and uncontroversial, the older generation defined the nature of rock and roll, indeed the nature of a generation, in terms of the more salient and controversial political messages in protest rock. "Despite the lack of political sentiment expressed in most rock songs," they wrote, "spokesmen of the older generation see the music as politically and socially subversive" (p. 48). Lull (1992) makes a similar point through the example of Pete Seeger's censored performance on the popular 1960s television show "The Smothers Brothers Comedy Hour." Seeger's folk music was anything but radical in its sound; it was his left-leaning lyrics that made the network censors sweat. So it is today—irritating as many adult critics find the sound of rap and heavy metal, it is the words that they catalogue and lament, that magazines and newspapers quote to illustrate popular music's latest disturbing turn, and that ultimately frame the public debate about popular music's social impact.

Lyrics also matter to kids. For one thing, if they did not, instrumental songs would be something more than an aberration on the *Billboard* charts. Indeed, it is most unusual to find even a single instrumental song or album in the top 100. Aside from the occasional breakthroughs by jazz pop artists like Kenny G or holiday music by Mannheim Steamroller, popular music comes with words. Even though the sound has primacy, lyrics obviously provide a crucial ingredient in the listening experience. Moreover, lyrics as sung, as interpreted by the singer, are not just spoken language, but part of the sound. No less than the electric guitar and the snare drum, the human voice is an instrument and performs melodic and percussive as well as discursive functions. Lyrics form part of the total musical gestalt that provides the emotional and social rewards discussed earlier.

Lyrics also play a cognitive role. They are attended to as language—interpreted for meaning, processed, discussed, memorized, even acted on. Moreover, although the research tends to show the primacy of affective gratifications for most teens, lyrics are mentioned as a primary gratification by a significant minority and a secondary gratification by most (Gantz et al., 1978; Roe, 1985). Even Rosenbaum and Prinsky (1987; Prinsky & Rosenbaum, 1987), whose work has been widely interpreted in the press as evidence of the irrelevance of lyrics, report that 17% of male adolescents (12 to 18 years old) and nearly 25% of females said they liked their favorite song because "the words express how I feel" (p. 85). In fact, this gratification was cited more often by the respondents than passing time or creating social atmosphere. For better or worse, considerable numbers of adolescents say they turn to popular music for guidelines on moral issues and social interaction, at least according to an interview study of Cleveland area high school students (Rouner, 1990). Students in the survey were asked to rank music against several other possible sources of moral and social guidance, including parents, teachers, friends, church leaders, and co-workers. They were also allowed to write in other sources not listed. Sixteen percent ranked music in the top three sources of moral guidance, and 24% placed music in the top three for information on social interaction.

To sum up, although lyrics are seldom the primary reason an adolescent chooses to listen or the primary criterion by which teens choose favorite genres, artists, or songs, they form an important element in the enjoyment of music and may become extremely important for certain youth, at certain times, and in certain circumstances. Nearly everybody has a special song or artist whose messages seem particularly relevant to a relationship, a mood, or a life experience, and listeners remember and dwell on these key lyrics (Lull, 1992). Most of the time these special songs are not high poetry about abstract social issues, but plain language about the concrete and everyday things that happen to young people. In his 1987 essay, "Why Do Songs Have Words?," Frith claims that much of what he calls the "pleasure of pop" comes from listeners' personal connections with these mundane themes. His comments about the uses of "silly love songs" are especially relevant here. According to Frith, even the most hackneyed and uninspired rock love "poetry" provides a source of imagery and language from which listeners can draw in their daily lives. In his words, they give music listeners "the romantic terms in which to articulate and so experience their emotions" (p. 102). Frith's argument receives empirical support from Rosenbaum and Prinsky (1987), who found that whenever adolescents said they liked a song primarily because of the lyrics, the song in question was invariably a love song, and usually one about a relationship just ended. Quite likely, the words from the "silly love song" helped them make sense of a difficult time.

The importance of lyrics varies from one era to another—the words were probably more salient in the 1960s and early 1970s than during the 1980s—and from one group of adolescents to another. Frith (1981) found in Britain that college-bound, middle-class rock fans took the words of their favorite music considerably more seriously than did working-class youth. Today's heavy metal fans are also deeply involved with the messages in the lyrics, which, according to one author, resonate with the "dismal condition of the world as they (see) it" (Arnett, 1991, p. 93).

For avid African-American rap fans, the lyrics provide the most important gratification, more important even than the beat and dancing (Kuwahara, 1992). Two general patterns seem to emerge from these and other studies. First, the more important music is to an adolescent, the more importance he or she places on lyric messages relative to other music gratifications (Reid, 1993). Second, attention to lyrics is highest among fans of oppositional or controversial music, whether it be 1960s protest rock or the heavy metal, rap, or alternative music of today. The more defiant, alienated, and threatening to the mainstream a music type is, the more attention its audience pays to the words.

MUSIC VIDEO USES

As reported above, watching music videos is for most adolescents an occasional diversion rather than a constant obsession, suggesting that the fears often expressed concerning the impact of music videos' powerful imagery may be exaggerated. Although we believe this conclusion to be essentially sound, it is countered somewhat by other factors. The most obvious consideration, of course, is the presence of visual information. The visual images and narratives of MTV clearly have more potential to form attitudes, values, or perceptions of social reality than does the music alone. Second, even though less time is spent watching music videos than listening to music, the fact that the time is spent watching and not merely listening means music video viewing is more likely a foreground than a background activity. If eyes are directed to a screen, less attention can be given to accompanying activities such as reading, studying, working, or socializing. Finally, we should not forget that averages conceal ranges— that is, although adolescents average less than 30 minutes a day viewing music videos, every survey reveals a segment of perhaps 5% to 15% who watch them several hours a day. These highly absorbed viewers obviously stand a much greater chance of being influenced.

A reasonable place to begin a discussion of music video uses is with the question: What matters most to the audience, the music on which the videos are based or the visual element added to the mix? Some writers and commentators reason from the energy and intensity of the visual element that the pictures matter most. Kinder (1984) has claimed that because music videos' uniqueness is based on its pulsing, discontinuous, dreamlike visual images, these images must be the "primary source of pleasure." Tetzlaff (1986) has stated quite firmly: "For the MTV viewer, the music is dominated by the visuals. The sound is familiar, mundane, repressed by the lo-fi speaker; the picture is novel, fast and loud" (p. 87).

In the end, it may not be possible to sort out whether the video viewing experience is better characterized as "TV plus music," as Kinder (1986) and Tetzlaff (1986) seem to suggest, or "radio plus pictures." It is interesting to note, though, the extent to which adolescents' self-reports of what they like about MTV place the music, rather than the pictures, in the foreground of the music video experience. Consider two studies in which students were asked what they liked about watching music videos. Table 3.5 shows some of the results of Sun and Lull's (1986) survey of approximately 500 San Jose, California, high school students and Christenson's (1992a) interviews with 100 fourth through sixth graders in Portland, Oregon. Both studies employed an open-ended format, although it should be noted they posed a somewhat different question— Christenson asked kids why they liked to watch or what they enjoyed about watching; Sun and Lull asked students to write down their reasons for viewing. We believe, however, that for most children and adolescents (indeed, probably for adults as well) the questions suggest the same task.

Both reports show the "music" in music video to be a central aspect of enjoyment. The "music itself" was the most frequently mentioned gratification in Christenson's study, whereas "music appreciation" took the top spot in Sun and Lull's results. Moreover, when visuals were mentioned, many students relegated them to an ancillary role; that is, visual images were appreciated because they shed light on a song's meaning. To be sure, other motivations and gratifications emerge—pure visual stimulation among them. In the Christenson study, for instance, visual stimulation (action, visual effects, animation) was mentioned nearly as often as musical enjoyment. (Because Sun and Lull combined visual stimulation and song interpretation into one category, their results do not allow visual stimulation to be separated out from other gratifications.) The two studies agree on the relative unimportance, at least at the conscious level, of motivations or gratifications relating to information or social learning. Adolescents do not seek guidance from MTV, except perhaps guidance about music itself.

As with music listening, studies of music video uses that employ predetermined lists of options in a closed-ended format point to a broader range of uses and gratifications than is usually indicated by open-ended responses. Brown and her colleagues (1986) presented adolescents with 19 separate reasons for watching music videos. The students used a 3-point scale (from "a lot" to "not at all") to indicate how much each reason

Table 3.5. Music Video Motivations and Gratifications.

4th-6th Graders (From Christenson, 1992b)

Question asked: What do you like about watching music videos?	% Who Mentioned[a]
The music itself: either sound or lyrics	36
Visual elements or visual stimulation	35
Interpretation of the meaning of lyrics	30
General terms used to describe entertainment ("They're funny," "neat,"...)	20
Audio-video combination	8
Miscellaneous other responses	17

9th-12th Graders (From Sun & Lull, 1986)

Question asked: Why do you watch music videos?	% Who Mentioned[a]
Music appreciation (the singer, song, concert)	23
General enjoyment/entertainment	19
Visual appreciation (including interpretation of lyrics & visual stimulation)	16
Pass time/habit	14
Information (mostly about music, concerts)	11
Emotional response	7
Social learning (learning from theme of video, fashion, to imitate musician)	5
Other (escape, conversation topic, ...)	6

[a]Percentages sum to more than 100% because students were allowed to give multiple responses.
Adapted by permission from "Preadolescent perceptions and interpretations of music videos," by P. Christenson, 1992b, *Popular Music and Society*, *16*(3), p. 67. © 1992; and from "The adolescent audience for music videos and why they watch," by S. Sun and J. Lull, 1986, *Journal of Communication*, *36*(1), p. 120. © 1986.

applied to them. The original 19 were reduced through factor analysis to this list, in descending order of importance:

- Diversion (they're exciting, good thing to do when alone, mood control)

- Attention to lyrics (think about the meaning of songs)
- Trend surveillance (learn to dance, see new fashions)
- Format preference (better than radio, TV)
- Social stimulus (something to do with friends, fill silence)
- Allow me to daydream (single item)
- Make me wish I were like some of the characters (single item)
- School of life (remind me of things happening in my own life, help me learn things about myself). (p. 25)

These results suggest that personal diversion and interpretation of song lyrics play a more important role than do social uses. They also confirm the unimportance of information or guidance motivations; as in other research (Christenson, 1992b; Hartman & Tucker, 1987; Sun & Lull, 1986), relatively few kids indicated that they turned to music videos for information about the world or how they should behave in it. The exception to this rule came in an area the authors call "trend surveillance." Almost 40% said they watched "a lot" in order to learn dance moves, and just over 25% watched "a lot" to learn about the latest fashions. In other words, when adolescents do seek information from music videos, the information has more to do with the details of fashion and courtship behavior than moral values, general knowledge about the world, or the conduct of social relationships.

Perhaps the most interesting contribution of the Brown et al. (1986) study is its analysis of some rather striking racial and gender differences. Blacks and females, compared to Whites and males, reported much higher levels of identification with the items included under trend surveillance and attention to lyrics. Black students, in fact, were almost twice as likely as Whites to say they watched music videos "a lot" for dancing and fashion information. Blacks were also more likely than Whites to use music as a stimulant in social occasions, to wish they were like characters in videos, and to use videos as a "school of life." Other research reports that females are more likely than males to watch music videos to relieve feelings of loneliness (Hartman & Tucker, 1987). These results, along with many others we have cited, point once again to the importance of race and gender in popular music. When there are differences, Blacks and females are more involved, both in terms of time and emotional investment, than Whites and males. Black females are the most involved of all.

THE ALLURE (?) OF SEX AND VIOLENCE

Given the abundance of sexual and violent imagery in music videos, many assume these elements form a major part of the genre's allure for young people. The research on responses to violent imagery does not suggest such an attraction. If anything, the presence of violence may be a turn-off. Hansen and Hansen (1990a) showed college students a set of videos with varying levels of sex and violence and found that higher levels of violence not only produced more negative responses to the video and song, but stimulated a host of intense negative emotions. As violence went up, students said they felt less happy, more fearful, and more anxious and aggressive. The negative effects of high levels of violence led the authors to pose the question: "If media depictions of violence have the potential to produce antisocial consequences and the viewer, in fact, does not enjoy it, why is there violence in rock videos at all?" (p. 233). To be sure, the effects of violence may not be quite as clear as the Hansens indicate. A similar study using college students found no significant effect of either violence or a violence-and-sex combination on evaluations of music videos (Zillmann & Mundorf, 1987). Even this latter study, however, contradicts the common wisdom that violence sells.

The effects of sexual imagery may depend on age. Christenson (1992a) found that many 10- to 12-year-olds believed that the sexual images and sexually explicit lyrics contained in some music videos were inappropriate for their eyes and ears. He asked kids if there was anything they did not like about music videos or whether there was anything in videos kids like them "shouldn't see." Half agreed there were such elements, and sexual content was by far the most frequently cited category of taboo material. (Some even said they were offended by the "nudity" in MTV, which in fact does not exist.) One suspects such misgivings are considerably less common among high school and college students. Indeed, by college the presence of sexual imagery appears to exert a strong attraction. Hansen and Hansen (1990a) found that videos with higher levels of sexual imagery not only received higher evaluations in terms of visual and musical appeal, but produced more positive mood states among viewers. Zillmann and Mundorf (1987) also reported increased appreciation of music videos with the addition of sexual imagery.

Interesting as these findings are, more research is necessary before the impact of sex and violence can be stated with precision. No doubt it depends on the type of sex or violence in question. Consensual sex will likely evoke a much different response than forced sex; explicit sex will produce different responses than implied sex; graphic depictions of violence will likely be more troubling for most kids than the sort of stylized, choreographed conflict displayed in many videos. Reactions to sex and violence also depend on audience differences. We have mentioned the importance of age as a complicating factor. Greeson (1991) reported different reactions to sexually explicit videos based not only on age (college students liked them less than high school) but also on social class (working-class kids liked them more than kids from a university town), church attendance (regular church-goers liked them less), and gender (males liked them more). Toney and Weaver (1994) also found that gender mediated reactions to soft and hard rock videos. Males expressed higher levels of enjoyment for hard rock videos and were less likely to be offended or disturbed by them. Females enjoyed the soft rock videos much more than did the males.

Finally, responses to violence and sex depend on individual attitudes and values. Bleich and her colleagues (Bleich, Zillmann & Weaver, 1991) reasoned that rebellious adolescents—those who defy being controlled by parents and other adult authorities and who tend to break the rules whenever they can—might be particularly attracted to rebellious, defiant, hard rock videos. They measured individual levels of rebelliousness in a sample of junior and senior high school students, then showed them two sets of music videos: three "defiant" videos (e.g., "Smokin' in the Boys' Room" by Motley Crue) and three "nondefiant" videos (e.g., John Fogarty's "Old Man Down the Road"). Contrary to the original hypothesis, rebellious adolescents did not respond more positively to the defiant videos than did nonrebellious students. On the other hand, rebellious kids gave quite different responses to the nondefiant videos, which they rejected quite strongly. We question, however, whether the "defiant" videos employed in this study provided a good test of the original hypothesis. Defiant though the videos may have been from the adult perspective, most students would see Twisted Sister, Motley Crue, and Aha (the three groups in the defiant category) as being closer to the musical mainstream than the defiant or rebellious fringe. In fact, even the nonrebellious students expressed a slight preference for the videos in the defiant category over the nondefiant ones. The study does, however, demonstrate that rebelliousness plays a role in forming reactions to softer edged and traditional music videos.

Solid evidence also exists that adolescents' sexual attitudes and values relate to their interest in music videos. A team of researchers from Central Michigan University (Strouse, Buerkel-Rothfuss, & Long, 1995) examined the relationship between sexual permissiveness and MTV use among 200 13- to 18-year-olds. In general, those with more permissive attitudes toward premarital sex spent more time watching MTV than those with less permissive attitudes. Interestingly, the relationship was much stronger for females than for males. The authors explain this difference by reference to research showing females' sexual behavior and attitudes to be more readily influenced by external social influences like MTV than that of males, who tend to be more governed by biological factors. Thus, assuming the correlation indicates MTV is influencing sexual attitudes (a big assumption indeed, as we discuss in Chapter 7), Strouse et al. argue that it should be stronger for females since they are more susceptible to influence. Strouse and her colleagues found that the relationship between permissiveness and MTV exposure also depended on family relationships. Among those reporting low satisfaction with their family life, MTV viewing correlated strongly with approval of premarital sex. Among those with positive family relationships, however, the amount of MTV viewing was essentially unrelated to permissiveness. Here the authors suggest, again based on the problematic assumption that MTV exposure is actually producing changes in sexual attitudes, that something about close family relationships helps to insulate adolescents from the impact. We should warn, however, that although these findings may be intriguing, a correlation between sexual permissiveness and MTV viewing might easily be produced by processes other than the influence of music video exposure. It is at least as likely, for instance, that the correlation indicates the operation of selective exposure; that is, permissive kids might simply be more attracted to MTV.

Keeping all the complicating factors in mind, we close with a few generalizations. First, it is clear that most adolescents take music videos far less seriously than do either the music industry or its critics. Music video viewing commands much less time than either music listening or television viewing, and the time expenditure seems motivated less by a quest for deep involvement than a need for transitory, light diversion. For most adolescents, MTV is just a way station in the process of remote control cable grazing. One can get a sense of where video viewing fits in the ecology of adolescent media use by observing what other types of media consumption correlate with it. Walker (1987) reported a negative relationship between the amount of time adolescents spend watching MTV and their exposure to television and motion picture violence, a finding that makes sense in the context of the studies of audience responses to music video violence discussed earlier in this section. However, Walker also found that higher levels of music video viewing went along with a heightened interest in romantic and comedy content in television and movies. The association with romantic themes makes sense, of course, given the information music and music videos provide on the subject of boy–girl relationships. The association with comedy viewing, we believe, underscores music video's role as light diversion. None of this precludes an influence on youth culture, or even the possibility that some youth are influenced in the ways many adults fear when they see the brash imagery of MTV. One thing is clear, though: music, not music videos, is the heavy equipment for adolescent living.

4

FRAGMENTED ROCK:
MUSIC PREFERENCES AND ALLEGIANCES

When you're growing up, you like rock and roll for one reason:
Because your parents don't.
—Jerry Kramer, Music Video Producer (1985)

In our experience, adults who maintain little or no contact with youth
culture or who, like most parents and teachers, contact it from the outside,
see all popular music as pretty much the same. If distinctions are made at
all, they are typically between "rock" and the two most visible and controversial current pop music genres, heavy metal and rap. Even this crude
differentiation is usually based not on any real exposure to the music but
on *Time* and *Newsweek* articles about dirty lyrics. A close look at youth
culture, however, reveals an astonishing variety of music genres and subgenres. Consider these trends:

- In 1950, radio formats did not exist as we know them now. Most
  radio stations broadcast a similar mix of music, drama, and comedy without specializing or targeting different audience segments. Today it is not difficult to find radio markets with as
  many as 30 different formats, most of them music, each very spe-
  cialized and aimed at a narrowly defined demographic segment.

- Just before rock and roll emerged in the early 1950s, *Billboard* magazine reported separate charts for only three categories of music: "Popular Albums," which included everything from the Mills Brothers' "Glow Worm" to the music from "South Pacific"; "Country and Hillbilly" (Tennessee Ernie Ford, Tex Ritter, Hank Thompson); and "Children's Albums" ("I Taut I Taw a Puddy Tat," "Bozo Has a Party," etc.). Now *Billboard* reports over 20 different charts, including the Billboard 200, Modern Rock (Alternative), Mainstream Rock, World Music, Gospel, Blues, Album Rock, Adult Contemporary, Dance/Club, Rap, R&B, Latin, Jazz, Country, and Classical.
- The annual Grammy Awards recognize more than 80 different categories, many representing distinct music genres, including all those just mentioned as well as World Beat, Heavy Metal, New Age, Latin Pop, Tropical Latin, Latin Jazz, Mexican-American, and Reggae.

The distinctions between radio formats and music types recognized by the industry by no means exhaust the divisions drawn in contemporary youth culture. A sense of the boggling fragmentation—or diversity, as the recording industry prefers to call it—is provided in a survey of college students' music preferences conducted by Peter Christenson and Jon Peterson (1988). The research on popular music tastes, they note, often ignores important variations by asking students to respond to only four or five music types. For instance, in one study college students were asked to rate these five categories: pop/rock, hard rock/rhythm and blues, classical, folk, and jazz (Skipper, 1973). The last three of these are essentially irrelevant to most adolescents—that is, although classical, folk, and jazz are not particularly disliked, they are seldom mentioned as favorites. The first two categories obviously have something to do with youth culture, but are badly in need of differentiation. Even in 1973, asking college freshmen how much they liked "rock/pop" or "hard rock/rhythm and blues" made about as much sense as asking how much they liked "steak/oysters."

After consulting students, music publications, and radio station music directors, Christenson and Peterson (1988) developed a list of 26 music categories, most of them different varieties of what many adults might define simply as "rock music." A sample of college students responded to each of these music types on a 5-point scale ranging from "love it" to "hate it." From most popular to least, the genres were mainstream pop, 1980s, 1970s, and 1960s rock, contemporary rhythm and blues, older new wave, Motown, 1950s rock, art rock, jazz, Southern rock, classical, reggae, psychedelic rock, soul, jazz fusion, folk, post-new wave, blues, 1970s funk, country pop, 1970s disco, heavy metal, Christian rock, hardcore punk, and Black gospel.

Protracted as this list may seem and obscure as some of its entries might appear to outsiders, only five of the categories were familiar to less than 80% of the students surveyed, and most were recognized by over 95%. Moreover, as the authors admit, their list could easily have been expanded. Any such list, no matter how inclusive, must be constantly updated. The most obvious omission from Christenson and Peterson's study was rap music, which in 1984 (the year the data were gathered) had yet to break onto the major music charts. Today, of course, rap is universally recognized and quite popular, even among middle-class White youth. A current inventory might include, in addition to rap and the 26 types used by Christenson and Peterson, these pop music styles: Top 40, contemporary hits, easy listening, album rock, soft rock, hard rock, classic rock, grunge, golden oldies, alternative, New Age, World Beat, progressive rock, protest rock, industrial rock, salsa, house, hip hop, ska, high life, technopop, synthpop, college rock, alternative, death metal, thrash punk, and a number of others. A colleague from West Virginia even suggested to us that no list of important popular music can pretend to be complete without including "hillbilly music."

Of course, not all youth are rabidly attached to a specific kind of music; like other dimensions of adolescent experience, the strength of music identity exhibits a wide range. Music taste and preference are a virtual obsession to some adolescents and a matter of considerable interest to most, but there are those to whom popular music and its distinctions are of little concern. Furthermore, long lists of popular music genres and subgenres probably exaggerate the number of distinctions and differences that really matter in adolescent culture. Some of the terms we have listed are essentially different words for the same thing—mainstream and Top 40, for instance—whereas others would be recognized by only a small number of adolescent pop music "experts."

Even with these qualifications, the diversity of music and the selectivity of music taste should be kept in mind for two reasons. First, assuming for the moment that music listening has some impact on adolescents, this impact will depend on the specific symbolic environment in which they immerse themselves. Different types of music are associated not just with a certain sound but also with a certain sorts of messages and philosophies. Three hours a day of death metal is a different thing than three hours a day of soft rock ballads, and the effects of the two ought to be different. Second, distinctions in music preference matter because of their linkage with individual and group identity: They tell us something about who adolescents think they are and how they function in their society. A kid whose tastes run to rap artists such as Coolio or Puff Daddy probably thinks of himself in different terms and associates with a different peer group than one who prefers the pop sound of Mariah Carey or Janet Jackson.

REDUCING THE CLUTTER

Although there may be 25, 40, or 100 genres of popular music that are meaningfully different in some way to someone, it is possible to simplify the array somewhat. As we have noted, some music "types" are really the same thing by a different name, and others do not really figure very much into teen culture. The density of the music map depends on age—a fourth or fifth grader may use only three or four categories, a high schooler a few more, whereas a college student may impose an even more elaborate classification scheme—but at any age certain music types or styles are chosen more often than others. In the industry as well as in adolescent conversation, terms like *pop, Top 40, rock, classic rock* (usually meaning rock of the 1960s and 1970s), *hard rock, heavy metal, alternative, rap,* and *R&B* (rhythm and blues) are used much more frequently than *thrash punk* or *ska*.

The complexity can also be reduced by looking for clusters or groupings among the various music tastes and styles. From the listener's standpoint, some types seem to "go together" (one suspects, for instance, that the soul or Motown fan will also tend to like contemporary R&B or 1970s funk) or "go apart" (heavy metal or Grateful Dead fans are quite likely to detest soft pop or disco). Attitudes toward different music types are not isolated from one another, but are structured and organized, grouped psychologically and sociologically into what one might call *metagenres,* that is, constellations of music styles and labels that coalesce in some way. Various principles may be used to form these groups—racial origin, danceability, instrumentation, dominant lyrical themes, and historical roots to name few—and individuals and groups may weigh these factors differently based on how they use music or where their own preferences lie. The research, however, points to some interesting general patterns and principles behind all the apparent diversity.

First, as we noted at the outset of this chapter, the clusters and groupings formed from within youth culture look much different from those constructed by outsiders looking in. A good example of this principle is found in the work of Fink, Robinson, and Dowden (1985), who used a statistical technique known as cluster analysis to reveal the embedded structure in the music tastes of a national general sample of 18,000 adults 18 and over—in other words, a sample composed mostly of youth culture outsiders. The analysis revealed four major groups of music: one including barber shop and sacred music; another combining country and bluegrass; a third incorporating opera, classical, and Broadway musicals; and a fourth that lumped together soul, rock and jazz. Our point is that this is obviously not the way an adolescent would see the terrain. First, the map acknowledges music types (barber shop, Broadway, opera, etc.) that simply do not exist for most adolescents (Smith, 1994). Second, and more important, it forces together genres that are worlds apart from the perspective of youth culture. When soul, rock, and jazz cluster together, as in this research, or punk, soul, rock, and jazz in another study of a general U.S. sample (Deihl, Schneider, & Petress, 1983), it is most likely not 18-year-olds talking, but the majority who are much older. For most adolescents, these forms have next to nothing in common.

The appropriate place to look for the deeper structure of popular music taste is in studies using adolescents as respondents. The empirical research in this area is widely disparate as to historical time frame, research method, and even country of origin, but most of it agrees on one fundamental dichotomy or tension: that between mainstream or Top-40 "pop" music and the harder sounding, more defiant music from the "rock" tradition. British sociologist Simon Frith (1981), who based his conclusions on a series of in-depth interviews with Yorkshire teenagers in 1972, was particularly emphatic on the importance of this distinction: "By 1972, the year I did my research," he wrote, "the rock/pop division seemed absolute, and the division of musical tastes seemed to reflect class differences" (p. 213). Among the teens Frith interviewed, "pop" music ("Bubblegum," "teenie-bop"), exemplified by the likes of Donny Osmond, Susi Quatro, and David Cassidy, was disproportionately a working class, female, and young taste. Unpretentious, often bland and banal "silly love songs with a more or less insistent beat," as Frith described it (p. 212), and usually released as singles rather than in album form, pop music was for dancing at the disco and hanging out on the street corner.

"Rock" music, on the other hand, tended to be preferred by an older group of middle-class males, either in or on their way to college. In its sound, rock music was harsher, louder, more aggressive, and less dance-able, at least for those who used music mostly for dancing. Its lyrics were less likely than pop lyrics to take up romantic themes and more likely to deal with political or personal identity issues. Rock was music for the foreground, not the background. According to Frith (1981): "[When] the Beatles and Bob Dylan met up with Elvis Presley, and rock 'n' roll and teenage pop got mixed up with blues and soul and funk and protest, the resulting records were at once exciting, intriguing, and real, and the audi-ence sat down to listen" (p. 213). Another British study roughly contem-porary with Frith (Murdock & Phelps, 1972) found that the two camps were recognized by fans and foes alike. Rock fans referred pejoratively to mainstream pop as "Bubblegum" or "moron fodder," and pop fans criti-cized rock for being "weird" and "messy," but both groups affirmed the crucial rock-pop distinction.

The rock-pop dichotomy applies in some form well beyond Great Britain in the early 1970s. Roe (1985) surveyed the attitudes of Swedish youth toward 10 kinds of music: country, punk, mainstream pop, reggae, new wave, rock, folk, 1960s protest songs, classical, and jazz. He then applied factor analysis to the data to uncover which types of music elicit-ed similar responses. Roe's analysis pointed to three underlying "factors" or clusters of music genres, one dominated by mainstream pop, another centered around new wave and rock, and a third combining classical, jazz, and folk. Different music labels (punk, new wave) reflected new times, but otherwise the first two categories seemed to carry much the same mean-ing as Frith's rock-pop distinction. The emergence of the third cluster documents a tendency found in various studies for more "serious," non-youth-oriented types of music to form a taste culture or metagenre of their own quite separate from the realm of pop and rock.

Christenson and Peterson (1988) also applied factor analysis to their music preference data obtained from U.S. college students and found that the original list of 26 music types could be boiled down only as far as eight metagenres. In other words, in this sample the underlying structure of music types remained differentiated and complex even after the appli-cation of factor analysis. Reasoning that gender-related differences in music use and preference might produce different underlying taste struc-tures, they then performed separate analyses for males and females. The major factors for males included: Black music (soul, Motown, contempo-rary rhythm and blues, funk, disco), "unhip" music (mainstream pop, folk, country pop), generic (1980s) rock, new wave/punk, American hard rock (including psychedelic rock, heavy metal, Southern rock, and 1970s rock), jazz/blues, classic rock (especially from the 1960s), and Christian music (including Christian pop and Black gospel). The categories for females were: Black music, mainstream pop (including generic 1980s rock), new wave/punk, American hard rock, classic rock, jazz/blues, Christian/country, and heavy metal.

These two lists contain both similarities and differences. Both genders seemed to perceive a cluster of music grounded in the racial origin of the performers, that is, a Black music factor composed of funk, soul, Motown, contemporary R&B, and disco. Both males and females combined into one group various music types of British origin—punk, new wave, and reggae. (For U.S. students, reggae is apparently associated more with its British than its Black origins.) Both groups also recognized the "classic" rock of the 1960s and 1970s, Christian music, and jazz-blues as distinct, coherent music categories. To be sure, males and females did not share the same feelings about the music in these categories—females, for instance, showed considerably more attraction than males to Black music —but they did agree on the basic clusters.

The music groupings also exhibited gender differences. First, although males included heavy metal with other kinds of "American hard rock" (1970s rock, psychedelic rock, Southern rock), females separated the two, placing heavy metal into a category all its own: "Females tend to dislike both the hard rock forms and heavy metal, but apparently for different reasons. For them—and not surprisingly, in view of the treatment of women in heavy metal lyrics and videos—metal stands alone" (Christenson & Peterson, 1988, p. 298).

Another set of music types coalesced around the term "mainstream," but this group also differed by gender. Males, who generally like mainstream pop much less than females and who tend to be much more ego-involved in avoiding the application of the word mainstream to their tastes, placed mainstream pop in the same category as country pop and folk music, neither of which enjoy much status among college or adolescent music listeners. In other words, for the males the mainstream category seemed really to be an "unhip" or "uncool" category, essentially a musical dumping ground. For females, however, "mainstream" seemed to be just another way of saying "current hits"; their mainstream factor, unlike that of the males, included both mainstream pop and 1980s rock, and excluded country pop and folk.

We should note that the number and nature of the groupings derived from cluster analysis or factor analysis depend on methodological considerations such as the length of the original list of choices, the size of the sample, and the nature of the population under study. Different categories will emerge for African-Americans and Whites, high school and college students, Southern and Northern teens. Christenson and Peterson studied Northeastern college students, the majority White, and their results may be limited to this population. Still, their study suggests two general conclusions: First, when the original array of music choices reflects the true diversity of popular music, preferences remain highly differentiated even after the application of statistical techniques designed to boil them down; and second, the underlying structure of music taste varies between genders.

WHERE DO PREFERENCES COME FROM?

An adolescent's music taste depends on a number of different influences. Peers, siblings, the mass media, personal experience, and personality characteristics all play a role in the formation of music preference. Physiological or genetic predispositions may even be involved. One study of college students, for instance, showed that those possessing a global need for arousal and new experiences—so-called "sensation-seekers"— were more attracted to high-energy rock music and less attracted to blander sound-track music than non-sensation-seekers (Litle & Zuckerman, 1986). One thing we know for certain: Differences in music preference are not random or idiosyncratic, but are shaped by social background and other environmental influences.

Indeed, one can predict music preference with some accuracy based on a mere handful of demographic and background variables. A 14-year-old, inner-city, Black male is almost certain to like rap and just as certain to detest hard rock. A 17-year-old, single-parent, drug-involved, White kid in trouble at school is quite likely to like heavy metal and very unlikely to like soft rock. Almost without fail, a popular, academically successful 15-year-old, White female will lean toward alternative or mainstream pop more than metal or hard rock. These rules have exceptions— kids, for example, who meet the profile but defy the general pattern or for whom influences other than race, gender, and age take precedence. Nor are the rules reflexive. One may say that given a youth is male, White, of lower income, and in trouble with school authorities, he will probably like heavy metal. One may not say that if he likes heavy metal, he is poor, in trouble at school, and so on. In fact, many if not most metal fans come from middle-income homes and are doing just fine in school.

Qualifications aside, the research consistently establishes the importance of various background influences in the development of music taste, and in the next sections we examine the more important ones. First, though, a comment is in order concerning the organization of this discussion. Partly in the interest of clarity, the various influences on music taste—parents, mass media, age, race, gender, social class—are presented in serial form and single file, as if each acted independently without regard to the others. As a result, most of the relationships discussed are bivariate relationships—between age and music preference, social class and music preference, and so on. Yet, as the research shows, music preferences relate to these other factors in more complicated ways. Research has examined some of these complicated interactions—we will find, for instance, that the relationship between gender and music preference depends on race, and that age interacts with social class—but unfortunately relatively few studies have examined the various multivariate relationships that no doubt operate. Indeed, the further exploration of such interactions is a necessary next step in the research.

PARENTS

Most of the research on adolescent music preferences focuses on issues such as social background, peer group membership, psychological attitudes and personal life experiences. Before we turn to these concerns, two frequently neglected influences should be mentioned—parents and the mass media. That parental influences should be ignored by researchers is perhaps not too surprising given the prevailing assumption that popular music is a prime staging area for the expression of intergenerational conflict. As we have discussed, however, many experts on adolescent development challenge the paradigm of deep generational conflict, proposing instead a model based on considerable parent–child harmony. There are hints that some of this harmony may extend even to popular music.

Many members of the first rock generation—those who grew up with the Rolling Stones, the Beatles, Jimi Hendrix, and the Who—now have children in junior high, high school, and college. It turns out that many of their teen- and college-aged children, far from branding the music associated with their parents' generation as "oldies," grace it with the more reverential term "classic rock." In many high schools and on all college campuses, in fact, classic rock is a widely acknowledged and highly popular musical classification. In one recent study of college students' preferences, eight of the nine artists most often cited as favorites were rock figures whose careers had begun in the 1960s and 1970s—artists like Pink Floyd, Bruce Springsteen, Led Zeppelin, Genesis, Billy Joel, Elton John, and the Beatles (Wells, 1990). In Christenson and Peterson's (1988) study of Pennsylvania college students, all but one of the older or "classic" music styles (e.g., Motown, psychedelic rock, and 1960s rock) scored well above the neutral point on the love–hate scale. (The one exception was 1970s disco, which, to the great dismay of pop music purists, is enjoying a 1990s revival.) Among males, in fact, 1960s and 1970s rock were the two most popular categories, both scoring higher than mainstream pop and 1980s rock.

This pattern does not necessarily signify a direct adoption of parental preferences and tastes. Very few teens, we expect, look to their parents for musical influence, and even fewer would admit it if they did. Nor does it mean parents and children generally agree on matters of musical taste; indeed, differences emerge even in preadolescence. In one study of preadolescents (Christenson, 1994), the proportion of kids who said they liked the music their parents listen to either "pretty much" or "a lot" decreased from over 30% of the third and fourth graders to only 9% of the fifth- and sixth-grade kids. Obviously a gap exists in most families, a very wide gulf in some (Smith, 1994). Still, it is difficult to reconcile the broad appeal, especially among middle class youth and college students, of "classic" rock with the traditional image of music as generational battleground. The influence of parents or of the parents' generation (these are different things, of course) is probably complex. For some kids, surely, it is direct and positive, essentially a form of modeling. For others the influence is reactive—no music will do unless it enrages their parents. In either case, there is an influence.

MASS MEDIA

Although the media clearly play a role in the development of music taste, we find surprisingly little published research relating adolescents' music preferences to other media exposure variables. The most obvious media influences are radio and MTV. It is taken more or less as gospel in the music industry that no song or album can become a hit without significant radio and MTV exposure, and without question such exposure influences the popularity of both individual recordings and music genres. The availability or unavailability of MTV or certain radio formats effectively dictates the extent of the local music menu and, presumably, the musical diversity to which adolescents are exposed. One would expect youth living in larger or more ethnically diverse radio markets to acquire more varied tastes than those from small towns or homogeneous communities.

This said, exposure on radio and MTV is by no means a necessary condition for a musician or music type to garner a loyal following. It is easy in these musically Balkanized times to cite artists, albums, even entire music genres that have gained considerable popularity with virtually no radio or MTV airplay. A striking example of this independence of taste from media exposure is Roe's (1985) finding that Swedish teens rated reggae—a style completely ignored by the government-run Swedish radio system—higher than any other music type, including mainstream pop. In the United States, stations specializing in rap or heavy metal music exist mainly in the larger urban areas, yet both music types attract ardent followings even in mid-sized and small communities. Many alternative musicians also attract their audience with very little radio exposure.

In fact, one could hypothesize among some groups of adolescents a *negative* relationship between radio/MTV exposure and music popularity. Particularly for kids alienated from the school culture or who wish to project an image of unconventionality and individualism, hearing a song on commercial radio or seeing a video in the MTV rotation may signal that the artists have sold out and the music has lost its edge. If the prom queen likes it, maybe it is time to move on to something that smacks a bit less of the mainstream. Recently a group of our students conducted an experiment that illustrates this phenomenon. Under the guise of doing music taste research for the college radio station, they asked classes of undergraduates to rate two recently released and completely unknown alternative rock songs. Before the songs were played, the respondents were instructed to read a brief biographical sketch of the artists. These sketches were identical on all questionnaires except for this difference: Half the students were also told that MTV had given the group a strong endorsement, the other half read the biographical information without any connection to MTV. It turned out that those who read the MTV endorsement rated the songs *lower* than the other students. This finding suggests that at least for college students MTV is more a negative than a positive guide to taste.

Of course, media other than radio and MTV provide information on popular music. For years, youth-oriented motion pictures have been closely identified with and often based on popular music, and for many teens movies provide exposure to music types out of their local mainstream. Small-town White teenagers hear more rap music and—for better or worse—get more of a glimpse of urban Black culture from one Spike Lee movie than they would from a year of local radio. Teen magazines also play an important part in the formation and the strength of music preference and allegiance, either directly or through a two-step flow of information in which pop music experts monitor music trends in pop music magazines and then transmit their knowledge to the less committed or well-informed majority.

Age is perhaps the elemental predictor of music taste because it is primarily age that separates those who listen to pop or rock from those who do not. Exaggerated though the generation gap notion may be, there are many obvious and major differences between the music preferences of adults and adolescents. As NBC researcher Horst Stipp (1990) noted, most adult-oriented music radio formats are just "time capsules" for different musical eras, and each format garners an audience composed primarily of people whose adolescence coincided with them. If one is unconvinced of the power of what Stipp calls the "puberty-music connection," a few visits to high school reunion parties should provide ample support for his thesis.

     Important age-related differences in music taste appear even within the period of late childhood and adolescence. The first of these is the almost instantaneous conversion upon entering school to pop or rock music of some kind, and a concurrent weaning from whatever was provided or encouraged by parents in the preschool environment. Of course, in many homes the preschool music environment is itself a rock or pop environment, if that is what parents and older siblings listen to. Yet even those with different home music influences quickly turn to pop or rock once they enter grade school. The nature and timing of the transition was demonstrated in a study by Greer, Dorow, and Randall (1974). Children ranging from nursery school through sixth grade were equipped with headsets, and for a period of 10 minutes they were fed either pop/Top 40 songs or classical and Broadway music. The children could continue to hear the music up to a maximum of 10 minutes as long as they held down a control button. The researchers reasoned that the more the children liked the music the longer they would depress the button. For those hearing the classical and Broadway tape, average listening (button-pushing) time started at about 90 seconds at nursery school, peaked at 3 minutes in first grade and then dropped off steadily to only 35 seconds among sixth graders. The age trend for pop listening was quite different; listening time was about a minute for nursery-school children, rose sharply to over four minutes among first graders and continued to climb through sixth grade.

The sixth graders in the study held the control button down an average of 9 out of a possible 10 minutes.

Survey data also confirm this migration to popular music. When we asked a sample of Pennsylvania grade-school children (Christenson, 1994) to name their favorite musicians or music groups, only a handful mentioned anything other than pop or rock musicians, even in the first and second grades. By the end of grade school, even this minimal level of interest in non-rock/pop had eroded. For instance, about 20% of the first through fourth graders cited a country musician, and 15% mentioned an "oldie" group from the 1960s or 1970s (usually the Beatles or the Beach Boys). By contrast, only 1 in 10 fifth and sixth graders mentioned a country artist, and not one referred to a 1960s or 1970s musician. Classical and jazz performers were virtually absent from the list regardless of age. In fact, grade-school children are almost as aware of the top hits as teenagers. When Stipp (1985) compared 6- to 11-year-olds with teenagers on their familiarity with top 10 hits, he found, as expected, that essentially all the teens had heard the songs before. Surprisingly, however, levels of familiarity were also very nearly as high—about 95%—among the younger children.

Age also affects the extent of differentiation on the music map. Although most preteens find a few terms such as *rap, rock, hard rock, pop rock,* and *oldies* sufficient to describe any important differences between music types, high school students may recognize 10 or 20 music subgenres and college students several more. In part, this trend results simply from increased music exposure and accumulated experience—the longer a child has listened, presumably, the more aware he or she will be of the extent of the musical menu—but it also reflects the changing nature of peer relations. Older adolescent society contains a more elaborate set of group distinctions than younger, and so it calls for a more elaborate set of cultural markers. Of all such markers, none is more important than music allegiance.

Older age groups also express less centrist or mainstream preferences than younger age groups. In Christenson's (1994) study of Pennsylvania grade-school children, for instance, only a handful of the first through fourth graders cited a favorite from outside the pop and rock mainstream. By comparison, nearly a third of the fifth and sixth graders named a "modern" or "progressive" group like the Police, Cars, or Talking Heads (the data are from the mid-1980s). The move away from the pop mainstream only goes so far, of course; although other preferences may make inroads, most studies still show Top 40 or "pop" to be the most popular type of music even in high school. In addition, the extent to which students move away from the mainstream appears to depend on social class. A survey of Canadian students reported by Jerome Tanner (1981) revealed an age-related decrease in the percentage of middle-class kids favoring Top 40, from 73% in junior high to 55% in high school. However, age made no difference among working-class students.

Does the age trend away from the mainstream signify an attraction to the alternatives or an avoidance of the conventional? Probably both. By definition, the "mainstream" will lose a certain share of the audience as other tastes develop; thus, devotees of reggae, World Beat, jazz fusion, alternative, and classic rock, for instance, may not dislike mainstream pop as much as they find it irrelevant. However, a process of conscious rejection takes place as well. As soon children are old enough to buy their first tape or CD, they realize that some music groups are cool and some uncool, and even if at first they like the way the uncool stuff sounds, they soon learn to steer clear of it. In college the process is played out in the form of a curious phenomenon one might call the "Madonna contradiction." Despite Madonna's phenomenal commercial success throughout her career, few college freshmen will admit publicly to owning any of her music. How can this be? What is happening, we think, is that all those Madonna albums purchased in junior high and high school have been stored safely in the bedroom closet back home. Madonna the sex kitten pop star is not thought to be an appropriate taste for liberal, independent, free-thinking college students, and so she is cast aside and replaced by the "alternative" or "classic rock" tastes felt to be more suitable on campus. (This does not necessarily mean college freshmen dislike Madonna; one of our students admitted taping a Madonna CD onto a blank cassette labeled "the Doors" and listening to it surreptitiously on her Walkman.)

Interestingly, despite its obvious nonmainstream reputation, heavy metal's popularity does not rise consistently with age. Rather, the relationship between age and the popularity of metal appears curvilinear, increasing at first during early and middle adolescence, then dropping off somewhat. The proportion of junior high school kids with a clear hard rock or heavy metal bent is about 25% overall, probably over 30% for boys. By the end of high school, however, the metal audience decreases to under 20% (Tanner, 1981; Wass, Miller, & Stevenson, 1989). By college, true heavy metal fans are rare indeed, probably making up less than 5% of all students (Wells, 1990). Granted, heavy metal is defined in somewhat different ways by different researchers, and college students differ from general samples of junior high and high school kids in social class as well as age. The important point, though, is that one may not argue, as some have, that heavy metal appeals solely or even primarily to older—and presumably less easily influenced—kids.

RACE

Of all the demographic and background predictors of music taste, race and ethnicity may be the most powerful. Entire genres of popular music are linked unambiguously and proudly with their racial and ethnic roots—R&B, soul, and rap with African-American culture, salsa with Hispanics, reggae with its Jamaican heritage. Although the association is not usually acknowledged as directly, contemporary hard rock and heavy metal are tied just as clearly to White youth culture. *Billboard* magazine recognizes the importance of these racial and ethnic origins by publishing separate charts for R&B, soul, rap, and Latin music in addition to its pop and rock charts. The racial and ethnic make-up of the listening audience—no surprise here—mirrors the origins of its musicians. Radio programmers are perfectly conscious of the strong relationship between race/ethnicity and music taste, and they stay close to their racial or ethnic home with their playlists and advertising strategies. Particularly in large radio markets, many stations are explicitly identified with specific racial and ethnic groups.

Perhaps because these racial and ethnic differences are too obvious to question, they have received surprisingly little attention in popular music research. What research there is, however, amply confirms the strong influence of race on music allegiance. A 1972 survey (Denisoff & Levine, 1972), for instance, showed race to be the most powerful of several central demographic predictors of music taste, including age, gender, social class, education, religion, and geographical location. More recent surveys reaffirm the importance of race, especially among males. In a study by Carol Dykers (1992), summarized in Figure 4.1, 70% of a broad sample of Black teenagers reported rap as their favorite music type, whereas 22% mentioned either pop rock or Top 10. Very few cited rock, heavy metal, punk, or country. With the exception of the pop/Top 10 category, the preferences of the White youth were distributed much differently: Both rock and heavy metal drew a quarter of the responses, and only 13% mentioned rap.

Racial differences can be even more dramatic in certain subgroups, as in one study of boys enrolled in an "optional" middle school for kids having trouble in standard school settings. Of the Black students surveyed, 92% said their favorite music was rap, only 2% heavy metal. In sharp contrast, 96% of the Whites cited heavy metal, and only one youth cited rap (Epstein, Pratto, & Skipper, 1990). To be sure, racial differences in music preferences are not this emphatic in all adolescent populations.

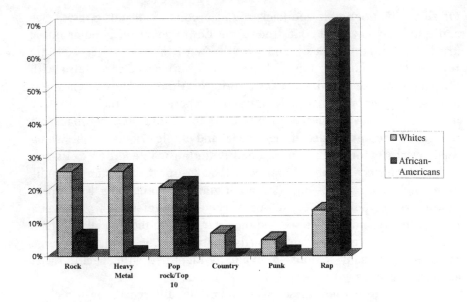

Figure 4.1. Favorite music of white and African American adolescent boys
Note: Adapted with permission from *Rap and rock as adolescents' cultural capital at school*, by C. Dykers, 1992.

Most of the youth in the survey came from lower income homes and were placed into the optional program due to academic and behavioral problems. Racial distinctions may be more sharply drawn in this sort of population to begin with, and they may have been sharpened further by the transplantation into an unfamiliar institutional environment.

Interestingly, strong as the racial differences are, they coexist with a significant amount of racial "crossover" listening, especially among middle-class Whites. From Billy Holiday to the Supremes to Snoop Doggy Dogg, no Black artist has risen to the top of the charts without attracting legions of White listeners. Consider, for instance:

- In Christenson and Peterson's (1988) study of Penn State students, contemporary rhythm and blues (R&B) ranked fourth overall, and second among females, of 26 music genres. Heavy metal, an unequivocally White music, came in fourth from the bottom.

- In our 1990 survey of 600 San Francisco area suburban 9th and 11th graders, rap tied for second place (with classic rock and "easy rock") out of 10 music genres. Only Top 40 rated higher.
- In a sample of suburban Portland, Oregon, 12- to 15-year-olds, rap was the highest rated music type, edging out pop and rock and scoring well ahead of hard rock and heavy metal (Christenson & van Nouhuys, 1995).

Race makes a difference, then, but how much difference it makes probably depends on other factors, and race has never made all the difference. Perhaps because it seems to be more a matter of exception than rule, crossover listening receives little attention as a distinct phenomenon in music preference. Obviously, though, crossover listening represents more than messy statistical error. The suburban White rap fan (just as the rare urban Black hard rock fan) is making a conscious cultural choice and a strong personal statement.

GENDER

Developmental psychologist Bernice Lott (1987) has argued that American adolescent society is really two cultures, one of boys and one of girls, each with its own values, style, and world view. If she is right, then within this rifted society, indeed pivotal to its maintenance, lies a corresponding polarization in popular music culture. So powerful is gender in determining music preferences that one music researcher has suggested the music industry might well junk its current taxonomy in favor of a system that distinguishes simply between "male appeal" or "female appeal" songs (Warner, 1984).

Three primary gender differences emerge from the research on music preferences. The first and most fundamental musical gender gap is the separation between pop (female) and rock (male) tastes. Whatever the historical era and whatever the population being studied, females exhibit greater attraction to the softer, more romantic, more mainstream forms (pop, disco, soft rock, Top 40), whereas males gravitate to the harder-edged rock forms (heavy metal, hard rock, punk, grunge, psychedelic rock). Second, males are more likely than females to adopt nonmainstream, fringe, or "progressive" music affinities (Christenson & Peterson, 1988; Christenson & Roberts, 1990; Dykers, 1992; Tanner, 1981; Wells, 1990). Third, and this obviously applies only for White youth, females have consistently shown more appreciation for African-American popular music such as soul, disco, funk, and R&B than males (rap may be an exception here, as we discuss later).

The gender gap in music preference appears as soon as kids develop an interest in popular music, but it appears to be especially pronounced among junior high and high school youth. The findings of Henriksen and Roberts (1990; see also Roberts & Henriksen, 1990) are typical here. As shown in Table 4.1, they reported significant gender differences for 7 of 10 music categories. Top 40 (or pop) showed the biggest disparity—females rated it 4.7 on a 5-point scale, males only 3.8—but differences also appeared for "easy rock," oldies, new wave (now itself a type of oldie), classical, and jazz, all of which were liked more by girls, and heavy metal, which was more popular with males. No gender differences turned up for classic rock, punk rock, or rap.

Table 4.2 shows previously unpublished results from a survey we conducted in Portland, Oregon, suburban middle schools in Spring 1995. The major difference between this study and that of Henriksen and Roberts is the introduction of alternative music, which was not sufficiently well established in 1990 to warrant inclusion. As the results show, at least in the suburban middle schools of Portland, by 1995 alternative music had jumped well above all other types, for both boys and girls. In most

Table 4.1. High School Students' Music Ratings by Gender in 1990.

	All	Males	Females	Difference?
Top 40	4.2	3.8	4.7	Girls higher
Easy (soft) rock	3.7	3.4	3.9	Girls higher
Classic rock	3.7	3.7	3.7	Not significant
Rap	3.7	3.6	3.7	Not significant
Oldies	3.6	3.3	3.9	Girls higher
New wave	3.4	2.9	3.7	Girls higher
Heavy metal	3.1	3.5	2.7	Boys higher
Jazz	2.8	2.6	2.9	Girls higher
Classical	2.7	2.5	2.9	Girls higher
Punk rock	2.5	2.5	2.5	Not significant

Note: Based on responses of 9th through 11th graders in suburban public schools in the San Francisco area; higher scores indicate greater liking. Adapted with permission from *Turn on, tune in, hang out: Music use in adolescence*, by L. Henriksen & D.F. Roberts, 1990, unpublished manuscript, Stanford University, Institute for Communication Research.

Table 4.2. Sixth through Eighth Graders' Music Ratings by Gender in 1995.

	All	Males	Females	Difference?
Alternative	4.2	4.1	4.3	Not significant
Pop	3.7	3.3	3.9	Girls higher
Rock	3.7	3.7	3.9	Not significant
Rap	3.6	3.7	3.6	Not significant
Hard rock	3.2	3.3	3.2	Not significant
Classic rock	3.1	2.9	3.3	Girls higher
Heavy metal	2.6	2.9	2.5	Boys higher
Classical	2.5	2.3	2.8	Girls higher
Country	2.1	1.8	2.4	Girls higher

Note: Based on responses from 231 sixth through eighth grade public middle school students in suburban Portland, Oregon. Scale ranges from 1 (Hate it) to 5 (Love it).

respects, however, these data confirm the picture from five years earlier. Pop (essentially a synonym for Top 40) and classical were preferred by females, heavy metal by males, with no differences on most other types. The basic pattern of females opting for the soft edge and males for the hard edge appears to hold for Black youth as well. Dykers (1992) reported that urban Black male adolescents were much more likely than females to cite rap as their favorite music (70% versus 46%) and much less likely to mention pop or Top 10 (22% versus 46%).

Surveys of college students show a somewhat more muted male versus female division in taste, but the gender gap exists even in the more liberal and gender-sensitive campus environment. Actually, there is at least a hint of a historical trend here. Research published during the earlier days of rock and roll (e.g., Fox & Wince, 1975; Skipper, 1973) generally produced quite general gender differences, not only on the critical rock–pop dimension but for a variety of nonrock music forms. In this earlier work, country, jazz, and blues consistently emerged as male and classical and folk as female domains. These differences, however, may have eroded somewhat over time. For instance, although Christenson and Peterson's (1988) study of Penn State undergraduates revealed the typical male preference for hard rock and the female attraction to mainstream pop and urban contemporary R&B, they failed to find differences for most other music types, including several that had previously seemed to separate the genders, such as country, jazz, classical, folk, and even heavy metal. A more recent survey of Temple University students (Wells, 1990) produced similar results—showing the standard differences on pop, rock, and R&B, but no differences on a host of other music categories, including heavy metal.

Overall, however, the essential gender differences in music taste have proven quite robust, and it is reasonable to speculate what might explain them. As we noted in our discussion of music uses in Chapter 3, females tend to use music in different ways and for different reasons than males, and these disparities in uses and gratifications logically imply different music preferences. Dancing, for example, tends to be more important to girls and so danceability becomes for them an important criterion of music taste, thus leading girls toward R&B and dance-oriented pop and away from hard rock and heavy metal.

The nature of lyric content also works to separate preferences by gender. Other things being equal, one might expect females to avoid music heavily laced with misogynist or macho-aggressive messages. The discourse of hard rock and heavy metal is decidedly a male discourse, and of a certain type. Simon Frith (1981), whose study of British teenagers led to some very strong conclusions on the connection between music and gender, coined the term *cock rock* to refer to such music:

> Cock-rock performers are aggressive, boastful, constantly drawing attention to their prowess and control. Their bodies are constantly on display (plunging shirts and tight trousers, chest hair and genitals), mikes and guitars are phallic symbols (or else caressed like female bodies), the music is loud, rhythmically insistent, built around techniques of arousal and release. Lyrics are assertive and arrogant, but the exact words are less significant than the vocal styles involved, the shrill shouting and screaming. What's going on at such "hard-rock" shows is a masturbatory celebration of penis power. Girls are structurally excluded from this rock experience: it speaks out the boundaries of *male* sexuality. (p. 227)

Frith wrote of British kids and White rock music in the early 1970s. Yet little in his description has changed, with the possible exception of the plunging neckline—today's "headbangers" simply go shirtless. Obviously, "cock rock" includes boys and excludes girls just as effectively here and now as it did there and then.

Of course, these causes of different music tastes have causes of their own. At bottom they can be understood only in the context of deeper cultural patterns of child rearing and gender-role socialization. The undeniable fact is that girls receive very different messages than boys: They are expected to be popular, beautiful, deferent, romantic, nurturant, and to *fit in*. Boys are expected to be independent, tough, aggressive, competitive, and to *stand out*. Whether adolescents can actually live up to these expectations or not, most feel the pressure to act them out, which includes making appropriate aesthetic choices. Boys will seek powerful, aggressive, defiant forms of music and avoid anything redolent of sentiment or conformity; girls will seek sociable, danceable, romantic, acceptable music and avoid the hard edge and the fringe.

These generalizations obviously are not absolute. One can find examples of gender "crossover"—heavy metal girls, male pop fans—as easily as racial crossover. Moreover, as we have noted, the size of the gender effect depends on other factors. The differences appear to be somewhat less pronounced among middle-class than working-class youth. Age, too, may affect the relationship between gender and music taste. Consider the following boy-girl comparisons for heavy metal in three roughly contemporary studies of middle-class White students, each using the same 5-point rating scale. In a survey of 6th through 8th graders, Christenson and van Nouhuys (1995) reported equally low ratings for heavy metal among boys and girls. Using 9th and 11th graders, Henriksen and Roberts (1990) found a gap of almost a full point, with boys well on the positive side of the scale (3.5) and girls on the negative (2.7). At the college level, Christenson and Peterson (1988) failed to locate any gender difference: As with the middle-school kids, males and females rated heavy metal music equally low. Taken together, these studies suggest an inverted U relationship between age and the strength of the gender gap, with the strongest gender effect precisely when it would logically be expected, that is, in the period of adolescence associated most strongly with the development of gender role identity and cross-gender relationships. At a broader level, the research suggests that gender differences in music taste may be more pronounced in groups with relatively rigid and traditional gender-role expectations, such as in working-class populations, and in groups for whom cross-gender relationships have a particularly high salience, as among high school-age adolescents. Where gender roles are defined more equally (e.g., on the college campus) or the boy–girl issue is not yet as salient, as in preadolescence, aesthetic divisions tend to be weaker or nonexistent.

Perhaps the most intriguing "nondifference" is shown in the case of rap music. As we have mentioned, rap is very nearly as popular in the suburbs as in the inner city, and recent research on middle-class populations shows it to be at least as popular with girls as with boys. This fact is difficult to explain in view of rap music's widely acknowledged misogy-nist and hypermasculine excesses. In a sense, rap is the "cock R&B" that corresponds to Frith's white "cock rock," and a simple rock–pop gender logic would predict a clear division in preference. Clearly, rap's populari-ty among White middle-class girls must be founded on something other than its messages about women. Why, then, do middle-class White girls like rap? First, an important aspect of rap's crossover appeal is that it arose and continues to flourish as a dance genre—its "message" is just as much for the body as the ear (Schusterman, 1991). Rap's danceability renders it extremely useful at adolescent social occasions, especially those that involve dancing. Because dancing is particularly important to girls, it is possible that rap's danceability counterbalances its lyrics. Second, and perhaps more crucially, for White girls (and boys) rap lyrics and messages may simply not carry much weight. As mere "cultural tourists" in the inner city, suburban girls may distance themselves from the "real" mean-ing of rap—the music is not about them or their neighborhood; they are not the "bitches" and "ho's" being exploited and put down. Thus, although rap lyrics may provide a source of amusement to female suburban fans, they may not identify closely with rap's cultural message, instead forming their response on the basis of other factors such as the music's fresh, hip sound and its usefulness in social settings.

If cultural tourism produces a detachment from the lyrics, then it makes sense that cultural involvement would increase the importance of lyrics. This may explain the sizable gender gap in African-Americans' atti-tudes toward rap music. African-American females live in the neighbor-hood and they know who the songs are about. Thus, the abusive treatment of females in rap may repel them at the same time that rap's racial identi-ty and usefulness as party music attract them. Writing in *Essence* magazine, a Black female college student described the resulting dilemma this way:

> A year and a half ago my girlfriends and I were grooving to the beats at a crowded house party in the 'hood. I was taking a break from my hip-hop hiatus because, frankly, I missed the music. And my sistas had reaffirmed to me the need to celebrate the genius of young Black musical talent. But as the party got groovier, someone slipped on "Gangsta Bitch"—the long, uncensored version—and we were aghast. Especially because the party noticeably livened and my Nubian sistas, who had previously lined the walls, now populated the floor, yelling out their "ho, ho, ho!"s. Most disturbing, though, was that I couldn't keep *my* toes from tapping to the beat. (T. Roberts, 1994, p. 62)

SOCIAL CLASS

There is an intuitive appeal to the idea that cultural preferences will relate to socioeconomic status or, to put it in the terms of U.S. sociologist Herbert Gans (1967), that a society will develop a stratified system of "taste cultures" in rough parallel with its general pattern of social stratification. Social status (defined in most studies as family income or parents' educational level) exerts a powerful influence on values, experiences, and cultural opportunities, and one might expect its influence to extend to music taste. For instance, to the extent that different types of music represent distinct and class-related views of the world, adolescents might identify with and adopt the music most closely in tune with their own social background. Music choices and social class might also come to be related through the process whereby different groups seek out distinctive combinations of cultural markers to identify themselves and set themselves apart from others. By this logic Miller beer, John Deere baseball caps (bill to the front), and Toyota 4x4 pickups go together and, as a set, stand apart from Heineken, Levi Cotton Dockers, and Volvo station wagons. In principle, one might expect music choices to play a similar role in marking social class distinctions among adolescents.

Reasonable as the theory sounds, however, the research provides at best a muddled picture of the relationship between socioeconomic status and adolescent music preferences. Certain early sociological studies, especially of British youth, revealed a close link between social class and music preferences. We have referred to Frith's characterization of the rock versus pop division between middle- and working-class British youth as "absolute." Another British study (Murdock & Phelps, 1972), roughly contemporary with Frith's work, failed to find class differences in the popularity of mainstream pop music, but did turn up sharp class differences in levels of attraction to soul or Motown, which were much preferred by working-class youth, and progressive/underground rock, which was a distinctly middle-class taste.

Most other surveys, though, produce either weak class differences or none at all. In Roe's (1985) research on Swedish adolescents, the only significant correlations between family background and music popularity were very modest ones for classical, folk, and jazz, each being slightly preferred by students from higher status backgrounds. None of the rock or pop categories exhibited any class differences. A few years later in Great Britain, J.M. Wober (1984) found a positive correlation between social class and a taste for Black music (note the reversal of earlier British research), but no differences in other music categories. U.S.-based studies indicate that social class has a much weaker effect than race, age, or gender (Lewis, 1992). To be sure, certain relationships do emerge rather consistently. In most studies, lower parental occupation and education tend to go with a preference for mainstream or Top 40, higher status with a taste for jazz, classical, "progressive" forms of rock, and world music. (In the United States, reggae music, a form that originated as a cry of protest from the Jamaican Black underclass, disproportionately attracts privileged White youth. In some high schools these upscale and often dreadlocked reggae fans are called "trustafarians"—that is, Rastafarians with trust funds.)

Still, the popularity of most popular music genres is independent of social class, and this extends even to the much-maligned heavy metal. Often branded by well-educated parents and music critics as a "working-class" taste, heavy metal turns out to attract the same level of popularity (or unpopularity) regardless of social class (Tanner, 1981; Wass, et al., 1989). The tenuous connection, especially in more recent U.S. research, between social class and music taste may be explained in a variety of ways. First, popular music genres rarely express anything resembling a coherent world view. When a clear ideology is expressed, as perhaps with heavy metal, its relationship to issues of social class is murky at best. Class distinctions, in other words, simply do not map straightforwardly onto music types. Second, as Frith (1981) points out, social class boundaries are less well defined and more easily permeated in the United States than in Britain. This, he argues, explains the weaker class differences found in the United States.

Finally, times may have changed. Regardless of country of origin, more recent studies tend to find weaker social class effects than earlier research. George Lewis (1992) has linked this trend to certain contemporary social and economic conditions:

> Under conditions of relatively high social mobility, greater discretionary income, easy credit, efficient distribution of goods, a high diffusion rate of cultural products, conspicuous consumption, and a greater amount of leisure time, the link between social and cultural structures becomes a question, not a given. (p. 141)

MUSIC PREFERENCES AND THE SCHOOL CULTURE

An adolescent's social standing is more than a simple matter of parental education or income. To a certain extent, at least, the elements that contribute to status in adolescent culture—physical attractiveness, academic achievement, athletic prowess, social and leadership skills, artistic talent, and so on—are developed and displayed in a school environment set apart from parents, home, and neighborhood. Thus, if one seeks relationships between adolescent social structure and aesthetic preferences, the appropriate measures of status and group membership are those grounded in the school culture rather than the home. Once that adjustment in the definition of "social class" is made, the connection between social structure and music affiliations becomes apparent.

Indeed, popular music orientation and preferences relate to school issues in a number of ways. In our earlier discussion of the social uses of popular music, for example, we mentioned the link reported by Brown and O'Leary (1971) between lower school performance and the choice of pop over "adult-encouraged" music. Other research suggests that the connection between music preference and school performance also depends on the type of popular music preferred. Keith Roe's (1984) examination of music use among Swedish adolescents provides one of the most detailed and informative perspectives on the relationship between school variables and music preference. Roe found that regardless of gender or social class the kids with lower levels of commitment to school and lower academic achievement tended to be drawn to "disapproved" and "oppositional" music forms such as hard rock and punk, whereas those with higher school commitment and achievement tended to prefer mainstream or soft pop.

Roe argues that the connection between school orientation and popular music taste arises from the process of academic evaluation, which inevitably separates students into two classes—the successes and the failures. This in turn leads to a polarized peer group structure based primarily on academic achievement and attitude toward school. The effects of this divided social structure are twofold, he claims. First, school orientation affects the extent of peer orientation. Adolescents who are doing poorly in school and who harbor anti-school attitudes become more highly peer-oriented—and correspondingly more defiant against the values and authority of parents and teachers—than those with positive school experiences and attitudes. Second, as a result of these relationships, Roe says, this alienated group develops a natural taste for disapproved, defiant cultural materials such as punk and heavy metal music. Logically, one would expect those kids who are performing well in the traditional, adult-approved ways to adopt "approved" or nonthreatening music, and this is what Roe found—that more successful, pro-school youth tended to adopt a taste for such music forms as classical, jazz, and mainstream pop. Moreover, this pattern applied regardless of social class. Indeed Roe concluded that social class bore almost no relationship to music preferences once school-based factors were taken into account. Most important of all, perhaps, is the direction of causation in the relationship between school orientation and music preference. Because the data came from a longitudinal study following the same students over three-year intervals, certain statistical tests could be used to settle some of the critical "which came first" issues that often plague surveys conducted at a single point in time. The results of these tests clearly indicated that it was early school achievement that led to later music choices, not the other way around. No evidence was found that early exposure to oppositional music exerted any negative influence on later school attitudes or achievement.

Music choices are an important way for youth to express what Grossberg (1984) has called "us–them" distinctions. The first crucial distinction is the one just discussed, that is, between "us," the youth, versus "them," the adults. However, music is also linked to the distinctions between the various subcultures that often develop in the school setting. Bradford Brown (1990) has distinguished between two types of peer groups: the "clique," who are the people one "hangs out" with, and the "crowd," a larger collective of individuals with the same "reputation" with whom one may or may not spend much time. Brown further notes the great importance, especially in early adolescence, of finding a niche in these groups. Interestingly, in his view, fitting into a niche in the crowd structure may actually be more important than finding a clique because the crowd represents one's status in the school culture. Brown argued that adolescents do not actively select a crowd to join; rather, they are thrust into it by their personality, background, interests, and reputation.

The adoption of a certain music style—that is, a type of music and a personal style to go with it—is one of the most powerful identifying markers in the school crowd structure. Indeed, many groups—"alterna-chicks," "punkers," "metalheads," "rastas," and so on—are defined primarily on the basis of music. The richest treatment of this issue comes from Frith's (1981) examination of teen subcultures in the British industrial town of Keighley. The key social distinction in Keighley was one familiar to the U.S. scene as well, that between the academically successful and college-bound students (the "6th formers") and the working-class youth headed for unskilled jobs (the "5th formers"). Frith observed marked differences between the two groups' music preferences and uses. The college-bound crowd much preferred "rock" to "pop"; indeed, the word *pop* was a strong pejorative for them. They tended to buy albums rather than singles, stressed the deeper ideological meaning of music, and saw music allegiance as a fundamental expression of individuality and resistance to convention. Working-class students, in contrast, bought singles more often than albums and related to the sound or the beat much more than the "message." Music to them was less a statement about the world than an escape from it. Nor were the distinctions limited to just these two. Frith noted a high degree of further differentiation into music and music-related cults—mods, teds, hairies, bohemians, hippies, Grebos—each militantly asserting its style and zeitgeist: "There is nothing in the USA to match the precision of white youth styles in Britain, where the slightest differences between groups are matters of passionate argument. The intensity of musical identity is most visible at a British show—everyone is dressed like the star" (p. 216).

Although the subcultures may be less painstaking in their attention to the details of style, divisions and crowds clearly exist on this side of Atlantic, and they are just as closely tied to music preferences. Tanner (1981) analyzed the relationships among music affiliation, social class, and commitment to school among Canadian public high school students. Like others before him, he found that those with high commitment to school were more likely to be Top 40 fans, whereas lower levels of school commitment disproportionately predicted a taste for heavy metal. The association was especially strong for working-class kids. Tanner concludes that working-class youth alienated from the mainstream school culture may be especially prone to adopt a music identity that takes a "tough, aggressive, even violent stance" (p. 9). Moreover, in his view, their embrace of heavy metal represents a conscious choice in a quest for a "cultural solution" to their low standing in the traditional school pecking order.

Recent U.S. studies find essentially the same pattern. In a 1992 survey of over 2,800 high school students in the Southeast, only 1 in 10 heavy metal fans expressed certainty that they would attend college, compared to 25% of pop and rock fans (Dykers, 1992). Similarly, Hakanen and Wells (1993) reported that adolescents' statements of whether they were an "A," "B," "C," "D," or "F" student were more strongly related to music taste than a host of demographic variables, including gender and parental education. The better students tended either to express indifference toward music or were inclined toward accepted forms: mainstream pop, classical, and jazz. Heavy metal was the overwhelming choice of those who saw themselves as school failures.

It is worth emphasizing that none of the authors whose research we have reviewed suggest that exposure to a certain kind of music determines success in school. The dominant view, rather, is similar to the position taken by Roe, that the primary factors are what happens in the family, the school, and the peer group. These determine one's position in the school culture, which in turn dictates certain patterns of peer association and cultural choices. Music affiliations function in this process in two different ways. First, an adolescents' chosen music can reflect, resonate with, and make sense of his or her personal and social experiences. In other words, the music expresses and reinforces who one is. Second, it tells others who a person is and what group he or she belongs to. As Graham Murdock (1989) put it in describing the British youth he studied: "Statements of musical taste were never simply aesthetic choices. They were also statements about self-image and social affiliation" (p. 244).

POLITICAL ORIENTATION AND MUSIC PREFERENCES

The pioneering work on the connection between political attitudes and music preferences was Robinson and his colleagues' (Robinson, Pilskain & Hirsch, 1976) study of 1960s protest rock listeners. The data came from a national survey of over 2,000 high school boys conducted in Fall 1966 and local surveys performed during 1969-1972. The authors raised the same question many parents asked at the time, that is, whether "protest rock," with its anti-establishment, anti-war, pro-drug and pro-free-love messages, had a tendency to attract or, as the authors suggest, *cultivate* an audience of like mind and habit. Their conclusion was that a connection did exist. Sharp differences in levels of drug use emerged between protest rock fans and nonfans. Of those who listed three or more protest rock albums (e.g., albums by Janis Joplin, Jimi Hendrix, and Crosby, Stills, Nash and Young) as their favorites, 56% said they used marijuana, compared to only 22% of those who reported no protest rock favorites. Corresponding differences emerged for amphetamine and LSD use, although overall levels of use were lower for these drugs. Robinson and his colleagues suggest, however, that drug use was not the real issue here. Instead, they argue that protest rock music and drug-taking were two important elements in a constellation of countercultural traits, which also included a strong anti-war stance, a favorable attitude to sexual freedom, support for racial equality, and a general openness and willingness to explore new ways of looking at the world. Unlike Roe and others, however, they saw music's role in these processes as potentially quite active. In their conclusions, in fact, they refer to the "possible role that the dissemination of rock music had in helping to create, sustain, and celebrate an atmosphere of social change through its legitimation of subcultural attitudes" (p. 132).

This notion that music choice depends to an extent on a general openness to new experiences has received little explicit attention in the research, but at least a hint of additional support comes from Litle and Zuckerman (1986), who reported that college students scoring high on a measure of "experience seeking"—that is, who were more likely to "seek sensation through the mind and senses and more open to a wide variety of experiences"—liked rock music more and "bland soundtrack music" (p. 576) less than those lower in this need. The second thrust of the Robinson et al. study—the link between music and political attitudes—has attracted more attention and considerable additional support. Three studies—each involving college students—bear on this issue. Two are from the early 1970s just following the Robinson study, and the third is from the mid-1980s, a time when many commentators were noting an apparent decline in both the political content of music and political awareness of students.

Mashkin and Volgy (1975) reported results from two separate surveys—one conducted during 1972–73 and the other in 1974—comparing the sociopolitical attitudes of rock, country western, and folk fans. Folk music listeners were the most likely and country fans the least likely to reject traditional gender roles. Folk and rock fans exhibited more political alienation (i.e., estrangement from politics and government) than country fans. Finally, folk and rock listeners were more likely than country fans to espouse what the authors call a "post-bourgeois ideology," or a "rejection of materialistic values in favor of more participatory, individual-worth values in society" (p. 453). Their 1974 survey, however, failed to reveal any such associations. The authors explained the discrepancy by noting a "profound change" in the lyrics of the three genres. According to their observations, by 1974 the three music types no longer differed in their incorporation of political content. The lack of audience differentiation, they argued, makes sense in terms of the absence of content differentiation. In our view, however, it is just as likely that the absence of significant relationships in the second study resulted from the small sample size, especially of folk fans (only 23 were included in the sample) and country fans (17 were included). The authors' explanation also presupposes that music's political or social meaning resides primarily in its lyrics, a proposition that we question in our later discussion of lyric themes.

In any case, another early 1970s study, this one employing a sample of over 700 college students, found a series of statistically significant associations between political orientation and music preferences. Fox and

Williams (1974) compared the music preferences of self-described liberals, moderates, and conservatives, and found: (a) conservative students liked mainstream pop/Top 40 and Easy Listening more than liberals did; and (b) liberals, more often than conservatives, favored classical, jazz, folk, blues, and protest music. The differences were particularly marked for blues and protest rock. Over 70% of the liberals said they liked blues versus 36% of the conservatives, and 52% of the liberals liked protest music compared to 17% of the conservatives. Political moderates fell into the middle range on both measures. All these relationships withstood statistical controls for age, sex, income, and other demographic variables.

In a later study, Peterson and Christenson (1987) asked whether the link between political and music affiliation had survived into the 1980s. They suspected, based on the apparent depoliticization of both music and youth during the period, that Reagan-era college students would form music affiliations for reasons irrelevant to their political or social outlook. Hence, they predicted no relationship between political stance and music choice. However, although the observed relationships tended to be in the weak to moderate range, some significant correlations between college students' politics and their music preferences were found. Students with liberal-left leanings tended to prefer music performed by Black musicians (soul, Motown, Contemporary Rhythm and Blues, jazz, Black Gospel) and genres with strong political identities such as hardcore punk and new wave. Conservatism, meanwhile, tended to accompany a taste for more generic music categories such as 1970s and 1980s rock. The strongest connection involved heavy metal. Among those who refused to categorize themselves politically—that is, those who circled "Don't know/don't care" instead of liberal, moderate, or conservative—42% said they either liked or loved heavy metal. Only 17% of those who checked off a political orientation indicated an attraction to heavy metal. This finding suggests a connection between attitudes to heavy metal and political alienation.

IS THERE A HEAVY METAL SYNDROME?

As we have seen, music preferences are not purely idiosyncratic or "free-floating" but are to a great extent predictable from demographic characteristics, school-based factors, political orientation, and the like. In other words, certain kinds of adolescents are drawn to certain kinds of music. We now turn to such personality and individual differences, with a special focus on the most controversial music types: heavy metal and rap music.

Due to the often controversial nature of heavy metal lyrics and videos, most of the research linking patterns of personality, social relationships and antisocial behavior with music preferences has focused on heavy metal music. This section explores whether a taste for heavy metal is, as some have suggested, associated with a consistent constellation of personal traits and tendencies and, if so, whether the pattern formed by these association may in any true sense be called a syndrome.

In the simplest terms, the question raised by alarmed adults and not a few social scientists is whether heavy metal fans tend to exhibit to a greater extent than nonfans the set of characteristics and attitudes suggested by the nature of the music—whether, for example, when compared to other youth, heavy metal devotees tend to be more suicidal, more defiant of mainstream authorities and norms, more likely to be in trouble in school and with the law, more at odds with their parents, and more likely to use illicit drugs. The simplest answer to the question is "Yes"; the research indeed confirms some of these predictions. Before turning to these results, however, recall some of the points we have already made regarding heavy metal music fans. We know, for instance, that almost all heavy metal fans are White, and so the comments in this section must be understood to refer to that racial group rather than African-Americans, Hispanics, or others. In addition, most (but not all) metalheads are males, and most are in the middle adolescent years rather than early adolescence or college age.

What is known about the heavy metal audience beyond these general demographics? First—and this becomes especially important in any speculation about the impact of the music—heavy metal fans are an especially committed, devoted audience. These are not casual listeners with just a loose identification with their chosen genre, but fans in the literal sense—they are "fanatical." Compared to other music types, ratings of heavy metal are likely to be more extreme; that is, kids either hate it or they love it. Few can take it or leave it. Those who love it are highly absorbed in their musical identity, both in terms of listening time (Wass et al., 1989) and a variety of other music-related behaviors. Arnett (1991a) reported that high school students who described themselves as "metalheads" owned an average of over 100 albums, 69% of them heavy metal. They spent over $38 a month on albums, concerts, equipment, and music paraphernalia—more than twice as much as a comparison group of non-metal fans—and attended an average of eight concerts a year versus three for the comparison group. Over 80% said they played an instrument (usually guitar), compared to only a third of the nonfans.

Equally important to any theory that might predict a link between the music's message and the personal characteristics of the audience, heavy metal fans are not just involved in the sound of the music, but also attend to the messages the music presents. Compared to nonfans, they express very high levels of personal identification with their favorite performers, say lyrics are more important to them, and claim a deeper understanding of the lyrics' meaning (Arnett, 1991a; Wass et al., 1989). Heavy metal fans are also more likely than other youth to adopt their favorite musicians as role models. When Arnett (1991a) asked a group of high school students to supply the names of people they admired, 60% of the metal devotees mentioned a favorite musician, compared to 13% of nonfans.

As might be expected in light of such high levels of involvement, heavy metal enthusiasts tend to be at odds with their parents and their school environment and closely allied with a peer group of other metal fans. They are more likely than other youth to come from families in which the parents are either divorced or living separately (Arnett, 1991b; Martin, Clarke, & Pearce, 1993; Wass et al., 1989) and express less satisfaction with their family relationships than other youth. A study of Australian high school students, for instance, found that those who preferred heavy metal were twice as likely as pop fans to describe their family relationships as "not close" (Martin et al., 1993). Similarly, Christenson and van Nouhuys (1995) reported significant associations between ratings for heavy metal and levels of agreement with such statements as, "I'd rather be with my friends than my family," "I spend a lot of time arguing with my parents," and "My friends know more about most things than my parents." Interviews with heavy metal fans tend to reveal either open or smoldering conflict with parents, and when relationships with parents are described as satisfactory, it is usually because the parents are permissive and let the kids go their own way (Arnett, 1991a). Heavy metal fans' relationships with school authorities tend to be strained as well, and they demonstrate less commitment to school, report more conflict with teachers and other school authorities (Christenson & van Nouhuys, 1995), and perform less well academically than those with more mainstream tastes. In fact, Hakanen and Wells (1993) found that heavy metal was the only type of music that predicted students' estimates of their performance in school.

What fills the gap in their social relationships is a strong bond with cliques and the broader heavy metal culture. As already noted, when adolescents are asked questions that pit parents against peers, levels of affinity for heavy metal music strongly predict peer orientation. There is no evidence that heavy metal fans see themselves as socially isolated.

Indeed, they are just as satisfied with the quality of their peer relationships as nonfans (Arnett, 1991a). Moreover, evidence exists that the peer group has a stronger hold on heavy metal fans than on most other adolescents, as indicated by positive correlations between students' attraction to heavy metal and how likely they are to say they would "go with their friends" rather than act individualistically (Gordon et al., 1992). In other words, although heavy metal fans may reject parental and school authority, they may be disproportionately responsive to the authority of the peer group.

Heavy metal listening is associated with certain patterns in personality, cognitive style, and belief systems. In a study of college students, Hansen and Hansen (1991a) reported that increased time spent listening to heavy metal music predicted a lower "need for cognition," that is, less interest in activities involving active, higher-level thinking. This makes sense, of course, in view of the negative relationship between heavy metal fandom and measures of academic performance and school commitment. Heavy metal listeners in the study also tended to demonstrate higher levels of Machiavellianism, implying, in the authors' words, "a greater likelihood of engaging in social behaviors that most people would judge to be manipulative, cynical, or amoral" (p. 344). This Machiavellianism seems consistent with research showing an association between attraction to heavy metal and lower levels of trust in other people (Gordon et al., 1992).

Arnett (1991a, 1991b) has claimed that heavy metal fans share an essentially libertarian belief system, an attitude that pretty much "anything goes," that the worst possible state of affairs is one in which authority figures, rules, and basic values interfere with the freedom to seek thrills and stimulation. Hard-core heavy metal fans, he suggests, are driven by a generalized tendency to seek sensations and thrills and a need to engage in a variety of risky behavior such as drug use and sexual and criminal activity, more or less "to see what it would be like" (see also Litle & Zuckerman, 1986). In accord with this thesis, Arnett reported differences between heavy metal fans and nonfans not only in their expression of sensation-seeking motivations generally, but also in their self-reports of specific reckless behaviors, including drunk driving, casual sex, and marijuana and cocaine use.

There is little question of a relationship between risky, reckless attitudes and behavior and the choice of heavy metal music. Using a scale of adolescent risk taking with such items as "I accept rides from people I don't know" and "I take part in dangerous activities," a group of Australian researchers found scores 25% higher for male heavy metal/rock fans than male pop fans. Self-reported frequency of delinquent behavior was 60%

higher than in the comparison group (Martin et al., 1993). According to Wass and her colleagues (Wass, Miller, & Reditt, 1991), youth in juvenile detention were three times more likely than regular high school students to claim heavy metal as their favorite music, and an overwhelming 96% of the Whites placed in an "optional middle school" for behavioral problems reported heavy metal to be their choice of music (Epstein et al., 1990).

An attraction to heavy metal predicts drug use as well. The Australian study mentioned earlier revealed 50% more admitted use of illicit drugs among metal/rock fans than pop fans. Arnett (1991b) has reported similarly wide gaps in a U.S. sample—50% of the heavy metal fans said they had used marijuana and 20% cocaine, compared to 16% and 0%, respectively, among those who did not like heavy metal. Finally, a study comparing chemically dependent youth with a sample of "normal" high schoolers (Eagle, Hawkinson, & Stuessy, 1989; see also King, 1988, for a similar comparison) revealed what the authors described as an "astounding" difference in music orientation, with heavy metal the almost unanimous choice of the drug-involved group. To illustrate, they provided this profile of "Billy," one of the drug-dependent kids in the study: "He listens to heavy metal and MTV about 5 hours a day, and even sleeps with it. Assuming that he sleeps an average of seven hours a night, Billy is exposed to heavy metal at least 12 hours of a 24-hour day, seven days a week—one-half of his total existence" (p. 5).

Although only a minority of heavy metal songs deal explicitly with Satanism, black magic, or witchcraft, such themes are far more prevalent in the genre than in other popular music, and evidence tentatively suggests an association between heavy metal listening and Satanic beliefs. Trostle (1986) found that street youth identifying themselves as "stoners" were much more likely than other youth both to prefer heavy metal and espouse belief in the existence of witches, voodoo, and the power of black magic. Among the college students surveyed by Hansen and Hansen (1991a), time spent listening to heavy metal was significantly associated with a tendency to say Satanic beliefs are widespread, a finding the authors interpret as an indication of more permissive attitudes toward the occult (see also Yee, Britton, & Thompson, 1988). Still, it is probably more accurate to say that the few adolescents who qualify as Satanists are likely to be metal fans than it is to characterize metal fans generally in terms of Satanic beliefs. Arnett (1991a) has suggested that, if anything, their religious or spiritual outlook is distinguished from other adolescents by an *absence* of religious belief, traditional or untraditional (Arnett, 1991a). Indeed, he has claimed that their very cynicism prevents them from taking Satanic messages too seriously. Most fans see the Satanic themes as just another marketing gimmick used to attract attention. As a savvy Slayer fan put it: "It's just a concept, . . . like other bands singing about sex" (Arnett, 1991a, p. 91).

Of course, heavy metal bands sing about sex, too, and in a way that many critics of the music find particularly demeaning, callous, and exploitative of women. It is natural, then, to ask whether any relationship exists between heavy metal affiliation and sexual attitudes and behavior. The research suggests a connection in this area as well. In one study, 54% of a group of high school-age heavy metal fans said they had had sex with a casual acquaintance, compared to 23% of nonfans (Arnett, 1991b), and other research shows a correlation between a taste for heavy metal and approval of premarital sex (Yee et al., 1988). More relevant to the specific nature of heavy metal music's treatment of women, Hansen and Hansen (1991a) found that the amount of time college students listened to heavy metal correlated with a "macho" personality. They identified two distinct elements of this sort of personality: (a) "male hypersexuality," indicated by levels of agreement with the idea that "young men need sex even if some coercion of females is required to get it"; and (b) level of general respect for women. Greater exposure to metal music was associated with more hypersexuality and less respect. In addition, those who listened to more heavy metal music gave lower estimates of the frequency of date rape and higher estimates of the rate of sexual activity in the general population than those who listened less. These attitudes, say Hansen and Hansen, also fit the macho personality. Finally, Christenson and van Nouhuys (1995) reported consistent positive relationships between middle-school students' attraction to heavy metal and various measures related to dating activity, such as whether the student had ever been out on a date, whether parents allowed dating, and how important it was to have a boyfriend or girlfriend. As they note, it is an open question whether "dating" meant anything to these younger students other than going out for ice cream, but the findings suggest a connection between heavy metal and interest in other-sex contact even as early as 11 or 12 years of age.

People have also expressed concern over the potential impact of heavy metal music's dismal, depressed view of the world and of its depiction (some have suggested glamorization) of depression and suicide. Obviously, with suicide ranking third after automobile accidents and homicide as a cause of adolescent death in the United States, the stakes are high here. Arnett has described the heavy metal world view in this way:

One can hear an echo in (heavy metal themes) of concerns with social issues from the music of the 1960's, but with this difference: the songs of the sixties often lamented the state of the world but promised a brighter future if we would mend our ways; heavy metal songs often lament the state of the world but do not provide even a hint of hope for the future. Hopelessness and cynicism pervade the songs. (Arnett, 1991a, p. 93)

Pursuing the implications of this attitude, a team of Australian researchers have explored what relation there might be between a preference for heavy metal music and adolescent risk factors for suicide (Martin et al., 1993). As Martin and his colleagues note, many of these risk factors are well established by existing research: Depression, feelings of hopelessness, previous suicide attempts, frequency of suicidal thoughts, drug abuse, and family problems all predict the likelihood of further suicide attempts. Their questionnaire data from over 200 Australian high school students suggest strongly that attitude toward heavy metal music fits among these other predictors of vulnerability to suicide. In general, those who preferred heavy metal or hard rock music reported higher levels of depression, suicidal thoughts, and more frequent infliction of self-harm. More specifically, 20% of the males and over 60% of the female heavy metal/hard rock fans reported having deliberately tried to kill or hurt themselves in the last six months, compared to only 8% and 14%, respectively, of the pop fans. Interestingly, these associations were all much stronger for females than males, prompting Martin and his colleagues to suggest that the relatively small percentage of female metal fans tend "to be more disturbed as a group, claiming more suicidal thoughts and acts" than male heavy metal zealots.

The reference to "disturbed" youth provides a good transition back to the question raised at the beginning of this section, namely: Is it legitimate to speak of a "heavy metal syndrome," that is, of a constellation of related traits with heavy metal at the focal point? Our feeling is probably not. True, a passion for heavy metal music tends to coincide with a variety of traits and behaviors: depression, suicidal thoughts, impulsiveness, drug use, delinquency, distance from parents and school, heavy reliance on peer influence, cynicism and amorality, sexual precocity and sexist attitudes, and so on. However, if there is a "syndrome" at work here, it is a "troubled youth syndrome," not a heavy metal syndrome. Leaving aside for the moment the question of whether popular music exercises any influence on adolescents' values and behavior (and we think it probably does), assuredly the consumption of heavy metal is not what brings together the various "at-risk," "troubled," or "alienated" characteristics with which heavy metal fandom is associated. Rather, the proper way to phrase the relationship is to say that White adolescents who are troubled or at risk in a variety of ways and for a variety of reasons gravitate strongly toward the style of music that provides the most support for their view of the world and meets their particular needs.

Perhaps the point can be further clarified by juxtaposing these statements: (a) most heavy metal fans are not particularly troubled or at risk; (b) kids who are troubled or at risk tend overwhelmingly to embrace heavy metal. In other words, whatever percentage one uses to estimate the proportion of heavy metal fans in the total adolescent population, they surely number in the tens of millions. Most of these kids are not on drugs, not in jail, not failing in school, not depressed, perhaps not even particularly at odds with their parents (except maybe when it comes to music). The correlations indicate that metal fans manifest these tendencies to a greater extent than their nonmetalhead contemporaries. However, it should be kept in mind that only in a few of the studies cited here have the correlations between attitudes to heavy metal and measures of personality and behavior risen above the .30 or .40 level. In other words, knowing that a youth loves heavy metal improves the odds of guessing certain other characteristics, but more uncertainty than certainty remains after the rule is applied. As we have said, the level of certainty is much higher if prediction runs the other direction: that is, if we know a youth is White, male, 15 years old, drug-involved, and in trouble with the law, then the odds are very high that his music of choice will be some sort of heavy metal.

We do not mean to imply that heavy metal music plays only a supporting role in this constellation of traits or that the music is merely peripheral in the lives of heavy metal kids. True, a parent whose child listens to heavy metal two or three hours a day but does not exhibit any other troublesome tendencies probably has little to worry about. Offensive as the music may sound from the bottom of the stairs, it will not turn the kid into a monster. However, in the presence of other traits—depression, animosity toward school, cynicism, and so on—a deep involvement in heavy metal may well be taken as a significant additional sign of trouble. Roe (1995) has coined the term *media delinquency* to refer to the close association between the cultural choice of what he calls "disvalued" media and other more standard forms of delinquency. As he put it: "*Both* the use that adolescents make of media contents that are socially perceived as disvalued and problematic *and* delinquency may be usefully conceived of as one dimension of the symbolic and behavioral reaction to failure and other problems at school" (p. 627). His position is essentially the same as the one we have proposed, that although "media delinquency" (such as the choice of heavy metal) may not *cause* problems in school or delinquent behavior, it is an essential part of the delinquent reaction to the deeper problems surrounding school failure and alienation from the mainstream adolescent culture. This point of view makes good sense in view of the seriousness with which most metal fans take their music affiliation. As Arnett (1991a) has pointed out, heavy metal music is central to the alienated and disaffected youth who seek it out. It provides a crucial source of personal identification and group solidarity, and articulates as no other set of cultural texts can their opposition to the cultural mainstream and their quest for alternative modes of self and peer acceptance. For many of these youths, listening to heavy metal is what matters most to them; indeed, it is often their primary source of solace. In other words, cases like that of Billy, which we described earlier, may not be as rare as one might think.

RAP MUSIC AND CULTURAL TOURISM

According to industry research, White listeners make up 60% of the rap music listening audience (Harrington, 1994), and Whites account for almost 75% of rap album sales (Lusane, 1992). For females and males alike, rap invariably emerges at or near the top of the list of music types for suburban White youth. Obviously, then, rap music occupies a much more central, mainstream niche in the adolescent culture than heavy metal. This "mainstreaming" of rap presents an interesting puzzle in view of the intense criticism it receives from parents, teachers, media critics, and other adult cultural authorities. Dramatically different as rap and heavy metal are in their sound, for many adults the two are as one when it comes to breaking the rules. Rap's singular ability to mobilize the protests of "legitimate" cultural authorities suggests that it, like heavy metal, might appeal disproportionately to kids on the margin, chafing from the shackles of school, home, and mainstream cultural norms. Even rap's most obvious difference from heavy metal, its urban African-American roots, suggests that it might occupy a marginal, minority status outside that culture. Rap musicians portray a dramatically different world than the one experienced by middle class youth. Indeed, rap lyrics often express the bluntest, most virulent hostility toward the White culture. Given all this, one might expect rap's appeal outside the inner city to be limited to kids who are at odds with their own community and its values. This, then, is the "rap anomaly": Despite its "bad boy" reputation and its "foreign" cultural roots, rap attracts a broad spectrum of White youth.

Why do so many suburban kids find rap attractive? First, whether adult authority figures like its lyrics or not, rap is arguably the freshest, most compelling sound in contemporary popular music. Like jazz, rhythm and blues, soul, and disco before it, rap follows a long tradition of innovation and mainstream acceptance of African-American music. Rock and roll itself traces directly back to Black rhythm and blues (Frith, 1981), and rap attracts White adolescents in the 1990s for some of the same reasons kids were drawn to rock and roll in the 1950s: novelty, energy, and a reputation for being rebellious and "on the edge." Of all the current popular music styles, the rap/hip-hop culture most defines the pop cultural cutting edge, thus providing adolescents concerned with "coolness" and peer status much crucial information on subjects such as the latest slang and the most recent trends in dance and fashion. Rap's incorporation by the mass media, especially in television situation comedies and broadcast advertising, further testifies to its broad appeal. Very few commercials aimed at adolescents feature heavy metal or even hard rock, but ads for products ranging from malt liquor to breakfast cereal capitalize on rap's catchy rhymes and rhythmic energy, thus infusing a sanitized version of rap music and dance style into mainstream culture.

In addition, we propose that the racial and cultural differences that at first seem capable of alienating the middle-class audience may in fact enhance rap's acceptability by allowing middle-class youth to buy into the music without buying into its message. Although middle-class White kids may appreciate rap's general tone of defiance, presumably they do not identify with the content of rap lyrics and the message of rap culture nearly as much as urban African-American youth do. Thus, for suburban White youth an involvement with rap music amounts to a form of "cultural tourism," a way to participate in rap's vibrancy without actually having to live in the inner city. This suggests, in turn, that middle class audiences may select or reject rap music based on style and sound rather than on content, with the lyrics performing more of a rhythmic function than a symbolic one.

Such a cultural tourism hypothesis receives support from the research. Kuwahara (1992) compared Black and White university students' reasons for liking or disliking rap music. The Black students placed a fairly equal emphasis on the beat and the message—indeed, "hardcore" rap fans,

most of them males, cited the music's message as the most important element in their enjoyment. They clearly identified with and participated in
rap's expression of Black male empowerment and resistance to dominant
cultural forces. Generally speaking, whether they liked rap or not, the
responses of the Black students indicated a high level of involvement with
its cultural meaning. White students, on the other hand, showed far less
involvement in their relationship to rap music. Most, in fact, wrote nothing in response to the question of why they liked or did not like rap, and
among those who entered a response none mentioned the lyrics or the
message of the music. Many listened to rap music simply because it was
being played somewhere in their environment—on the radio, for instance,
or in a neighboring dorm room. Their attitudes toward rap were essentially dismissive—it was entertaining, amusing, different, but not to be given
any close attention. Thus, although Kuwahara did not put it in these terms,
the contrast between Black and White students is consistent with a contrast between cultural immersion and cultural tourism.

Working with 12- to 15-year-old suburban youth, Christenson
and van Nouhuys (1995) provided a comparison between the predictors
of heavy metal and rap "fandom." Their findings, too, seem consistent
with a distinction between a high involvement–cultural immersion mode
of music affiliation versus a low involvement–cultural tourism mode.
Levels of affinity for heavy metal were associated with precisely the sorts
of factors that would be expected based on a cultural immersion model.
That is, in line with the reputation of the music (and consistent with prior
research), heavy metal fans reported considerably more peer (versus parent) orientation, less positive attitudes toward school and higher levels of
conflict with parents and school authorities than did nonfans. In other
words, these White suburban youth seemed to base their responses to a
culturally proximate White rock form at least partly on how much they
identified with the music's anti-establishment themes.

Rap affiliation, on the contrary, was largely unrelated to the sorts
of attitudes and orientations one might expect based on its reputation.
That is, despite rap music's open defiance of adult and mainstream cultural values, it held no special allure for those who rejected the importance
of school or saw themselves in conflict with school and parents. The main
difference between rap fans and nonfans was that fans were more interested in the opposite sex and more interested in spending time with their
friends (as distinct from actively arguing with their parents). In other
words, those who liked rap appeared to be farther along in the basic adolescent processes of establishing independence from the family and form-

ing satisfactory peer and other-sex relationships (Feldman & Elliott, 1990), but they did not appear alienated from adults or marginalized in their own peer culture.

Apparently, then, although many White youth express an attraction to rap, they maintain a detachment from its political and social discourse. In essence, they play the tourist's role. If this is true, what are the implications of this cultural tourism? First, given the apparent lack of direct identification with rap's messages, it seems unlikely that exposure to rap music or rap culture will have much direct impact on the values and behavior of young White listeners. If the music is not *about* them, presumably it will hold few important lessons *for* them. The most likely influence, other than on dancing, fashion, and style, may be to form their conceptions of contemporary African-American culture. For many White teens the mass media—especially music and music videos—provide the primary source of information about the inner city and the people who live and work there. If, like other travelers, these suburban rap tourists arrive at new "understandings" of the place they have visited, they must, like other tourists, base these understandings on the small sample to which they have been exposed. Clearly this presents a problem—rap may be an authentic expression of the lives and experiences of the musicians who perform it, maybe even the neighborhoods they live in, but it provides at best a limited and distorted snapshot of urban African-American experience.

If we could be assured that these young White cultural tourists knew that Black America was not equivalent to gangsta rap, maybe the distortion would not matter as much. Unfortunately, rap fans, both White and Black, assign great authenticity and credibility to hardcore gangsta rappers. More "positive" (less violent, misogynist, sexually explicit, racist) rap music is often ridiculed as a prettied up, sanitized version of the real thing, what Lusane (1992) has called "rap lite." Positive, "liberal" rap has turned out to be a commercial failure. Music companies are perfectly aware of the limited market for innocence and often take special care to highlight and even embellish recording artists' police records in order to enhance their street credibility (Samuels, 1991). If the music companies are right that young listeners equate the hardcore of rap with the inner core of African-American experience, then the impact of crossover rap listening may be more to cultivate negative racial stereotypes than to advance cross-cultural understanding.

5

THE MESSAGES
IN THE MUSIC

When I want you, in my arms
When I want you, and all your charms
Whenever I want you, all I have to do is dream.
—Everly Brothers (1958)

Hey, we want some pussy!
—2 Live Crew (1990)

Most of the criticism now being directed at popular music and music videos stems from something in their "content." With the popular song, this means lyrics—sometimes specific words, sometimes more general images or portrayals. With music videos, of course, visual information gets most of the attention, but the issues involved span the same range from the specific (e.g., how women are dressed) to the general (e.g., how women are treated in relationships). Different people worry about different things, but it would not take any of us very long to find something in the messages and imagery of music media that we would just as soon not have young people hear or see. Given these concerns, a review of popular music content is in order.

We believe that the words and images in music media carry implications for adolescent socialization. Still, some qualifications and warnings must be introduced at the outset of the discussion. First, to a large extent the "message" of popular music, for those who love it as well as those who hate it, resides not in certain words or pictures but in the "sound"—the melodic and rhythmic qualities that differentiate popular music from other music and pop music genres from one another. The child and adolescent fans who love it ground their music preferences and purchase decisions first and foremost on these auditory elements of style, not on the complexion of the messages or stories conveyed in the lyrics. Indeed, what most of us probably think of as the story or the "message" is often—perhaps usually—ignored during the music listening or video viewing process.

As for those who hate it, it is worth recalling that the constituencies who pressed most urgently for the eradication of rock and roll in the 1950s aimed their criticism and outrage not at the lyrics, which were about as sappy and sentimental as anything out of Tin Pan Alley, but at the throbbing sexual implications of rock's rough, primitive, musical structure and the provocative physical gyrations these "jungle rhythms" produced in performers and audience alike. In the 1950s, the Iranian government actually banned rock and roll, but not on the basis of the ideology expressed in its lyrics. Rather, Iranian authorities were alarmed by reports of a rash of hip injuries incurred by frenzied dancers (Ward, Stokes, & Tucker, 1986). What was radical, then, about early rock and roll was the way it sounded, not the stories it told. Today, when many people say they hate pop, rap, or heavy metal they more often express a visceral response to the musical style than a rational objection to the images or themes embedded within it.

One should also keep in mind that music and messages about music come through various channels other than stereos, radio stations, and the MTV network. To be sure, these "primary" music media attract most of the criticism and nearly all the research. Even so, it should be noted in passing that movies, talk shows, album cover art, pop magazines, rock concerts, even posters and t-shirts are all, in a sense, "music media"—that is, they are part of the extended music culture and are involved in its discourse—and all of them deserve more attention from social commentators and social scientists than they have received thus far.

Any discussion of music content should also be tempered with a healthy respect for the importance of context in music use. The songs and videos themselves provide some important contextual information: Stylistic variables such as rhythm, melody, or vocal inflection can radically alter the meaning of a certain lyric or picture. The meaning of a song depends on a host of circumstantial factors—the performer who sings it, the site of the performance, with whom one listens, and so on. Everybody can think of a song that had a special impact on them because of the people and setting originally associated with it, and everybody can think of a familiar song that assumed a completely different meaning when it was redone by a new performer. As for the importance of the performance context, one need simply recall comedian Roseanne Barr's notorious Dodger stadium rendition of the "Star Spangled Banner" at the 1991 National League playoffs. She screamed, she bellowed, and at the end she spat on the ground and scratched her crotch. She got the words right, though.

Having said all this, we still argue that "content" matters. First, for a significant number of listeners, the meaning of lyrics (or the "message" of a music video) is every bit as crucial in their pleasure as the melody or beat. Even for the majority who would rank other music qualities higher in importance, lyrics, themes, and meaning are central at certain times and under certain circumstances. Depending on their own experience and what they observe casually around them, people mistakenly tend to view the music listening process in one of two stereotypical ways. In one view, music functions mainly to manipulate atmosphere or mood, while lyrics (which according to this perspective are often unintelligible and uninterpretable anyway) are more or less ignored. The other perspective sets music much more in the foreground and posits rapt attention to lyrics and obsessive involvement with their meaning.

This clash of viewpoints emerged in an interesting way during a talk on popular music we gave to a group of California pediatricians. During the discussion period following the lecture, one 45-year-old physician objected vehemently to any suggestion that lyrics might influence listeners. "If music has any impact at all," he said, "it can't be from the lyrics, because everybody knows that kids don't pay any attention to them. At least mine don't. They're just after the emotional high and party atmosphere they get from the music. Besides," he concluded (and here a palpable tone of personal violation crept into his voice), "the volume is always cranked up too high to understand the words anyway." At this a colleague of his countered by recalling times when she had seen music listeners pay the keenest attention to lyrics. During her high school and college days, she said, she and her friends would spend hours intricately unraveling the deep meanings of their favorite songs. "If lyrics are ignored," she commented, "how come so many kids are able to sing hundreds of pop songs word for word?"

Obviously, the dichotomy is false: Both images of music listening reflect reality. Sometimes lyrics do remain in the background—for that matter, the music that carries the words often plays a background role. Other times, though, the words and what they mean matter a lot. In fact, recent developments in the music industry may boost listener attention to lyrics. One is the common practice of including a full transcript of the words along with a new cassette or CD, a practice that was quite unusual 15 or 20 years ago. Once in printed form, of course, the words become more accessible to interpretation and analysis. The other development is the current climate of controversy surrounding sexually explicit, violent, and Satanic messages. Ironically, the public uproar surrounding these messages may bring lyrics and their meaning closer to the center of the music experience than they might otherwise be.

THEMES AND PORTRAYALS IN MUSIC LYRICS

Like literature, film, television, and other forms of artistic expression, popular music touches on a prodigious array of subjects. Love, death, work, play, sports, smoking, drinking, drugs, homes and home towns, war, peace, fathers and sons, starvation, obesity, capitalism, dogs (the Beatles' "Martha My Dear" was reputedly about Paul McCartney's Australian sheep dog)—all these and thousands more subjects have provided grist for the popular songwriter's mill (see Cooper, 1991, for an overview of the range of themes). And the range in tone and treatment is as broad as the range in subject matter. The lyrics that head this chapter, for instance, are both about male–female relationships, but there is a pretty wide gulf between "All I have to do is dream" and "Hey, we want some pussy!"

Dramatic as they can be, however, such examples of topical range and extremes in treatment are poor indicators of what adolescents listen to on a day-to-day basis. The critical question is not what merely exists but what prevails in the discourse of popular music. Informal observation and argument by example can be useful in detecting gross (in a couple of senses) trends; that is, we can probably trust our intuition that the mere existence of lyrics like 2 Live Crew's "Hey, we want some pussy" or Slayer's "I feel the need . . . to fuck this sinful corpse" signal some sort of change in the nature of popular music lyrics. However, casual observation may too easily be used to offer support for any point of view. If one wanted to argue that popular music has always been sexually explicit, selected examples from the blues of the 1930s or 1940s could easily be found to illustrate the proposition—for example, these lines from Bessie Smith's "Empty Bed Blues" (Johnson, 1928):

> He's a deep deep diver, with a stroke that can't go wrong;
> He's a deep, deep diver, with a stroke that can't go wrong;
> Oh, he can touch the bottom, and his wind holds out so long.

Examples of Platonic romanticism in the music of the 1990s could be trotted out just as easily to show that music is as innocent and sweet as it ever was.

In short, not much is settled by selective reference to extreme examples, and so when possible we base this chapter on quantitative content analyses—studies that draw on large, representative samples of music or music videos and employ clear, consistently applied definitions and categories. Of course, such research cannot settle all issues. Content analyses usually focus on message characteristics that are readily observed and easily agreed on, thus they may not be particularly well suited to the unraveling of implicit, unconscious, or latent themes. Yet this limitation may not be as critical as it seems. Messages or themes so abstruse or subtle as to be undetectable by standard content analytic techniques are probably of little relevance in a discussion of what really reaches most children and adolescents. Young listeners pay attention to lyrics but their information processing is generally not very deep or analytical. The simple, straightforward themes are the ones most likely to get through. As we discuss in Chapter 6, when lyrics or video narratives are the least bit complicated or allegorical there is very little agreement among listeners on what they "really" mean.

BOY MEETS GIRL

Those who say pop music has somehow "always been that way" are right in at least one respect. Now, as always, the most common theme is the boy–girl issue—courtship, romance, falling in and out of love, and increasingly in recent years, sex. However, once the analysis extends beyond the global level, important historical trends emerge in both the frequency and the tone of the portrayals.

In terms of frequency, the last 50 years or so have seen a general downward trend in the predominance of love and courtship themes. The earliest systematic research on popular music lyrics focused on Hit Parade songs from 1941–42. At that time, over 90% of popular songs revolved around themes of love and romance (Peatman, 1944). Over a decade later, sociologist Donald Horton (1957) examined the lyrics of 235 top hits from 1955 and put the proportion about love and romance at about the same level. Horton classified the great majority of these as "songs in the conversational mode," that is, addressed by the singer directly to the object of desire or torment (e.g., "Baby I Need Your Lovin'," "Baby Please Don't Go").

By the mid-1960s, however, love themes began losing ground to other concerns. Applying the same sampling method and thematic categories as Horton, communication researcher James Carey (1969) found the proportion of songs from the 1966 charts about love and romance to have dropped to 70%. In other words, 30% were about different subjects. Because the major difference between the 1955 and 1966 pop charts was the replacement of older music forms with rock and roll, Carey concluded that this greater thematic range was a fundamental phenomenon of rock and roll music. A spate of content analyses between the late 1960s and the early 1980s traced a further erosion of the dominant position once held by romantic themes. By the early 1980s, in fact, only about 50% of the songs on the *Billboard* charts dealt unambiguously with love, romance, or sex (Hyden & McCandless, 1983; Rice, 1980). Curiously, in view of the apparent urgency of recent content-related controversies, there are no published analyses of lyrics in the 1980s and early 1990s careful and thorough enough to provide a solid basis for gauging current trends. Previously unpublished data from Roberts and his students (Roberts, Kinsey, & Gosh, 1993), however, suggest that love and romantic themes returned to a somewhat higher level in the 1980s and early 1990s. They analyzed the primary themes in the Top 40 hits for each even-numbered year from 1980 through 1990, a total of 240 songs in all. The results in Table 5.1 indicate that over 70% of the songs were built around a love relationship theme, with only minor fluctuations during the decade. Dance and music themes appeared in about 7%, social and political issues in 5%, identity and growing up in 5%, and loneliness in 3%. The remaining 8% covered a variety of miscellaneous topics, none occurring in more than a handful of songs.

Of course, the concern about popular music content has not arisen from its natural predilection for love and courtship but from the directions such themes have taken. Different critics object to different things. Some lament the displacement of Platonic love by overt sexual depiction, others bemoan the sad and pessimistic portrayal of relationships, still others worry about the stereotypical way in which lyrics describe the women (and sometimes the men) involved in the relation-

Table 5.1. Major Themes in Top 40 Songs from 1980-1990.

Theme	1980-82 (%)	1984-86 (%)	1988-90 (%)	Overall (%)
Love relationship	72	66	79	73
Dance, music	6	9	7	7
Social & political issues	4	8	4	5
Identity, growing up	5	8	0	4
Loneliness	4	4	3	3
Miscellaneous	9	5	7	8
(N of songs)	(80)	(80)	(80)	(240)

Note: Figures based on the top 40 songs on the year-end *Billboard* charts in each even-numbered year from 1980-1990. Percentages may not add to 100 due to rounding.

ships. Whatever the specific complaint, though, it is clear that the way popular music deals with the boy–girl issue has changed significantly.

The most obvious trend has been toward more emphasis on the physical, sexual aspects of love and less on the emotional. Popular music—and this will surely surprise no one—has become a good deal less romantic than it once was. A more detailed comparison between Horton's (1957) analysis of mid-1950s lyrics with Carey's (1969) later replication illustrates the nature of this change. Horton identified five distinct stages in the way popular songs played out what he called the "drama of courtship":

1. *prologue,* in which the singer wishes or dreams about love abstractly with no particular love object in mind
2. *active courtship,* that is, the seeking or wooing of a specific person as yet unattained
3. *honeymoon,* or the happy-in-love, glad-I-found-a-girl (or-boy)-like-you phase
4. *the downward course of love,* in which outside forces (usually either parents or the cruel, unfaithful love object) threaten an existing relationship
5. *all alone,* pining away for a lost love.

Of these, the courtship phase was most frequent, accounting for about 40% of the songs in Horton's sample, with the "all-alone" phase close behind at 30%. About one song in six dealt with the downward course of love, and the honeymoon and prologue stages were least frequent, neither appearing in more than 10%.

A decade later, Carey (1969) noted several changes in the way pop music dealt with love and sex issues. First, when he applied Horton's classification scheme to the love-related lyrics of the 1960s, Carey was unable to find an appropriate category for a quarter of the songs in his sample. They concerned love in the most general sense, but the treatment did not really fit any of the stages Horton had described. As for those that did fit Horton's categories, Carey observed a number of changes in emphasis and treatment. The prologue phase had essentially disappeared. By the 1960s, when boy met girl they plunged straight into courtship. Moreover, the songs about courtship painted a more active, less fatalistic picture than in 1955, with the outcome of the relationship much more in the singer's own hands and less in the hands of fickle fate or a disinterested lover. Finally, the honeymoon or happy-in-love stage was far less romantic and rarely displayed any expectations of commitment or exclusivity in relationships.

Carey much preferred this new dialogue to the old. As he saw it, the old double standard so common in 1955 had been at least partially cast aside in favor of more equality in relationships, and issues related to love and sex were at last being exposed to open and frank discussion. "Love," he wrote, "is basically physical—people are animals, but happy animals" (p. 726). Current observers may well look back with a certain wistfulness on the examples he provides of this carnality (all lyrics quoted in Carey, 1969, pp. 725-726):

the Supremes ("Love is Like an Itchin' in my Heart," 1996),

> Love is like an itchin' in my heart,
> Tearing it all apart
> Just an itchin' in my heart, baby I can't scratch it.

the Troggs ("Wild Thing," 1967)

> Wild thing, I think you move me
> But I wanna know for sure. . .

the Mamas and Papas ("Somebody Groovy," 1966),

> Oh, please please believe me
> I need someone to relieve me.

Needless to say, the evolution toward more explicit treatment of physical love did not stop in the mid-1960s. An analysis by Richard Cole (1971) tracked the same trend into the early 1970s, providing illustrations such as the Rolling Stones' unambiguous "I laid a divorcee in New York City..." from the song "Honky Tonk Woman." In 1982, a research team at the University of Florida published a 30-year trend analysis of music lyrics under the title: "Popular Songs Emphasize Sex, De-emphasize Romance" (Fedler, Hall & Tanzi, 1982). They placed the top five hits for each year between 1950 and 1980 into one of three categories, depending on whether the relationship described was primarily: emotional, focusing exclusively on a strong, emotional bond; physical, focusing on sexual attraction or pleasure; or balanced between the two.

The trend from emotional to physical was dramatic. In the 1950s, 90% of the songs about relationships were described as either "very" or "somewhat emotional," 7% balanced, and only 3% either very or somewhat physical. In contrast, only about 40% of the songs in the 1970–80 decade were essentially emotional in their approach, with the rest either balanced or primarily physical. "By the 1970's," the authors conclude, "lyrics had become so explicit that no one could doubt their meanings" (Fedler et al., 1982, p. 14). The examples they cite seem to bear out their conclusion—song titles such as "Let's Get It On," "Kiss You All Over," and "Do You Think I'm Sexy," and lyrics like these from Rod Stewart's "Maggie May" (1971): "You turned into a lover and mother what a lover, you wore me out/All you did was wreck my bed, and in the morning kick me in the head."

The study of top 1980s hits to which we referred earlier also provides some insight into trends in sexual explicitness, as Figure 5.1 shows. Roberts, Kinsey & Gosh (1993) divided their 240 songs into three categories: those that made no references to sex, those with implicit references to sex (e.g., "Let's go all the way"), and those with explicit sexual references. The results showed that, if anything, the overall frequency of sexual references decreased slightly during the 1980s. Much more striking, however, was the change over the decade in the relationship between implicit and explicit sexual language. In 1980 and 1982, 40% of the songs contained implicit language, and only 4% had explicit language. By 1988 and 1990, implicit references to sex decreased to about 20% and explicit increased to 15%. In other words, although references to sexual activity did not increase during the 1980–1990 period, the language used to describe it became more direct.

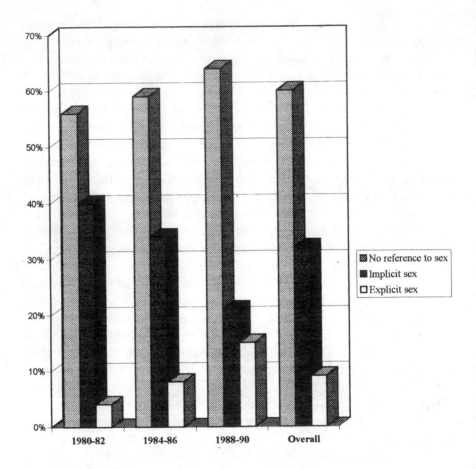

Figure 5.1. Proportion of top 40 songs with references to sex, 1980-1990

Note: Figure based on the top 40 songs on year-end *Billboard* charts in each even-numbered year from 1980 to 1990. Percentages may not add to 100 due to rounding.

Regrettably, very few studies have compared the content of different styles and genres of popular music. This omission matters because of the increasing Balkanization of the pop music map, with its fragmentation into quite distinct, even antagonistic genres and subgenres. As we discussed in Chapter 4, few adolescents listen unselectively to the *Billboard* top hits. Rather, they actively seek (or studiously avoid) specific music types: pop, heavy metal, reggae, rap, classic rock, alternative, World Beat, college rock, roots rock, Latin, R&B, and so on. Content analyses that ignore these divisions say rather little about what specific segments of the adolescent population really listen to.

In 1980, Ronald Rice published a rare exception to this pro-crustean tendency. Rice compared lyrical themes from top songs on four separate *Billboard* charts: pop (which at the time included rock), rhythm and blues (or R&B—primarily contemporary popular music by Black performers), country and western, and easy listening (EZL). Considering first the two music types youth are most likely to favor, songs off the pop charts were significantly more pessimistic about romantic relationships than R&B hits. Songs dealing with the downward course of the relation-ship or being left alone outnumbered "honeymoon" songs by a ratio of three to two within the pop category. R&B lyrics were much more opti-mistic, with honeymoon songs considerably outnumbering "left alone" or "downward course" songs. Both R&B and pop were distinguished from country and EZL by their frequent incorporation of "dance" themes—this was, after all, the "Saturday Night Fever" era.

Interestingly, although lyrics have become more frank and openly sexual, we find no evidence that popular music has become generally less sanguine about romantic relationships over the years. Indeed, songs with gloomy or desperate overtones have always held a slight edge over happy, positive portrayals, and the trauma of courtship (the desperate search, the wondering if you are loved, the obsessive dwelling on the departed loved one who has forsaken you) has always been a staple of music's discourse on love. For songwriter as well as listener, something about the sad times, about "losing your baby," simply seems to call for a song. Singer-song-writer John Prine made a telling comment on this connection during a 1991 interview on the public radio program "Fresh Air." Host Terry Gross had complimented his most recent release, comparing it favorably to one of his early albums, thus implying that intervening efforts had been somewhat less distinguished. Prine acknowledged the point with: "Yeah, both albums came just after I got divorced."

IMAGES OF WOMEN AND MEN

Two decades ago, feminist critic Marion Meade (1972) wrote that: "Rock music, in fact the entire rock culture, is tremendously degrading to women" (p. 173). Obviously, many of today's observers would agree. Indeed, some of the fiercest attacks on popular music's cultural messages arise from the feminist perspective. From this camp, the offensive thing about recent lyrics is not the reduction of love to sex but the increasingly exploitative and abusive treatment of women in sexual contexts. To be sure, it is easy to find examples of this sort of treatment in recent lyrics and music videos—we provide a few ourselves later in this chapter. However, the systematic research on gender-role portrayals in popular music lyrics tends to draw a more nuanced picture than comments like Meade's might suggest. Wilkinson (1976) examined a sample of 200 popular songs from the years 1954–68 for signs of sexism or gender stereotyping and was forced to conclude that the roles and characteristics of women were not dramatically different from those of men. Men and women, for example, were equally likely to be the primary actors or initiators in relationships. If anything, certain patterns contradicted standard stereotypes: Men often cried, begged, pouted, expressed dependence and need, acted submissively, and "played the fool," and women were portrayed overall as less dependent and vulnerable than men (Wilkinson, 1976).

A comparable study of 110 popular songs from 1972–82 (Hyden & McCandless, 1983) confirmed Wilkinson's observation that both genders often displayed emotional vulnerability and dependency, but some gender differences emerged as well. Males, for instance, were more often associated with characteristics such as initiative and competence and expressed loneliness more often than females. Females showed more warmth, acted more seductively, and interestingly enough, were portrayed as more powerful than men. The authors concluded that the late 1970s and early 1980s popular music they studied incorporated a seemingly contradictory view of women: passive and childlike yet powerful and seductive.

A research report in the November 1985 issue of *Sex Roles* (Cooper, 1985) provides both good and bad news for those concerned with the portrayal of women in popular music. The study tracked trends in female images over the 30-year period from 1946 to 1976. The good news was a significant decline in portrayals of women as dependent and submissive. In the 1940s, almost 40% of the songs about women presented them as highly needful or "clingy," compared to only 20% thirty years later. At the same time, however—and in line with the general trend from Platonic to physical love—the proportion of songs referring to women's physical characteristics (hair, eyes, skin) increased sharply over the period. Finally, the study corroborated the increasing tendency of rock music to portray women as dangerous seductresses. The data revealed a dramatic increase over the three decades in references to women as evil, threatening, and conniving. Rather than applauding the assertive modern woman, many rock musicians—both male and female—seemed to fear and resist her emergence.

Some of these findings make more sense when one considers that from the earliest days of rock and roll at least 60% and at times as much as 75% of the top popular music performers have been male. Of the 240 songs analyzed by Roberts, Kinsey, and Gosh (1993), almost two in three were performed by solo males or male-only groups (see also Denisoff & Peterson, 1972; Hesbacher & Anderson, 1985; Wells, 1986). Inevitably, then, issues of love and courtship are much more often framed from a male perspective than a female one. This imbalance complicates the picture of gender-role portrayals, especially in studies (including all that we have cited to this point) that take no account of the singer's gender.

Consider a first-person portrayal of a woman in a relationship with a man. Even if she were to describe herself in the song as emotional, devoted, desperate, and so on, the meaning of these qualities would be much different than if a male singer were assigning them to her. The nature of the source, in other words, clearly alters the meaning. It would seem important, then, to separate songs sung by female artists about themselves from those sung by male artists about a woman. Actually, given the specificity of popular music taste, an ideal approach would differentiate by both gender and genre. To put it more concretely, if one is concerned with the images of females or male–female relationships a 15-year-old boy is most likely to encounter and identify with, it makes little sense to give any weight to soft rock ballads sung by women.

Unfortunately, the only content analysis to combine these two elements is now over 15 years old and of limited value as a measure of current portrayals and images (Freudiger & Almquist, 1978). One finding from the study, though, is worth noting: At least in the 1970s, songs sung by men portrayed the opposite sex in much more glowing terms than songs sung by women. Although the portrayals of women in male-perspective songs varied in some specifics by genre (in soul music, for instance, women were less submissive than in country music), women were seldom portrayed negatively. Songs from the female point of view not only tended to portray men stereotypically as aggressive, demanding, active, and so on, but were highly critical in doing so. This does not mean, of course, that the songs by males were enlightened and noble. In country music, especially, but in many pop and rock songs as well, women are often extolled for their dependency and submissiveness, a form of praise most women could quite happily do without. Nor does it mean that songs by women (many of which are written by men) are hypercritical or unfair. The male subjects may richly deserve the opprobrium heaped on them. Clearly, though, the gender of the voice matters in all this, and it ought to be considered more often and more seriously by content analysts.

We find, then, both similarities and differences in the way popular music portrays men and women. The similarities, such as the frequent reference to both men and women as emotional and needy, probably derive in part from the natural tendency, mentioned earlier, for popular songs, no matter who sings them, to adopt a sad or at best bittersweet tone. In fact, the finding that the men in popular songs are often allowed to reveal emotion, uncertainty, and dependence is really what one might call a "first-person effect." That is, because song lyrics tend to refer to the first person as emotional, desperate, lonely, sad, and so on, and because most songs are sung from the male perspective, males often appear vulnerable. As for the gender differences, no doubt some of them arise from real differences in gender-role expectations and gender stereotyping. Popular music lyrics, like the content of all media, will reflect these cultural patterns. Yet the overall impression from the studies of pop and rock music cited here is that, although stereotyping certainly exists, the values and images embedded in music seem to be somewhat less rigidly stereotypical than in other popular media.

RECENT TRENDS IN SEX AND SEXISM

Given the lack of very recent content analyses, it is impossible to be precise about current trends, either in sexual explicitness or in sexism. It is clear, however, that the limits have been pushed much farther in the last few years. Compare, for instance, the Rolling Stones', "I laid a divorcee in New York City," which is certainly clear enough, with 2 Live Crew's 1989 line "Nibble on my dick like a rat does cheese." The former is clear enough, maybe, but it is far less graphic and vivid. We have already provided a few examples of this new trend, and many more can be found in newspaper and magazine articles running under headlines such as "X-rated" (*Time*, May 7, 1990), "Singing Dirty" (*Portland Oregonian*, March 25, 1990), "The Rap Attitude" (*Newsweek*, March 19, 1990), and "MCA, Seagram Assailed for Graphic Lyrics" (*Billboard*, December 21, 1996). Ironically, the best source of offensive lyrics short of buying the albums used to be the Parents Music Resource Center (PMRC), who until recently argued its point about "porn rock" by compiling and distributing an exhaustive compendium of sexually graphic, misogynist, violent, and Satanic music lyrics.

In case some readers have missed out on all this, we offer a sampling. Consider these excerpts from various groups over the past decade or so:

Rushed her in the room, sat her on the bed
Grabbed her by the ears as she gave me head
Then I turned her over, got it from the back
The pussy was sorry so the bitch got slapped.
   ("S & M," 2 Live Crew, 1988—rap)

Evil dick likes warm, wet places,
Evil dick don't care about faces,
Evil dick likes young, tiny places,
Evil dick leaves gooey, telltale traces.
   ("Evil Dick," Body Count, 1992—rap)

The blade of my knife faced away from your heart
Those last few nights
It turned and sliced you apart
Laid out cold, now we're both alone,
But killing you helped me keep you home.
   ("You're All I Need," Motley Crue, 1987—hard rock/heavy
      metal)

Now I ain't looking for a love that lasts
I need a shot and I need it fast
If I can't have her, I'll take her and make her.
   ("I Want Action," Poison, 1988—hard rock/heavy metal)

Panties round your knees, with your ass in debris,
Doin' dat grind with a push and a squeeze;
Tied up tied down, up against the wall
Be my Rubbermade baby, an' we can do it all.
   ("Anything Goes," Guns N Roses, 1987—hard rock)

Got me a big old dick and I like to have fun,
Hold it against your forehead I'll make you suck it.
Maybe I'll put a hole in your head, you know, for the fuck of it,
I can reduce you if I want.
   ("Head Like a Hole," Nine Inch Nails, 1994—alternative rock)

Obviously, popular music has not always been exactly *this* way, never mind the Stones' laying a divorcee in New York City, Marvin Gaye's "getting it on," or the orgasmic background breathing in Donna Summer's late 1970s disco hits. These new lyrics would simply have been unthinkable 20 or even 10 years ago.

Current research cannot answer precisely how prevalent such lyrics are or the number of youth who are hearing them. It is clear, however, that the music industry's common disclaimers that such lyrics come only from a few marginal groups and that the problem of offensive lyrics is small in relation to the entire universe of recorded music make no sense in terms of what teenagers listen to. True, if one considers all releases—classical, jazz, New Age, polkas, Broadway musicals, big band, country, ethnic music, and so on—only a tiny percentage are sexually explicit. For that matter, most album releases are purely instrumental. Yet these other music categories account for very little of adolescent music listening. As for the marginality argument, maybe one could say back in 1985 when the Senate Commerce Committee held its hearings on the porn rock issue that the critics were dredging up some rather arcane groups (Mentors, Bitch, Piledriver, and Impaler). However, there is nothing obscure today about Guns N Roses, Poison, Metallica, Ice-T, Dr. Dre, Snoop Doggy Dogg, and Nine Inch Nails. Indeed, many mainstream pop artists—(the artist formerly known as) Prince, George Michael, Michael Jackson, and Madonna, for example—have for years produced songs with lyrics not much less graphic than the rap and heavy metal that now gets most of the criticism in the press.

One measure of the incursion of graphic sex into the current music mainstream is the excellent chart performance of "stickered" albums. For the past few years it has become standard practice in the recording industry to identify tapes or CDs with potentially offensive lyrics with a "PARENTAL ADVISORY: EXPLICIT LYRICS" warning sticker or label. Because the decision to sticker an album is exercised by the record companies themselves, parental advisory warnings are applied "conservatively," that is, only to the strongest, most graphic material. Lyrics with even the slightest ambiguity tend to escape unscathed, as do those with a mere smattering of four-letter words. Even so, stickered albums routinely do well on the *Billboard* charts: In fact, the second hottest album of 1991, Guns N Roses' *Use Your Illusion I* (total 1991 sales over 4 million), sported a parental advisory label. In Summer 1994, one of our students examined a random sample of over 1,000 CDs in Portland-area record stores and found 8% overall bore parental advisories. For certain music types, however, the rate was much higher: 13% of the heavy metal albums and 58% of the rap albums were stickered (van Nouhuys, 1994).

Of course, that albums with parental advisory labels achieve successful sales does not mean explicit sex or degradation of women have become the norm in popular music lyrics. Even today, most pop and rock songs contain lyrics with traditional, romantic themes. We doubt, for instance, if the trend since 1990 has taken the proportion of top hits with explicit sexual references much beyond the 15% or so found by Roberts and his students (Roberts, Kinsey, & Gosh, 1993). Strangely, the hard and soft edge coexist side by side on today's music charts. Ice-T raps about anal intercourse even as pop star Michael Boulton croons "Love is a wonderful thing, makes ya smile through the pouring rain." Yet the claim can no longer be made that the hard edge exists only at the outer edge. Indeed, in Summer 1997, no fewer than 5 of the top 25 albums in the United States carried a parental advisory sticker.

Interestingly, one increasingly popular new genre—"alternative music" (or "modern rock," as it is called in the *Billboard* charts)—contains very few references to sex, graphic or implicit. Quite the contrary, compared to other styles of popular music, alternative music incorporates a relatively low level of concern with romantic relationships in general. Hare and Christenson (1996) examined the lyrics of a random sample of 50 songs from Billboard's 'modern rock' charts and were unable to discern any clear thematic focus for most of them. These examples illustrate the ambiguity found in many of the lyrics:

> I thought I knew all it took to bother you,
> Every word I said was true, that you'll see,
> How could it be I'm the only one who sees your rehearsed insanity
> I still refuse all the methods you've abused,
> It's all right if you're confused, let me be.
>   ("I'll Stick Around," The Foo Fighters, 1995)

> I'm just a mutt and nowhere is my home,
> Where dignity's a land mine in the school of lost hope,
> I've panhandled for life because I'm not afraid to beg,
> Hand me down your lost and founds of second hand regret.
>   ("No Pride," Greenday, 1995)

> Take off your coat, your silver is tarnished,
> Lady in darkness, the cat is old and still,
> Keep all your makeup packed on your head,
> Invite all the demons, the truck stops in the bed.
>   ("Same Dress, New Day," Tripping Daisy, 1995)

To the extent any primary themes could be determined in "alternative" lyrics, they include: first, a concern for relationships, that is, many references to a "you," but to a "you" that could as easily be a father, a friend, or a stranger as a romantic partner; and second, a concern with, even an agonizing over, issues of personal identity. The best two words to describe the themes in alternative music may be ambiguity and angst—a diffuse feeling of confusion, anxiety, and uncertainty about one's place in the world runs through most alternative songs. We discuss in our next chapter the "problem" of interpretation, that is, the wide range of meanings both adolescents and adults assign to music lyrics. Alternative lyrics seem especially open to these disparate readings. One thing about them is clear, however: They are usually not about sex.

POLITICAL AND SOCIAL THEMES

Overtly political themes were rare in pre-rock popular music. In his analysis of early 1950s music, for instance, Horton (1957) judged only 12% to be about anything other than love or romance, and these few were essentially apolitical, consisting mostly of religious, comedy, and dance themes. Beginning in the late 1960s, though, a significant number of songs with consciously political or social messages began to penetrate the pop charts. In fact, much of the early empirical research on rock and roll was stimulated by the perception that popular music was suddenly saying something about social injustice and war instead of getting a girl, that is, saying something important enough to warrant "serious" academic research. Popular music's political voice was relatively clear and strong during the late 1960s and early 1970s. Yet even during the golden age of "protest rock" the number of songs concerned in any obvious way with political or social issues probably never exceeded 1 in 10 (Freudiger & Almquist, 1978), and we see little evidence that this figure has changed dramatically since. In their analysis of 1980–1990 top songs, Roberts Kinsey, and Gosh (1993) found that only 5% conveyed themes related to political and social issues. Still, given the place of political and social themes as the largest "non-love" category and the common perception, both within the rock community and without, that political music has the power to move young minds, the evolution of political and social protest lyrics deserves some attention.

For most of the period since the 1960s, the dominant politics of rock has been liberal/progressive—peace, love, equal rights, United States out of Central America, save the tropical rain forest, and so on—a "politics of Woodstock," as it were. Of course, this liberalism was always laced with a healthy dose of libertinism, especially when it came to sex and drugs, but it has generally been a politics of the left. The high water mark of the politics of Woodstock came in the late 1960s and early 1970s, but it lives on, partly through new recruits (especially in alternative rock), but also through a cadre of 40- and 50-something rock legends like Paul Simon, Sting, Jackson Browne, Michael Jackson, and Bruce Springsteen. Classics in the mold include Marvin Gaye's "What's Goin' On," John Lennon's "Give Peace a Chance," Bruce Springsteen's "Born in the USA" and Michael Jackson's 1991 release "Black or White."

The new politics, like the new sex, is disproportionately associated with rap and heavy metal. There are, of course, immense differences between rap and heavy metal, but in the present context they share this: In both, open expressions of social hostility and intolerance increasingly supplant the progressive tradition of peace and tolerance. The politics of Woodstock, then, is giving way to what we call a "politics of attitude." Just as in the case of sexual content, one encounters in the politics of attitude an acrimony and meanness of spirit never before encountered in popular music: Blacks excoriate non-Blacks, Whites vilify non-Whites, and both berate homosexuals, with the venom played in often brutal terms.

Even the music industry has become embarrassed by the politics of attitude, indeed sufficiently so to attempt some strategic distancing from it. In January 1990, CBS Records President Walter Yeltnikoff responded to the outcry over alleged anti-Semitic lyrics in Public Enemy's album *Fear of a Black Planet* with an internal memo, reading in part: "A number of recordings have recently been released which have stirred strong reactions . . . suggesting that these songs validate and promote bigotry and intolerance. . . . When the issue is bigotry, there is a fine line of acceptable standards which no piece of music should cross" ("Yeltnikoff issues," 1990).

In this case, CBS did not pull the album nor discourage its distribution and purchase, and it quickly rose to the top of the charts. Industry embarrassment may have led to stronger pressures, however, in the case of Ice-T's 1992 release of "Cop Killer," a song that included the lyrics "Die, die, die, pig, die" and "I'm about to dust some cops off." The public outcry surrounding the song was probably multiplied tenfold by the timing of the release just after the Los Angeles riots. Ice-T bowed to public and corporate (in this case Warner Records) pressure and withdrew the song from his group's *Body Count* album, raising issues of free expression that some find as troublesome as others find the lyrics. Regardless of this particular outcome, however, similar messages are certain to recur, and they will just as surely evoke strong reaction.

The politics of attitude appears not just in fringe acts but in the work of many of the very hottest artists in the industry, and the trend is not limited to rap and heavy metal. In 1990, Madonna was denounced by the Anti-Defamation League for lyrics in her "Justify My Love" single that seemed to suggest Jews were agents of Satan (Britt, 1992). A similar outcry in 1995 forced Michael Jackson to change the phrases "Jew me" and "Kike me" to "Do me" and "Strike me" in his song "They Don't Care About Us" (Smith, 1995). The top-selling White, hard rock/heavy metal band Guns N Roses has developed a special reputation for intolerance with lyrics such as:

> Police and niggers, that's right, get outta my way
> Don't need to buy none of your gold chains today. . .
> Immigrants and faggots, they make no sense to me
> They come to our country and think they'll do as they please
> Like start some mini-Iran or spread some fuckin' disease.
>   ("One in a Million," 1988)

Sometimes political messages (if we include expressions of bigotry in the category) mix with personal vendetta. In his 1991 album *Death Certificate*, Ice Cube not only railed at his estranged group NWA for hiring a Jewish manager, he even specified the proper remedy for the offense:

> Get rid of that devil, real simple,
> Put a bullet in his temple.
> Cuz you can't be the niggers for life crew
> With a white Jew tellin' you what to do.
>   ("No Vaseline," 1991)

In the same song Ice Cube exhorts his former comrades to lynch their new lead performer, and elsewhere on the album *Death Certificate* he refers to the tension between Korean-Americans and African-Americans in this way: "Oriental one-penny motherfuckers, pay respect to the black fist, or we'll burn your store right down to a crisp." These sentiments rose to such a level of offensiveness that even the generally forgiving editors of *Billboard* magazine issued an appeal to record stores to "strongly protest" the album. The week after the editorial appeared, *Death Certificate* rose to number 3 on the U.S. album charts.

These are not the only trends to attract attention from those concerned about popular music's role in adolescent socialization. Indeed, virtually any category of lyric could be seen, from some perspective or other, as a tear in the social fabric. Of the many possible points of controversy, though, a few have risen to prominence. In the balance of this section, we consider: violence, Satanism/occultism, suicide, and subliminal messages.

VIOLENCE, SATANISM, AND SUBLIMINAL MESSAGES

Parents and citizens' groups complain almost as much about violent lyrics as they do about sexual ones. Examples have already been provided of violence toward women and what one might call "people of difference," and violent imagery surfaces in various other contexts as well. Portrayals of gang or street violence are often the central theme in rap music (e.g., from Dr. Dre, "Rat-a-tat and a tat like that/ Never hesitate to put a nigger on his back"), and increasing levels of violence characterize other genres as well, particularly "death metal" and grunge (Wilson, 1994).

We do not know in specific terms what proportion of songs incorporate violence, although it is probably not a great proportion in the very top songs. Only 8% of the songs in our 1980–1990 top 40 analysis contained references to violence, and violence or death formed the primary focus in fewer than 1% (Roberts, Kinsey, & Gosh, 1993). But that study's time span ended about the time rap—the genre that has been most criticized for its violence—broke into the mainstream. If anything, the level of violence expressed in "gangsta rap" has increased in past few years. The other main source of violence in pop music, heavy metal, seldom breaks into the top 40, and so few heavy metal songs were included in the data collected by Roberts et al. (1993). Thus, it seems likely that the Roberts et al. study provides a low-end estimate of the frequency of violent themes and imagery in music lyrics. Whatever the frequency, a number of important questions about the specific form and nature of violent lyrics remain unanswered. We do not know, for instance, in what settings the violence tends to occur, whether it usually succeeds or fails, or who the victims usually are, all important issues in predicting the effects of media portrayals of violence. Most important, of course, we do not know how it is interpreted and what, if any, influence it has. We do know, though, that it appears quite frequently in certain genres, that it is prominent in the work of some of the most popular musicians, and that it appears to be on the rise.

Essentially the same holds for suicidal and Satanic or occult representations: They exist, they are not solely fringe phenomena, and they seem to have the potential to influence young listeners. Both of these types of themes are identified almost exclusively with heavy metal (or hard rock bordering on heavy metal) music. Indeed, a fascination for the morbidly bizarre defines certain heavy metal bands even more than violence and sex. *Billboard* writer Ethlie Ann Vare (1984) described the connection this way:

> Yes, metal takes heat from all sides. And not without reason. Slayer's recent Metal Blade release really does have sides labeled "6" and "66" instead of "1" and "2." Metal videos are full of women in cages, tattered clothing and collars. Motley Crue's album cover is a penta-gram. And what do you suppose the name Black Sabbath [a heavy metal group] connotes: a Tupperware party? (p. 1)

Often, two or more of the trademark heavy metal themes are woven into the same album and often into the same song, as in this airy tidbit from the song "Necrophiliac" (1985) by Slayer:

> Satan's cross points to hell, the earth I must uncover,
> A passion grows to feast upon
> The frozen blood inside her.
> I feel the urge, the growing need,
> To fuck this sinful corpse,
> My task's complete, the bitch's soul
> Lies raped in demonic lust.

Although they appear much less frequently than violent, sexual, and Satanic messages, lyrics with suicidal themes have also drawn criti-cism from parents and others concerned about the influence of music. Surely all would agree that suicidal messages, if they have any influence, pose a threat to the welfare of adolescents. One classic suicidal refrain comes from Ozzy Osbourne (also known to bite off the heads of live ani-mals during his performances), whose song "Suicide Solution" (1987) is alleged to have contributed to several teen suicides:

> Make your bed, rest your head,
> But you lie there and moan,
> Where to hide, suicide is the only way out.
> Don't you know what it's really about?

An intriguing and controversial connection between music and suicide involves the old subliminal message bugaboo. In 1989, the British hard rock band Judas Priest was sued by the parents of two teenage Nevada fans who, after a day of drinking, drugs, and listening to Judas Priest's album *Stained Class*, attempted to blow their heads off with a 12-gauge shotgun. One boy died; the other was permanently disfigured. Their parents claimed that the two had been pushed over the edge by subliminal messages in the album, particularly by the words "Do it," which they claimed had been subliminally embedded in one of songs. The judge dismissed the case—no harmful intent on the band's part could be shown, nor could hours of sophisticated audio reprocessing reveal the existence of the reputed subliminal goad. Still, the impact of suicidal messages, intended or unintended, manifest or subliminal, continues to be of concern.

Of special concern to those who believe in the influence of subliminal messages is the process known as "backward masking," an audio technique in which messages are recorded (or according to one theory inserted by the Devil himself) in reverse, thus camouflaging their Satanic intent and rendering defenseless the subconscious minds of young listeners. Playing music backward, people claim to have heard the words "Satan, Satan, He is a god" in a song by Black Oak Arkansas; "Decide to smoke marijuana" in Queen's "Another One Bites the Dust," "I love you, said the devil" in the music of the Rolling Stones; "Turn me on, dead man" on the Beatles' *Sergeant Pepper* album; and scores of other incantations to sin and devil worship from artists ranging from AC/DC to the BeeGees (McIver, 1988, pp. 52-53). Not all alleged "subliminal" material is backward masked. Believers in the power of subliminal persuasion, many of whom are not Christian fundamentalists (many, in fact, are liberal college students), claim to be aware of many *forward* examples that are inaudible at normal volume, acoustically distorted, recorded very fast or slow, or otherwise rendered unintelligible under normal listening conditions.

Forward, perhaps. Straightforward, no. In the Judas Priest case, for instance, the court was ultimately unconvinced that the words "Do it" were even on the album. Something was there in the background, but what? Recently we played the contested passage to our students and only one or two out of an entire class claimed to hear anything like "Do it," even when they were led to expect it. Some subliminal or backward messages unambiguously exist and have been introduced purposely, often simply to poke fun at the entire controversy (Walker, 1985). An album by Pink Floyd, for instance, contained the backward statement "Congratulations, you've just discovered the secret message!" However, after a thorough review of the issue, McIver (1988) concluded that most alleged examples of the practice were more imagined than real:

> [There are] undoubtedly real messages and images, embedded either to tease the fundamentalists, as a gimmick to arouse interest and increase sales, or perhaps even because the artists or technicians actually believe in their efficacy. . . . Except for this small percentage of deliberate subliminals, most examples seem to be simply constructions or projections by the more imaginative (paranoid?) listeners . . . who then coach and exhort their followers to see and hear the same messages and images. (p. 58)

Even if all subliminals could be established as real, there is no solid scientific evidence that they have any persuasive or cognitive impact or even that listeners are biologically capable of perceiving and processing them during normal listening (Walker, 1985). In any case, the manifest content of lyrics played forward at normal volume levels provides more than ample material for analysis without resorting to subliminal messages.

MUSIC VIDEOS

We assume no reader has completely escaped seeing at least a few minutes of MTV, and so we will not attempt a definition of the music video form here. In fact, a good measure of the uproar over the values and imagery in music videos arises from the difficulty of avoiding them. Audio media can stay safely up in the kids' bedroom and the nasty lyrics right there with them. Music videos are much more public. They appear on the same living room TV set as "Oprah" and the nightly news, and only the most vigilant of remote control cable grazers can avoid them entirely. Obviously, music videos attract special attention because of the visual element. Offensive and troublesome as some lyrics may be, the attitude prevails that, when it comes to influencing adolescents, words are one thing, pictures quite another. Many parents and media critics would agree with Tennyson that "things seen are mightier than things heard."

From a purely aesthetic standpoint, there is nothing revolutionary about setting pictures to music. Hundreds of Hollywood movies over the years have contained more or less free-standing songs with visualization, usually based in dance (Gene Kelly, Fred Astaire, and Ginger Rogers), but often accompanied as well by dramatization or extravagant visual display. By the simple definition "pictures to music," the definitive music video may still be Disney's 1940 animated classic *Fantasia*, which was re-released a few years ago in a promotional campaign calculated to capitalize on the film's status as the archetype of the music video form. Music visualization played a central role in the teen movies of the 1950s and 1960s, many of which were little more than thinly plotted vehicles for stylized music performance sequences by teen idols such as Elvis Presley, Frankie Avalon, or the Beach Boys. The pre-MTV zenith of rock music visualization arguably came in the two classic Beatles movies *A Hard Day's Night* (1964) and *Help!* (1965). The latter, especially, anticipated much of the zaniness and absurdism that has come to characterize contemporary music videos.

At the same time, it would be silly to deny the differences between Gene Kelly's curbside dance to "Singin' in the Rain" (1952) and the bizarre pyrotechnics of contemporary MTV. Music videos are an identifiable and unique popular artistic genre, a bedazzling, bombastic, often fragmented and surrealistic audio-video gestalt. Sometimes they tell a story, but just as often they present an elliptical and dream-like sequence of images lacking any apparent narrative structure. At times music videos make logical thematic connections between lyrics and visuals, but just as often the video component takes off in its own direction, unconnected to anything in the song but the beat. These and other distinguishing formal features—unorthodox camera angles, quick cutting, computer manipulation, and so on—mark a sharp distinction between the contemporary music video and previous examples of music visualization. Presumably, these differences in form make differences in meaning: A kiss, a rape, a fistfight, a murder, are not the same thing in the rock video context as they are in a motion picture or television show.

Just as critical to an understanding of the nature of music videos as these formal characteristics, though, is the distinctive economic function of music video. Whereas Gene Kelly's "Singin' in the Rain" sequence or the Beatles' cavortings to the songs in *Help!* were designed to add entertainment value to a cultural product sold directly and straightforwardly to the consumer, the essential function of music videos is a bit more ambiguous. In one sense, they operate as "pure" commercial entertainment; that is, they generate revenue through sales and rentals or, by virtue of their ability to attract and hold viewers, through the sale of product advertising on cable TV channels. At the same time, though, music videos are consciously designed and distributed with a promotional purpose in mind, functioning as advertisements for the music and the artists. So central is the commercial function that many assume no group or recording can hope to succeed without a video boost. (Indeed, the conventional wisdom has it that music videos were primarily responsible for the revival of stagnant recording industry revenues in the 1980s.)

Regardless of whether one accepts the argument that the music industry would languish without the hype injected by music video, it is easy to agree with media critic Patricia Aufderheide's (1986) observation that the "music video format always amounts to wall-to-wall commercials for something" (p. 62) or with Tetzlaff (1986) when he wrote that "MTV places fashion at the center of everything" (p. 87). An hour of the cable channel MTV (the undisputed king of music video channels) unfolds commercials within commercials after more commercials. The videos promote the artists and their music, the paid commercials (many of which are distinguishable from music videos only by their length) hawk consumer goods, and the gushy "V.J." patter touts MTV's programming and the music stars who appear in it. Even MTV's short "news" segments serve up a bubbly sort of "infotainment," essentially promotional in nature, seldom seriously critical of the music industry, its products, or its personalities.

Within the videos themselves, one is confronted by a relentless onslaught of fashion statements and consumer goods ranging from ruby nose rings to million-dollar yachts. Virginia Fry and Donald Fry (1986) of Wichita State University have characterized this cavalcade of commercial imagery as a "supermarket of styles," and propose that many young MTV viewers, after first selecting a certain stylistic or music subculture to join (e.g., rap, punk, or heavy metal), use music videos to learn the various markers of that style: what clothes to wear, how to arrange their hair, what accessories should go with the image, and so on. The only consumer information missing from most videos is the brand names. (In many boutiques and department store apparel sections today, a sort of tailor-made MTV is played, usually on several monitors. These videos are distinguishable from the "real thing" only because brand names *are* included.)

That product images and fantasies of wealth should be such essential ingredients should not surprise us in an age when kids happily shell out $30 for a t-shirt not despite but precisely *because* it advertises Guess, No Fear, Esprit, or Nike. Glamorized images of the things 15-year-olds dream of having figure as prominently into music videos as sex and violence. Indeed, one team of researchers concluded an investigation into MTV content by highlighting what was originally a peripheral concern in their research: "Perhaps the most staggering implication of our study," they wrote, "is found in the way rock videos glorify luxury and material wealth" (Vincent, Davis, & Boruszkowski, 1987, p. 755). At a certain level, this seems natural; after all, who could seriously conceive of a popular art for teenagers in which all clothing was modest and conservative and all cars were Honda Civics? Natural or not, though, this aspect of the form should not be ignored. For those inclined to speculate on the influence of music videos, their profound commercialism offers as likely a place as any to begin the search.

SEX AND VIOLENCE IN MUSIC VIDEOS

By far the majority of the criticism leveled at music videos is prompted by their sexual and violent imagery. Indeed, should anyone seriously doubt the prevalence of either, a few minutes of MTV should quickly settle the issue. This, too, seems natural enough—sex and violence have long been mainstays in U.S. popular media, and no segment of the population is more fascinated with them than teens.

Most studies of violence and sex in music videos distinguish between "performance" and "concept" videos. Performance videos depict an ostensible concert or studio performance of a song, with the video component consisting of shots of the musicians lip-synching the words, simulating the playing of their instruments, and gyrating on stage, all this intercut with shots of crazed, pulsating, fist-waving swarms of 16- to 18-year-olds. Not that performance videos are produced with stylistic restraint—on MTV, less is definitely not more—but underneath all the swish pans, fisheye lenses, tight close-ups of body fragments, multiple superimpositions, colorization, and frenetic cutting, the device is to show the music group doing its work.

Concept videos also tend to feature the musicians as central characters, but rather than lip-synching or mock-playing instruments, they enact characters in a drama. In some cases the drama offers a coherent story of some kind, usually grounded (however loosely) in the lyrics—boy meets girl, falls for girl, is spurned by girl, and so on. These are sometimes called "narrative" videos. In contrast, "conceptual" videos present not a story or progression of events but an impressionistic stream of images. Audio-video connections are abstract and nonthematic, that is, based on musical properties like rhythm, instrumentation, and sound "color" rather than on lyrics. In any case, it is concept videos that rouse the ire of most critics and form the focus of most content analyses. In reality, of course, performance and concept are properly seen as dimensional poles rather than two neat categories. Most videos are hybrids: that is, most performance videos incorporate at least a few non-performance-related video inserts, and most concept videos show the artist in some sort of performance mode, however stylized.

But on to sex. If one were to search for a metaphor or motif that would embrace the greatest possible number of rock videos, one could do no better than the "Dream Kegger": Rich Beverly Hills parents out of town, 10 luscious babes for every horny guy, unlimited booze ("kegger" refers to a party with a keg of beer), wanton carousing, and so on. The same general theme characterizes many rap videos. Needless to say, the main business of this dusk-to-dawn Bacchanale is chasing (and getting) girls (or boys). As with music lyrics, sex and courtship comprise by far the largest thematic category of music videos. One analysis of music video themes found that close to 50% were about love and sex, 20% carried social protest themes, and nearly 25% seemed to lack any central theme at all (Brown & Campbell, 1986).

Partly due to this thematic ambiguity and partly because visual stimuli seem to lend themselves better to micro-level analysis than do lyrics, most content analyses of sexual content in music videos focus on images or patterns of portrayal rather than underlying themes or messages. These studies find a lot of sexual imagery. It should be made clear, however, that the sex in music videos, however provocative and stimulating it may be, is not of the sort that would be slapped with an "NC-17" or even an "R" rating if it appeared on a movie screen. Videos contain little sexual intercourse and virtually no complete full-frontal nudity (Vincent, 1989). Rather, sex on MTV consists primarily of bikinis and lingerie, pouty looks, flirtation, suggestive dancing, necking, undulation, crotch-grabbing, and snaking up against street lamps: in other words, it is a matter of titillation more than consummation.

How much of all this one defines as "sexual" obviously depends on what is included in the definition. A study by communication researchers Barry Sherman and Joseph Dominick (1986), for instance, found that three quarters of concept videos contained "sexual acts," but by far the most common varieties were flirtation and nonintimate touching (e.g., holding hands), one or both of which occurred in 55% of the videos. Intimate touching, such as stroking or caressing, appeared in about 20%, and hugging and kissing each appeared in about 10%. A similar analysis conducted by Richard Baxter and his colleagues (Baxter, DeRiemer, Landini, Leslie, & Singletary, 1985) obtained essentially the same results: Sexual behavior appeared in 6 out of 10 videos, but almost all of it took the form of light physical contact, sexually suggestive dance movements, or provocative female attire. More recently, Tapper, Thorson, and Black (1994) found "sexual appeal" imagery, that is, the presence of implicit or explicit sexual images or symbolism, in about 30% of the videos sampled off various television channels. The 30% figure, however, masked large differences between genres: About 50% of the pop, soul, and rap videos contained sexual appeal imagery versus 23% of alternative, 14% of classic rock, and only 8% of heavy metal videos. Women are somewhat more likely to behave sexually than men, but sexual behavior is common for characters of both genres. Indeed, content analysis of videos from the year 1990 conducted by Sommers-Flanagan and her colleagues (Sommers-Flanagan, Sommers-Flanagan, & Davis, 1993) led to the conclusion that "the most salient MTV message is, whether you are male *or* female, *act sexual*" (p. 752; emphasis in original).

Although videos are unquestionably less morally conservative than other popular media, their sexual imagery is still overwhelmingly heterosexual and mainstream in nature. No study has reported more than a few isolated cases of overt sadomasochism, exhibitionism, sexual bondage, or other "taboo" or "deviant" sexual behavior. Like other sexual behavior, nontraditional sex tends to be shown through implication and in nonintimate contexts. For example, although the Sherman and Dominick (1986) study found a third of all "sexual acts" on MTV occurred in a same-sex (e.g., female to female) context, almost all fell into the category of flirtation and nonintimate touching. Same-sex kissing made up only 10% of all kissing. Similarly, whereas the Baxter research detected some sort of androgynous physical appearance in over 20% of the 62 videos analyzed, only one video depicted homosexual courtship or dating.

From this account of the research, music videos almost sound prudish and un-sexy. They are not, of course. The sexual repertoire may stop short of intercourse, but sexual fantasy is a key ingredient in the "dream kegger," and there is little question that the sexual imagery in music videos is increasingly graphic, sensual, and erotic. Comparing videos from the mid-1980s to those of the early 1990s, Burns (1994) concluded that the essential shift was from "rock-and-roll sex" (leering, posing, and so on) to "movie sex," characterized by sensuous kissing and embracing. Even if one is not troubled by the frequency of sexual depiction or the level of eroticism, many find room for concern in terms of the portrayal of women. A fair share of gorgeous male models preen and strut on MTV, as a glance at most Madonna videos will confirm, but the overwhelming majority of music videos are by male performers, and in most of these the women preen and strut for the gaze of men, not the other way around.

Indeed, the differences between male and female portrayals seem to be clearer and more far-reaching with music videos than with music lyrics. A study by Seidman (1992), for instance, demonstrates not only that women are much more likely than men to wear provocative clothing and be the objects of sexual pursuit, but shows strong gender differences in occupational status and personality characteristics as well. Seidman's research team formed judgments about the job status and character traits of nearly 1,000 characters appearing in 192 MTV clips. Almost all the job roles were filled by the stereotypically "appropriate" gender. Over 90% of the police, soldiers, and athletes and 100% of the scientists, politicians, and managers were male, and similarly high proportions of "female" occupations—for example, hair stylist, dancer, telephone operator—were filled by female characters. All but 2 of 14 character traits applied in the study showed significant gender differences, and most of those differences were in line with traditional cultural stereotypes: Male characters were more likely to exhibit adventurousness, aggression, and dominance; female characters were more affectionate, fearful, and nurturing.

Vincent and his colleagues examined both the extent of gender stereotyping and whether levels of sexism changed during a period of increasing feminist criticism (Vincent et al., 1987; Vincent, 1989). They selected a random sample of over 200 MTV concept videos, half from 1985 and half from 1986–87. Each video was placed in one of four categories, from most sexist to least:

- "condescending," in which women were treated uniformly as less than full people, that is, as sex objects, dumb blondes, whimpering victims;
- "keep her place," granting women some strengths and skills but within stereotypically female roles
- "contradictory," with a roughly equal balance between traditional, subservient roles and independence
- "fully equal," in which the female characters were treated equally and nonstereotypically.

During both of the time periods studied, "condescending" videos appeared more frequently than any other type. Thus, at least by Vincent's definition, MTV was offering up a great deal of sexist imagery, a conclusion that is hardly surprising. However, the situation changed over the two-year time span. Whereas in 1985 "condescending" portrayals outnumbered "fully equal" ones by a margin of 57% to 13%, the gap narrowed to 41% to 38% two years later. Vincent qualified this finding by observing that even in the 1986–87 period over 50% of male artist videos treated females in a condescending way (only 10% of those with female lead performers did so). Moreover, he acknowledged the impossibility of establishing any cause–effect link between the apparent change in portrayals and the heavy public criticism of the industry during the mid to late 1980s. Still, those inclined to be concerned about the way music videos represent women would presumably welcome any trend of this sort. The key question is whether the trend continues to the present. Given recent developments in popular music, especially in rap, this seems doubtful. A 1995 study comparing 20 rap videos with 20 alternative videos reports that 60% of the rap videos contained images that objectified women's bodies, and 55% contained "macho" images. The corresponding figures for alternative music were 35% and 25%, respectively (Utterback, Ljungdahl, Storm, Williams, & Kreutter, 1995), thus suggesting that genre makes as big a difference with music video content as it does with lyrics (see also Tapper et al., 1994).

What does the research show about violence and aggression in music videos? Although they differ in some important methodological areas, the various relevant studies all find violent imagery to be nearly as much a staple for music videos as sex. In 1984, the National Coalition on Television Violence (NCTV) published data indicating that some form of violent or hostile behavior occurred about 18 times an hour in MTV programming. Of the 62 videos Baxter and his colleagues (1985) examined, over half (53%) contained representations of violence or crime. About 25% of the videos showed physical violence against people, 1 in 6 incorporated dance movements that mimicked violence, and about 10% displayed guns, chains, knives, or other dangerous weapons. Homicide appeared in only 2 of the 62 videos.

Sherman and Dominick (1986) also looked at violent content. They excluded performance videos from the analysis and applied a more restrictive standard than either the NCTV or the Baxter study, counting only "overt expressions" of violence. This ruled out, for instance, mere threats (NCTV included them) and nonviolent crimes (Baxter included these). Even by this tougher standard, 56% of 166 concept videos contained at least one violent act. As in the study by Baxter et al. (1986) most of the violent behavior was hand-to-hand combat—punching, pushing, wrestling—rather than weapon-assisted assault. When violence did occur, it typically incurred no consequences. Only 12% of the violent acts led to injury and 3% resulted in death.

In 1989 Cleveland State University researchers Pamela Kalis and Kimberly Neuendorf examined a random sample of MTV videos for the presence of "aggressive cues," that is, events or objects representing physical harm. Perhaps because of this expanded definition, or perhaps because of a historical trend toward more violence in videos (Baxter et al. and Sherman and Dominick performed their study in the mid-1980s), they reported a much higher frequency of violent imagery than previous research. Three fourths of the concept videos in the sample included one or more aggressive cues. Equally interesting, though, is that nearly one in three *performance* videos also portrayed aggressive content. This finding points out the vagueness of the distinction between performance and concept videos and challenges the logic of excluding performance videos from content analytic studies. Kalis and Neuendorf (1989) also performed a shot-by-shot analysis of the visual prominence of aggressive imagery. They found that whereas only a limited percentage of shots (13%) and total screen time (about 10%) was devoted to violent or aggressive imagery, the images that occurred tended to be visually prominent, that is, shown in close-up or extreme close-up (see also Seidman, 1992). In sum, although precise estimates vary from one study to the next, it is clear that violent behavior and imagery are common in music videos. Moreover, both casual observation and research results indicate that such portrayals are not on the decline (Tapper, Thorson, & Black, 1994).

Both critics of the music media and social researchers have expressed special concern about violence against women. In 1984, NCTV head Thomas Radecki claimed on the basis of his research that "the intense sadistic and sexual violence of a large number of rock music videos is overwhelming; it is surpassed only by Hollywood's glut of revenge and slasher movies" (quoted in Zuckerman, 1984, p.1). However, our reading of the research on sexual violence provides some comfort, cold though such comfort may be in view of the many other manifestations of misogyny in popular music and music videos. Generally speaking, the patterns of aggression and victimization in music videos reflect the demographics of the medium. That is, because males outnumber females by about two to one on the screen, most violence ought to be male on male, and content analyses bear out this expectation: Male characters make up a large majority of both the perpetrators and the victims of violence in music videos. In fact, the primary violation of these gender demographics arose in the form of disproportionate levels of woman-on-man violence. Kalis and Neuendorf observed that only about 20% of all male violence in videos was directed against females. In comparison, over 60% of all female aggression was aimed at males. A dark cloud may surround this silver lin-ing in that this peculiar pattern probably reflects the prevalence, especially in hard rock and heavy metal videos, of what Sherman and Dominick (1986) dubbed the "predatory female" stereotype, a stereotype that feeds on and into male resentment and fear of strong, independent women. Overall, however, whether out of conscience or a feeling that blatant vio-lence against women might not get aired (this seems to be one issue on which the in-house censors at MTV draw the line), videomakers seem to chart a course away from graphic violence against women.

Thus far we have stressed the content areas that have received the most attention from critics and researchers. Obviously, though, con-sumerism, violence and sex do not exhaust the array of themes and images in music videos. Related to violence, but still conceptually distinct from it, are the frequent portrayals—especially in hard rock, heavy metal, and rap videos—of frustration, anger, rage, and defiance against symbols of authority. One does not have to watch MTV for very long to see examples of adolescent nose-thumbing at parents, teachers, businessmen, police, politicians, or other symbols of power and money. Some might say that is what rock and roll was originally all about. Indeed, Susan Bleich and her colleagues (1991) have argued that among rock music's many themes "none is more obtrusive . . . than that of adolescent defiance of freedom-curtailing impositions by persons or institutions in power" (p. 351). Some of the rage and rebellion is more or less free-floating—in one study from the early days of MTV nearly half of all the concept videos analyzed con-tain "nihilistic" images (Davis, 1984)—and much of it is quite targeted, often shading into social protest.

Somewhere between 20% to 25% of music videos incorporate themes of overt political or social protest, a considerably higher propor-tion than with song lyrics. Most themes are straight out of the traditional politics of Woodstock, that is, oppression of the little man by big business and big government, the horrors of war, and so on (Wadsworth & Kaid, 1988). In fact, music videos often convert romantic, apolitical songs into political or rebellious video statements. The mutation may simply be a matter of what works well on the screen: Violent social conflict allows for more striking visual imagery than diffuse rock poetry. The higher politi-cization of videos versus lyrics may also result from the fact that the peo-ple who write the songs often have little to do with the production of the video. Perhaps, when nobody is looking, the 40-to 50-year-old music company A&R people and Hollywood videographers who make the important decisions in music video production seize the opportunity to reassert the tradition of Woodstock.

THE FOREST OR THE TREES?

University of Massachusetts professor Sut Jhally has claimed that the female objectification and exploitation so frequently seen in music videos cultivate a social climate conducive to rape and other mistreatment of women. To illustrate his case Jhally (1994) has edited together an impressive collection of what he considers misogynist MTV images and added through narration some dramatic statistics on violence against women. Jhally calls this hour-long video onslaught of breasts, buttocks, seductive pelvic thrusts, and simulated rape scenes *Dreamworlds: Desire, Sex, and Power in Rock Video*, and he sells or rents it on a nonprofit basis to individuals or groups interested in the effects of sexist imagery in music videos.

Jhally might well be criticized for jumping the gun with his strong claims. We are unaware of any direct evidence either supporting or refuting his theory about the effects of MTV on the incidence of rape. Perhaps the most important question, though, is whether Jhally is playing fair with his criticism. In a column under the heading "Sex, Lies and the Trouble with Videotape," *New York Times* popular music writer Jon Pareles (1991) accused both Jhally's work and a similar video expose of porn rock produced by the Parents' Music Resource Center, *Rising to the Challenge* (Vision Videos, 1988), of two types of deception: unrepresentativeness, that is, being unfairly selective in their process of collection and reporting; and decontextualization, lifting images from their original surroundings. According to Pareles: "Watching 'Dreamworlds' makes it clear that academics are just as prone as fundamentalists to misunderstand rock video" (p. H–31).

The charge of unrepresentativeness is assuredly true. Pareles is quite right to say the sort of exploitative and violent imagery compiled by Jhally and the PMRC do not characterize *all* music videos. However, as Pareles is himself no doubt aware, both *Dreamworlds* and *Rising to the Challenge* are political rhetoric, hence they play by a different set of rules than systematic, quantitative content analyses. Political rhetoric is by nature selective and biased: It can be little else if it is to be the least bit effective. To be sure, such rhetoric must be examined for honesty and accuracy. If, as Pareles maintains, the two videos claim to be representative, then this claim should be examined. If, to the contrary, they claim only to illustrate the existence of a problem or to call attention to certain things without pretense to telling the whole story, then they may be forgiven for their selectivity.

To emphasize the second charge, that of decontextualization, Pareles wrote: "'Dreamworlds' uses the illusory logic of video: it tears images out of context, then proceeds as if juxtaposition equals logical connection" (p. H–31). Perhaps, but as Pareles himself seems to be aware, an irony exists here: His definition of Jhally's transgression might just as easily be a definition of music videos themselves. The uniqueness of music video as an aesthetic form rests largely on this very process of ripping apart and stitching back together. This does not make Pareles' charge wrong, nor does it relieve people like Jhally, the PMRC, or the researchers whose work we have cited from paying as much attention to context as they possibly can. Yet a legitimate question arises about the true importance of the sort of contextual information Pareles refers to.

Many music videos are so disjointed and inscrutable that possibly the narrative context in which one finds sexual, violent, racist, or for that matter positive, images matters less than the images themselves. Some of the content analyses reported in this chapter have characterized the broad thematic focus or thrust of music texts; others have pursued more micro-level analyses. The studies of music videos, especially, have tended to focus more on molecular issues–the frequency and nature of specific kinds of events, vignettes, and images–than on stories and themes taken as a whole.

The question, obviously, is: Which level of analysis is more appropriate? This issue would not matter much if the macro picture corresponded perfectly to the micro. In fact, the two levels of analysis can yield sharply divergent impressions. It could be argued, for instance, that even in recent years most music media messages, when viewed from the widest angle, remain reasonably well in line with conventional, mainstream notions of what is important and right. Taking this view, Leming (1987) has noted that when sexual promiscuity is portrayed in popular music, it is just as often treated as a road to unhappiness than as a solution to loneliness. Leming has also challenged the common assumption that the music media are fundamentally countercultural in nature. Because teenagers are more conservative and conventional than popular representations often make them out to be, one should expect the media texts they produce and consume to reflect this conservatism.

But Leming is looking at the forest. A narrower angle of view reveals a different picture. Even if many songs do paint a reasonably romantic and traditional picture of boy–girl relationships, many others contain graphic sexual lyrics. Even if most videos fail to challenge traditional norms and symbols of authority, many others display themes and images of defiance and rebellion. Forest versus trees issues arise even within specific songs or videos. If in the end a song portrays casual sex as a road to unhappiness, the casual sex nonetheless occurs along with the language used to describe it. If a music video, taken as a whole, makes a strong anti-war statement, it may still be riddled with violent imagery. Moreover, song titles may give a different impression than song lyrics. The title phrases "I Want a New Drug" by Huey Lewis and "Born in the U.S.A" by Bruce Springsteen may be as close as many listeners ever get to the lyrics' meaning: Yet a thorough reading of the lyrics reveals the former to be anything but pro-drug and the latter far from patriotic.

Music lyrics and music videos, then, operate at different informational levels. Whatever their deepest message or "definitive" interpretation, embedded within them is a wealth of simple behavioral description and example—snapshots and vignettes of how people meet, talk, dress, fall in and out of love, treat old people, express joy, deal with stress and frustration, and even how they can sing and dance and grab their crotch all at the same time. Obviously these bits and pieces appear in a textual context, and that context matters. But the context that matters most may not be the complete, deeply read moral or message of the narrative, assuming there *is* a narrative. Rather, the most important context of music messages rests in the lives and minds of the kids who listen and watch. Perhaps the most important thing to bear in mind in any discussion of the content of music and music videos is that messages and effects are not synonymous. If today's music contains historically unique levels of sex or violence, that does not determine how those messages influence kids. Many factors intervene between content and effect. We now turn to some them.

6

MAKING SENSE OF POPULAR LYRICS

I don't listen to the words, only how the song
sounds. I don't give a damn what they say.
   —Southern California teenager (1987)

The old chestnut about the 5-year-old who loved Sunday School because
she got to sing a song about a bear named Gladly is probably apocryphal.
It endures because, dubious origin or not, it is a good story based on an
easily recognized kernel of truth. The cuddly little Teddy named Gladly
("Gladly, the cross-eyed bear") elicits smiles and knowing nods because
people recognize that children often misinterpret the "real" meaning of
things—in this case, the opening line of a well-known Christian hymn
expressing the singer's willingness to carry Jesus' cross ("Gladly the cross
I'd bear"). We suspect it also endures because it expresses a fundamental
truth that extends well beyond children. Anyone—child, adolescent, or
adult—may attribute meaning in ways that can surprise, delight, enrage,
or simply mystify others.

MAIRZY DOATS AND MONDEGREENS

Consider these "nonsense lyrics" made popular in the mid-1940s:

Mairzy doats
En dozey doats
En little amzee divy
A kiddelee divy two,
Wooden u.

Anyone close to 60 years old, give or take a few years, should recognize those lyrics. They are transcribed here precisely as the older of the two authors of this book sang them for 20 years, enjoying them as a nonsense verse taught to him by his parents during his preschool years. Imagine his surprise when the "real" words were revealed:

Mares eat oats,
And does eat oats,
And little lambs eat ivy;
A kid'll eat ivy too,
Wouldn't you?
  ("Mairzy Doats," 1943)

Almost 40 years ago, Silvia Wright (1954) coined the term *Mondegreen* to describe such misunderstandings of songs and other verbal expressions. Recounting her childhood fondness for the English ballad "The Bonny Earl of Murray," she described how this story of two slain lovers moved her to tears:

Ye Highlands and ye Lowlands,
Oh, where hae ye been?
They hae slain the Earl Amurray,
And Lady Mondegreen.

Indeed, as good poems and songs are meant to do, the ballad led the romantic young Ms. Wright to create a vivid and elaborate image of what must have transpired:

I saw it all clearly. The Earl had yellow curly hair and a yellow beard and of course wore a kilt. He was lying in a forest clearing with an arrow in his heart. Lady Mondegreen lay at his side, her long, dark brown curls spread out over the moss. She wore a dark green dress embroidered with light green leaves outlined in gold. It had a low neck trimmed with white lace (Irish lace, I think). An arrow had

pierced her throat; from it blood trickled down over the lace.
Sunlight coming through the leaves made dappled shadows on her
cheeks and her closed eyelids. She was holding the Earl's hand. . . . It
made me cry. (p. 48)

Among the other cold, hard realities of adulthood with which Ms.
Wright ultimately had to deal, of course, was that her ballad, beautiful and
sadly romantic though it was, was not the poem printed in Percy's *Reliques*.
There was no Lady Mondegreen. After the *Earl of Murray* (not Amurray)
was killed, they *laid him on the green*. Wright ultimately confronted that
fact, but much to her credit saw no reason to give in to it, arguing that her
version of the ballad was superior and labeling any such reinterpretation a
"Mondegreen." Over the years, the word "Mondegreen" gradually has
come to signify any mishearing of a popular song, phrase, or proverb.
    Jon Carroll (1992a, 1992b), a columnist for the *San Francisco
Chronicle*, has made something of a cottage industry of collecting
Mondegreens. The task has been made immensely easier for him by rock
'n' roll, which provides, he wrote, "a veritable hotbed of lyric confusion"
(1992b, p. E–12). Perhaps Weird Al Yankovic's parody of the hard rock
group Nirvana ("Smells like Nirvana") captures the real point of many
rock lyrics: "Sing distinctly? We don't wanna/ Buy our album, we're
Nirvana." We assume most rock lyricists really do want to say something,
but if they do, the following mishearings reported to Carroll by his readers give one pause: "There's a bathroom on the right" ("There's a bad
moon on the rise," Creedence Clearwater), "You and me and Leslie"
("You and me endlessly," The Rascals), and "Cheese and Flies—Soup with
Stars" (Jesus Christ, Superstar"). To this list we can add those compiled by
Pauline Yoshihashi (1993), a staff reporter for the *Wall Street Journal*:
"Jane's a fool" ("Chain of Fools," Aretha Franklin), "Its hard to find nice
things on a four-sided cow" ("Poor Side of Town," Johnny Rivers), or our
favorite, "The girl with colitis goes by" ("The girl with kaleidoscope eyes,"
from the Beatles' "Lucy in the Sky with Diamonds").

RESEARCH ON THE INTERPRETATION OF MUSIC LYRICS

Logically, the potential for lyrics to influence attitudes, values, or behavior depends on what sense the listener makes of them. Returning to the
example with which we opened this chapter, a hymn about assuming the
burden of Jesus is not likely to deepen the religious beliefs of a child who

thinks the words are about a visually impaired bear. Similarly, for a heavy metal lyric or music video to influence teenagers to experiment with drugs or premarital sex or to worship the devil, the youngsters presumably must interpret the song in terms of drugs, sex, or Satan. Indeed, to be truly influenced, it is reasonable to assume that they would have to go further and connect the meaning to their own lives. To what extent does this occur? What do we know about how adolescents process and understand music lyrics and music videos?

CONSTRUCTING MEANING

Earlier we noted that interpreting a message is as much a process of construction as discovery. The meaning of any message derives from both the content of the message and the experiences and expectations people carry around inside their heads. One need glance only briefly at the dramatically different interpretations many *Newsweek* or *Time* cover stories elicit from various readers in the "Letters to the Editors" section for evidence of the "constructive" nature of meaning. And who has not been shocked to find their favorite movie or music panned by a close friend? Given the vast array of people's experiences and expectations, small wonder that diverse interpretations of events and messages emerge.

Many empirical studies show that viewers interpret the same TV shows quite differently depending on such factors as age, gender, intelligence, level of cognitive development, race and ethnicity, socioeconomic status, religiosity, mood, prior attitudes and values, and so forth. Individuals' backgrounds and experiences exert tremendous influence on the sense they make of any message. For example, experiments conducted at the Institute for Child Development at the University of Minnesota (Collins, 1983) have shown that children from middle-class families understand TV shows featuring middle-class characters better than shows featuring lower-class characters. Children from lower-class families understand programs featuring lower-class characters better than do middle-class children. In the same research, 8- and 9-year-old children's expectations about what constitutes appropriate behavior for women strongly influenced their perceptions of TV shows featuring either "traditional" or "nontraditional" female leads. Children with a more traditional view of women's roles better understood the actions of more traditional female characters, and vice versa.

There are similar variations in comprehension of popular music lyrics. Typically, researchers use one of three general strategies to exam-

ine whether and how youngsters understand music lyrics: (a) they compare listeners' (or music video viewers') understanding of a song with
some "definitive" interpretation, (b) they compare and contrast interpretations offered by different groups of listeners to the same song, or (c)
they examine how listeners process (make sense of, interpret, think about)
song lyrics without regard to the "actual" narrative meaning of the lyric.

COMPARISONS WITH "DEFINITIVE" INTERPRETATIONS

The most common approach to assessing comprehension of song lyrics is
to compare youngsters' understanding of songs to presumed definitive
interpretations made by "expert" adults. An "expert" adult can be the lyric
composer, a parent, someone who criticizes pop music, or simply the person conducting the research. In any case, most studies of this type make
two crucial assumptions: first, that there is a correct meaning; second, that
this meaning is relatively obvious. Much of the critical comment about
rock lyrics encountered in the popular press typifies this kind of "Father
knows best" approach. That is, "Here's what the song obviously means.
Now, let's see if the kids get it."

   Some of the earliest examples of this strategy looked at adolescents' understanding of social protest lyrics. In the mid-1960s, the diffusion of social and political protest messages from folk to popular music
lyrics engendered a good deal of adult outrage, some of it strikingly akin
to attacks currently aimed at sex and violence in popular music lyrics.
Researchers wondered to what extent these lyrics were understood by
young listeners. In 1965, R. Serge Denisoff and Mark Levine (1971) questioned 400 college-level sociology students about the meaning of the
protest rock song "Eve of Destruction." This song, an explicit political
dissent characterizing humankind as nearing the brink of nuclear annihi-
lation, had just reached the top of the national charts, the first protest song
to achieve such popularity:

> The Eastern world it is explodin'
> Violence flarin' and bullets loadin'
> You're old enough to kill, but not for votin'...
> If the button is pushed, there's no running away.
> There'll be no one to save, with the world in a grave
> Ah you don't believe we're on the eve of destruction.
> Take a look around you boy, bound to scare you boy,
> Ah, you don't believe we're on the eve of destruction....
>   ("Eve of Destruction," Barry McGuire, 1965)

During the autumn of 1965, when anti-war demonstrations hit many college campuses, "Eve of Destruction" was well known to most college students. In the San Francisco Bay Area, where Denisoff and Levine conducted their study, the song had received abundant air play, elicited significant amounts of comment and criticism, and had sparked a campaign to ban it from the air waves. Given the somewhat liberal political views characteristic of sociology students (not to mention San Francisco Bay Area students), it was reasonable to assume that most respondents would be familiar with the song. Familiarity, however, failed to breed understanding. According to Denisoff and Levine (1971), P.F. Sloan, who wrote the lyrics, said they meant that "reality" is nuclear weapons being "a cloud hanging over me all the time," implying that "if the world is full of hate, we have to change it to love" (p. 120). Yet when students were asked to interpret the lines, "take a look around you boy, bound to scare you boy," only 14% knew that they were supposed to be afraid of the threat of nuclear destruction. Another 45% showed partial understanding, 23% revealed no understanding, and 18% did not respond at all (some of the nonrespondents had not heard the song; others simply could not offer any interpretation). Clearly, not many students were "getting" Sloan's intended message.

A few years later, John Robinson and Paul Hirsch (1972), then at the University of Michigan's Institute for Social Research, published a similar study of 430 Michigan high school students' understanding of several social protest songs. The students came from both rural and urban environments and diverse racial and socioeconomic backgrounds and included 8th and 11th graders. The song lyrics purportedly focused on drugs ("Incense and Peppermints," "Lucy in the Sky with Diamonds," "The Condition My Condition Was In"), indifference ("Ode to Billy Joe"), sex ("Heavy Music," "Gimme the Green Light"), and hypocrisy ("Skip a Rope"). The news media provided the "correct" interpretations of some of the songs in this study. For example, "Lucy in the Sky with Diamonds," an alleged LSD anthem, had aroused a good deal of comment and controversy in the press (the Beatles always denied any such intent). The meaning of some of the other songs simply "appeared obvious" to Robinson and Hirsch. For instance, they characterized "Heavy Music" as "the most blatant and straightforward" sexual song "we have encountered" (p. 227).

As in Denisoff and Levine's (1965) research, the students in this study showed little comprehension of the presumed meaning of the lyrics. Depending on the song, from 10% to 30% of the teenagers wrote "correct" interpretations. Another 20% to 60% gave "inadequate descriptions," and the remaining youngsters either did not know or refused to answer. Robinson and Hirsch (1972) also found that understanding depended on listeners' background characteristics. Not surprisingly, older teenagers, those with better grades, those who listened to music more frequently, and those who reported they were usually more attracted to the meaning of a song's lyrics than to its sound were more likely to know the definitive meaning of the songs. Students gave a fascinating variety of interpretations of specific songs. For example, when explaining "Green Light," middle-class adolescents tended to say the singer wanted a date with the girl, but those from working-class families said "he wanted the girl to go all the way." Robinson and Hirsch concluded that teenage listeners to popular music make up a composite audience comprising many social groups. Although those groups typically have different music preferences, when they do hear the same songs they tend to give strikingly different interpretations. We discuss this pattern more fully later.

More recent studies also find similarly low levels of "correct" lyric comprehension. In the mid-1980s, Rosenbaum and Prinsky (1987) interviewed 266 teenagers from Southern California. The kids, who came from both private and public schools, were asked to name their three favorite songs and then to explain what they were about. Over a third could provide no interpretation whatsoever of the songs. Indeed, many made it quite clear that they simply did not pay much attention to lyrics:

- "I don't listen to the words, only how the song sounds. I don't give a damn what they say."
- "[It's] a punk song—it's not supposed to mean anything."
- "I have no idea. Do you listen to the words of songs when you're dancing?" (p. 82)

As for the other two thirds of the respondents, when Rosenbaum and Prinsky compared their own judgments to the students' interpretations, they found very little understanding of the lyrics—even of favorite songs.

Unfortunately, like Denisoff and Levine (1965) and Robinson and Hirsch (1972), these researchers also failed to explore the specific nature of the adolescents' "misunderstandings." We say unfortunate because simply to ignore youngsters' readings of song lyrics when they conflict with the researchers' interpretations dismisses a great deal of potentially valuable information. What if, for example, a substantial number of teenagers concurred on an interpretation deemed incorrect by the researchers? Indeed, what if the teenagers in question had conducted this study? We suspect their conclusion might well have been that adult researchers manifest very little understanding of popular songs.

THE PROBLEM OF MEMORY

Obviously, assumptions about what constitutes the "correct" meaning of any song lyric—indeed, the assumption that there is a single, correct meaning—pose fundamental problems. We return to this issue later. First, however, we consider one other important weakness in several of these studies—their reliance on listeners' memory. Studies such as those we have just described confront students with two tasks: (a) remembering the lyrics, and (b) saying what they mean. Success on the second task largely depends on successful fulfillment of the first. In other words, regardless of whether students are asked about songs selected by the researchers or about their favorite songs, they must first remember the lyrics before they can explain their meaning. In studies like Rosenbaum and Prinsky's, students' low levels of understanding may have as much to do with an inability to recall specific songs as with a lack of comprehension.

Researchers have addressed the memory problem either by having youngsters listen to songs just prior to explaining the meaning of the lyrics, by presenting written transcripts of the lyrics, or both. For example, Patricia Greenfield and her students conducted a study of youngsters' interpretations of two hit songs: "Born In the USA" by Bruce Springsteen and Madonna's "Like a Virgin" (Greenfield et al., 1987). Immediately after listening, 10 students each in the 4th, 8th, and 12th grades, and 25 college undergraduates answered questions about specific phrases from the songs, and then described each song's overall meaning. Their responses to "Born in the USA" are particularly interesting because of the way the rather upbeat title and refrain tend to belie the song's seemingly indisputable tone of disillusionment and despair. Here are some of the lyrics the youngsters were asked to interpret:

> Born down in a dead man's town.
> The first kick I took was when I hit the ground.
> You end up like a dog that's been beat too much,
> Till you spend half your life just covering up.
> Born in the USA
> I was Born in the USA
> I was Born in the USA
> Born in the USA.

Got in a little hometown jam,
So they put a rifle in my hand,
Sent me off to a foreign land
To go and kill the yellow man.
Born . . .

Come back home to the refinery,
Hiring man says, "Son, if it was up to me."
Went down to see my V.A. man.
He said, "Son, don't you understand now."
Born . . .

Down in the shadow of the penitentiary,
Out by the fires of the refinery,
I'm ten years burning down the road,
Nowhere to run, ain't got nowhere to go.
("Born in the USA," Bruce Springsteen, 1984)
Reprinted by permission. Words and music by Bruce
Springsteen. Bruce Springsteen Music. © 1984.

The results summarized in Figure 6.1 clarify why the researchers characterized comprehension of the song as "surprisingly low." Even though participants had just listened to the song and were presented written excerpts in the questionnaire, only 40% even attempted to answer all the questions about the lyrics. Not surprisingly, older students answered specific questions about the meaning of "home town jam" (presumably a problem the singer had in the town where he grew up) and "yellow man" (a North Vietnamese or Viet Cong soldier) much more accurately than fourth and eighth graders. Younger children, who tend to interpret most messages in highly concrete terms, gave quite literal answers. To one fourth grader, the yellow man was "a man who fell in yellow paint and it splashed on him"; for another, he was a man who "has a yellow mask." However, misinterpretations, albeit more abstract, metaphorical ones, also occurred among college students: "A yellow man is any kind of Communist!" (Greenfield et al., 1987, p. 320). When confronted with the task of describing the song's overall theme—that is, "the general feeling Bruce Springsteen has about living in the USA"—participants of all ages fell into the same error. Even high school seniors and college students failed to mention any kind of disillusionment. Indeed, regardless of age, a substantial number of youngsters tended to take the lyric's catch phrase, "Born in the U.S.A.," at face value, interpreting the song as a statement of pride in birthplace rather than disillusionment.

Greenfield et al. (1987) found similar age differences in interpretations of "Like a Virgin." Students were asked to explain this reference to "wilderness":

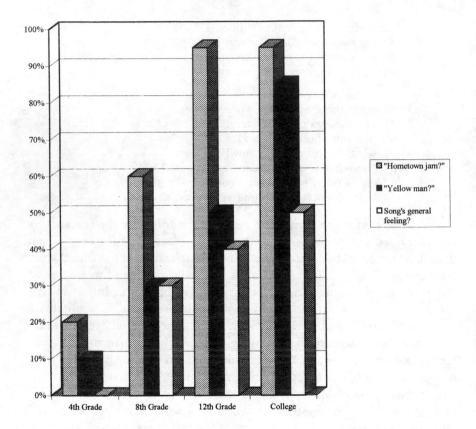

Figure 6.1. Percent in each grade giving correct answers about "Born in the USA"

Note: The three questions and associated answers were: "What is a 'hometown jam?'" (answer: trouble the singer found himself in where he grew up); "Who is the 'yellow man?'" (answer: a North Vietnamese or Viet Cong soldier); "What is the general feeling that Bruce Springsteen has about living in the USA?" (answer: disillusion). Adapted by permission from "What is rock music doing to the minds of our youth? A first experimental look at the effects of rock music lyrics and music videos," by P. Greenfield et al., 1987, *Journal of Early Adolescence, 7,* p. 318. © 1987.

I made it through the wilderness, somehow I made it through—
Didn't know how lost I was until I found you . . .
("Like a Virgin," Madonna, 1984)

Fourth graders read the lyrics quite literally, speaking of the wilderness as "hills and trees." College students, who are far more capable of understanding metaphor, referred to "rough times" and "emotional loneliness." As for comprehension of the overall theme, Greenfield and her colleagues reported that although only 10% of the 4th graders "correctly" understood the song, 50% of the 8th graders, 60% of the 12th graders, and 80% of the college students met their standard. The researchers attributed much of the poor showing of the youngest to their ignorance of the word *virgin*. They also speculated that the better performance of the older students, as well as the greater overall accuracy of comprehension for this song (compared to "Born in the USA"), was because the title "accurately summarizes the song and serves as a kind of encapsulation of Madonna's feelings" (Greenfield et al., 1987, p. 320). Unfortunately, Greenfield and her students never provided their reading of the "correct interpretation" of the song any more explicitly. This is an important oversight given that many of their conclusions are based on the assumption that "correct" interpretations exist.

James Leming (1987) attempted to address both the memory problem and some of the difficulties inherent in establishing a "correct" meaning by which to judge the accuracy of listeners' interpretations. He interviewed 58 11- to 15-year-olds from predominantly rural communities who were attending a summer camp for "academically talented" youngsters. Groups of students were assembled in an informal setting, where they were served soda and snacks. After answering questions about their music use and preferences, the youngsters listened to three Top 40 hits from previous years: "Physical" (Olivia Newton John), "Material Girl" (Madonna), and "I Want a New Drug" (Huey Lewis and the News). They were then asked to identify the songs and artists and to express in writing their interpretation and evaluation of the songs, the artists, and each song's theme or "value message."

Leming took a different approach from most other researchers in determining the "correct" meanings of the songs. Rather than relying on his own interpretations, he assembled a panel of judges to establish a standard meaning. Twenty public school teachers, most of whom had teenage children of their own, provided written interpretations of the three songs' lyrics and "value messages." Most of the teachers concurred that

"Physical" suggests casual sexual activity with no sense of marriage, commitment, or sensitivity:

> I took you to an intimate restaurant
> Then to a suggestive movie
> There's nothing left to talk about
> 'Less it's horizontally.
> Let's get physical, physical, I wanna get physical.
>   ("Physical," Olivia Newton John, 1981)

The panelists also agreed that "Material Girl" says clearly that only suitors who possess material goods and are willing to shower them on a woman deserve attention:

> They can beg and they can plead,
> But they can't see the light,
> That's right.
> 'Cause the boy with the cold hard cash
> Is always Mr. Right.
> 'Cause we're living in a material world
> And I am a material girl.
>   ("Material Girl," Madonna, 1984)

It is interesting to note, however, that there emerged no clear adult consensus regarding the meaning of "I Want a New Drug."

> I want a new drug,
> One that won't hurt my head,
> One that won't make my mouth too dry
> Or make my eyes too red.
> One that won't make me nervous
> Wondering what to do,
> One that makes me feel like I feel
> When I'm with you.
>   ("I Want a New Drug," Huey Lewis and the News, 1983)

About half the teachers interpreted the song literally, that is, as about the hunt for a drug with no side effects. However, the other half felt the song had little or nothing to do with drugs. They viewed the drug reference as a metaphor for a search for love.

Table 6.1 shows that even less consensus emerged from adolescents than from the teachers. Just under half the teenagers gave a love-related, metaphorical interpretation to "I Want a New Drug." Another quarter explained the song in terms of drugs, and the remainder—nearly a third—were unsure how to interpret it. Two thirds agreed with the teachers that "Material Girl" espoused materialism as an important factor in personal relationships, but almost a tenth interpreted the song as rejecting materialism in human relations. The remaining quarter indicated they were unsure of the song's meaning. Finally, whereas over a third of the youngsters thought "Physical" advocated sexual relations, another third heard a plea for physical exercise, and a little over a quarter were unsure or gave responses that could not be interpreted.

Although adult and adolescent interpretations converged somewhat, there were also some striking differences. Several teenagers found socially desirable values in both "Material Girl" and "Physical" that the adult panel completely overlooked. Leming (1987) concluded that the study shows that adolescents' interpretations "of the value message in songs shows considerable variation between songs and within a given sample of adolescents" (p. 379). We would add that this variation, as well as the sharp differences between what adults and teenagers read into the

Table 6.1. Teenagers' Interpretations of Three Songs.

Physical	36% saw the song as advocating sexual relations;
	36% interpreted the song as a pitch for physical exercise;
	28% were either not sure of the meaning or their response couldn't be interpreted.
I Want a New Drug	26% said the song advocates drug usage;
	45% said it was a love song;
	29% were unsure.
Material Girl	67% saw it as espousing materialism as an important factor in personal relationships;
	9% interpreted the song as rejecting materialism in personal relationships;
	24% were unsure.

Adapted by permission from "Rock music and the socialization of moral values in early adolescence," by J. Leming, 1987. *Youth and Society, 18,* pp. 376-377. © 1987.

songs, points as much to the richness of lyric meanings as to any deficit in adolescent understanding.

MULTIPLE MEANINGS

Clearly, the studies discussed thus far raise questions about whether it is even possible to identify the "correct" meaning of a song. To their credit, both Leming (1987) and Greenfield et al. (1987) attempted to eliminate memory as a possible explanation for youngsters' poor interpretive performance. However, neither researcher adequately comes to grips with the possibility of multiple meanings; rather, they assume song lyrics have a single (or at least dominant) meaning that adult experts can discern. This assumption ignores frequent instances when even expert adults disagree about meaning—indeed, disagree to the point where interpretations seem almost diametrically opposed. Leming's panel of school teachers were not the only adults confused about the dominant meaning for a song. Consider what Bruce Springsteen might have thought when, during the 1984 presidential campaign, Ronald Reagan invoked "Born in the USA" as an example of a patriotic and optimistic view of America ("Hey, Baby," 1992; Hillburn, 1985) or, more recently, when *The Ultimate Encyclopedia of Rock* (1993) wrote of the "Born in the USA" album: "Perfectly encapsulating the concept of the mid-eighties American dream, the album was patriotic, rousing, and yet had real soul" (p. 215).

We do not deny that there are cases when meaning seems clearly discernable by almost any standard. 2 Live Crew's "Hey, we want some pussy" and George Michael's "I want your sex" strike us as rather straightforward, and we suspect there would be little dispute over what Ice-T means when he sings:

> I got my 12-guage sawed off;
> I got my headlights turned off;
> I'm 'bout to bust some shots off;
> I'm 'bout to dust some cops off.
>   ("Cop Killer," Ice-T, 1992)

Nevertheless, it is more common by far for songs to invite different interpretations. After all, why should some listeners not envision a buckskin-clad Madonna wending her way along a forest track as she sings of "[making] it through the wilderness," even as others read the phrase as a metaphor for loneliness? In our view, the *Washington Post* headline, "Rock Lyrics: Parents Worry but the Young Aren't Listening" (Gladwell, 1991, p. A3) misses the point. The young *are* listening, but as often as not they tend to hear quite different things—different not only from adults but also from one another.

COMPARISONS BETWEEN GROUPS

As with our earlier discussion of Mondegreens, empirical research also provides many amusing examples of children's "misinterpretations." Typically, however, the studies go no further than presenting examples, ignoring the interesting question of what sense these so-called "incorrect" listeners have made of the lyrics. Even if incorrect by adult standards, such interpretations can provide interesting insights into the mental world of the child. For instance, given the somewhat antiquated grammatical structure in the hymn we mentioned in the first sentences of this chapter, it may not be unreasonable for children to construe "Gladly the cross I'd bear" as a celebration of a myopic Teddy. When some listeners interpret a lyric in one way and others in another, the more interesting question concerns not right or wrong interpretations, but the *nature* of the differing interpretations.

Earlier we described Robinson and Hirsch's (1972) finding that adolescents from middle-class families interpreted "Green Light" as about a guy who wants a date with a girl, whereas adolescents from working-class families felt "he wanted the girl to go all the way." It seems reasonable to hypothesize that something about the different experiences and expectations of youth from different social backgrounds led to differences in their reading of the lyric. This suggests another approach to understanding lyric interpretations—that is, to compare interpretations of the same lyric given by different groups of youngsters. This approach assumes that children with different capabilities, backgrounds, needs, desires, interests, or experiences will attribute different meanings to lyrics, that youngsters from similar subgroups will give similar interpretations, and that the nature of the differences between subgroups can help explain why songs are interpreted in different ways.

Age is an obvious criterion for identifying different groups within an audience. We have already noted that grade-school children tend to give much more literal interpretations of songs than do adolescents and college students. Indeed, during preadolescence, as little as one or two years can make a big difference in how children construe songs.

Christenson (1992b), for example, interviewed 9- through 12-year-olds about a Billy Ocean video, "Get Outta My Dreams, Get Into My Car." When asked what the video was about, a bare majority of the youngsters (51%) mentioned any kind of romantic attraction or relationship. However, clear differences emerged between younger and older children's interpretations. Most 12-year-olds made sense of the video in terms of its abstract focus on the male–female relationship ("It's about a guy who likes a girl and wants to know her better"). Nine- and 10-year-olds, on the other hand, tended to focus on concrete events and details ("It's about a guy who wants to take a girl for a ride in his car"). Some of the younger children read it as simply a song about a man and his car.

Research on children's cognitive development tells us that the years from 9 through 12 are a period of steady movement away from "concrete logical operations," in which the tendency is to focus on concrete details and the relationships between concrete facts, toward more "formal operations," which are associated with increasing ability to deal with abstractions and the relationships between relationships (Flavell, 1977). In this context, Christenson's findings suggest that differences in cognitive development as well as in social background may produce differences in how children interpret the messages of music media, even within the preadolescent years.

Race and gender provide two other clear-cut markers for different life experiences, hence, different perspectives on lyrics. Jane Brown and Laurie Schulze (1990) examined how race and gender influenced college students' responses to two of Madonna's music videos, "Papa Don't Preach" and "Open Your Heart." Their study can serve as a prototype of the group comparison approach, so we describe it here in detail. As Brown and Schulze noted, large and often contradictory variations characterize adult responses to Madonna and many of her songs. *Playboy* magazine views Madonna as a trailblazer in the "commodification" of sex, having "put sopping sex where it belongs—front and center in the limelight" ("Madonna, the Lee Friedlander sessions," 1985, p. 122). Others, however, see her as a major symbol of feminist power *combating* the commodification of sex. Tama Janowitz (1987) wrote in *Spin* magazine: "Madonna is not . . . selling sex, she is representing power" (quoted in Brown & Schulze, 1990, p. 90). Commentators differ as much on the meaning of Madonna's musical products as they do on the meaning of her persona. One of her earlier hits, "Papa Don't Preach," was branded by the New York City affiliate of Planned Parenthood as "a potent message to teenagers about the glamour of sex, pregnancy and childbearing," even as it was praised by the California chapter of Feminists for Life in America as a positive, prolife song (cited in Brown & Schulze, 1990).

Brown and Schulze reasoned that different categories of young listeners would also have quite different interpretations. Specifically, they identified three group characteristics that might correlate with different interpretations of the themes in Madonna's music: gender, race, and "fandom," that is, the degree to which listeners defined themselves as Madonna "fans." As we noted earlier, substantial evidence indicates that both racial and gender differences predict quite different responses to mass media in general (Comstock & Cobbey, 1979; Greenberg et al., 1989), especially in music uses, gratifications, and preferences (see Chapters 3 and 4). Race and gender differences in adolescent sexual attitudes, norms, and behavior are also well documented. Males, for example, report earlier, more frequent sexual activity than females. Black girls who become pregnant out of wedlock can expect more favorable reactions from the baby's father, their families, and their peers than can White girls in the same situation. A variety of social, political, and economic factors have been posited to account for these differences, but regardless of the cause, or causes, there is good reason to expect them to affect interpretations of songs about male–female relationships (Brown & Shulze, 1990).

"Fandom," the "expressed appreciation and enjoyment of a particular popular music star," served as a third way to categorize listeners. The researchers wondered whether responses to a song might differ depending on whether a favorite artist delivers it. Perhaps, they speculated, fans might respond to favorite performers in the way that audiences often respond to celebrity product endorsements. Nonfans, presumably, would be more critical in their interpretations.

To test these notions, Brown and Schulze (1990) showed two videos to students from a Northeastern college, a predominantly White Southern college, and a predominantly Black Southern college. The first, "Papa Don't Preach," recounts how a young woman falls for a young man, becomes pregnant, then struggles with how to tell her father that she intends to keep the baby. The second, "Open Your Heart," portrays Madonna dancing before an all-male audience in a typical big city, porn-shop peep show. In the course of the narrative, Madonna notices, establishes a relationship with, and finally dances with a young boy who has somehow wandered into the show. Ultimately, she leads him out of the porn palace back to a (possibly) more innocent world. The students were asked several broad questions to assess their responses to and understanding of the videos: "How did this video make you feel?"; "What images stick in your mind?"; and "What do you think this video is about?" More specific questions followed. For example, about "Open Your Heart" they asked: "Who is the woman and why is she dancing?"; "Who are the people watching the dancer and why are they there?"; and "What would you say happens to the little boy and the woman?" The students were also asked if the videos made them think about anything in their own lives or the lives of an acquaintance and whether they thought the video was "trying to tell them anything."

One set of research assistants read through the questionnaires in order to develop categories for the many open-ended responses that the students used to describe the videos. Once these categories were defined, another group of assistants read through the questionnaires a second time, assigning students' responses to the appropriate categories. For instance, they were asked to decide whether a response mentioned pregnancy, abortion, marriage, father–daughter relationships, and so on. These responses were then analyzed according to students' race, gender, and "fandom."

The expectation that gender and race would influence interpretations received strong support. As Table 6.2 shows, well over half the White students said the central theme of "Papa Don't Preach" was teenage pregnancy. Among Black students, however, only 21% of the males and 40% of the females saw pregnancy as the primary issue. Indeed, only 43% of the Black males and 73% of the black females even mentioned teenage pregnancy in any of their comments about the video, compared to 85% of the White males and 97% of the White females. For many of the African-American students, father–daughter relationships emerged as the video's central issue. Almost half the Black students focused on this issue, compared to only a quarter of the Whites. Moreover, when attention was limited to only those students who mentioned pregnancy in their open-ended responses, Black males were far less likely than any other group to refer either to abortion or to marriage in the future. Brown and Schulze suggest that their focus on the father–daughter theme may have precluded consideration of marriage.

Regardless of race, males were more likely than females to discuss the video in terms of the portrayed teenagers' relationship. White males were the most likely to predict that the young couple would marry and establish a life outside the home; Black males were least likely to anticipate this outcome. Females were more likely to imagine either no marriage or a subsequent divorce, with Madonna eventually returning home to live with her father.

Table 6.2. Reactions to "Papa Don't Preach" by Race and Sex.

	Black Male (%)	Black Female (%)	White Male (%)	White Female (%)
Mentioned pregnancy[a]	43	73	85	97
% of those also mentioning:				
Abortion	8	21	28	29
Marriage in the future	25	54	65	51
Primary theme:				
Teenage Pregnancy	21	40	56	63
Boy/girl relationship	21	5	15	5
Father/daughter relationship	43	50	22	25
Independent girl/decision making	14	5	7	8

[a]Not all coded categories included.
Reprinted by permission from "The effects of race, gender and fandom on audience interpretations of Madonna's music videos," by J.D. Brown and L. Schulze, 1990, *Journal of Communication, 40*, p. 95. © 1990.

"Fandom" had only a minor effect on interpretations of "Papa Don't Preach." Only 11% of participants (35 of 332) designated themselves as Madonna "fans." The majority (62%) expressed moderate or neutral views toward Madonna, and 27% registered definite dislike. (Madonna appears to polarize college students much as she polarizes critics. Those who like her, like her very much—"Madonna is God," wrote one young woman. Those who do not like her, dislike her intensely—one liked Madonna "as much as slamming my fingers in the car door.") Conclusions based on so few "fans" require caution. Nevertheless, it appeared that being a fan and a female combined to produce somewhat more ideological interpretations of "Papa Don't Preach." Female fans voiced pride in the stand Madonna seems to take in the video. One commented on her being a "female making her way to the top," another on her taking "a stand on an issue." Male fans, however, focused on Madonna as an attractive woman rather than perceiving her as making a statement.

"Open Your Heart" evoked confusion, discomfort, even disgust among the students, regardless of race, gender, or fandom. Brown and Schulze (1990) speculated that student discomfort with the video probably stemmed from its sexual content and their unfamiliarity with the setting of the video (only half of the Northeastern students and fewer than 15% of the Southern students identified the peep-show setting). Even so, as with "Papa Don't Preach," interpretations of "Open Your Heart" depended on race and gender. Almost half the White students named pornography, sexual perversion, or women-as-sexual-object as the song's primary theme; just 20% of the African-American students made such comments. Males were slightly more likely than females to view sexual love as a primary element. Among African-Americans, half the males and almost 30% of the females failed to find a clear theme in the video compared to 11% of the White students.

Gender differences in responses to "Open Your Heart" were especially striking among those who identified themselves as Madonna fans. Female fans embraced the ending, viewing it as an escape into innocence, but almost without exception they also interpreted the video as primarily "pornographic," portraying women as sex objects to be ogled by "sleazoid" males. Female fans were almost unanimous in their discomfort and anger at what they viewed as an appeal to what Brown and Schulze call "patriarchal pleasure." Most declared that the only people they would show the video to were males: "a frustrated male friend . . . a perverted old man . . . any human male." Male fans, however, were generally comfortable with the video. White males, in particular, openly mentioned their erotic attraction to Madonna, often focusing their reactions on her body and her dancing, expressing pleasure that the video aroused "sexual excitement" and made them feel "turned on." No female fan mentioned Madonna's body as something she liked about the video.

According to Brown and Schulze (1990), females in general and female fans in particular tended to interpret "Open Your Heart" from the point of view of the dancer, constructing scenarios explaining how and why she acted as she did and often creating a psychological and social identity for her that "resisted patronizing her as the bad girl/whore" (p. 99). Conversely, males interpreted the video primarily as a commentary on men and read the story from the perspective of the male characters in the video—"guys who can't open their hearts up to their wives or girl friends so they go to peep shows" (p. 99).

Clearly, the social class differences in interpretation reported by Robinson and Hirsch (1972), the age differences found by Christenson (1992b), and the gender and race differences we have just considered (Brown & Schulze, 1990), all produce large variations in the way that subgroups of adolescents interpret music. At the same time, however, these studies also point to similarities in meaning assigned by youngsters within distinct groups. For example, the differences in interpretation indexed by gender, race, and fandom in Brown and Schulze's work leave little doubt that the experiences, perspectives, social allegiances, and backgrounds that different individuals bring to a music video strongly influence the meaning they assign to it. In other words, although there is a good deal of variation in how songs and music videos are interpreted, the meanings they elicit are not random. In all the studies we have considered, groups of adolescents who come from similar backgrounds and have similar experiences agree on roughly similar interpretations.

A FOCUS ON THE INTERPRETATION PROCESS

The interpretation of a song or video involves more than a simple assignment of meaning. It includes all the mental processes engaged during listening or viewing—attention, thoughts generated by the song or video, memories that might be elicited, connections listeners might make between the song and their own lives, and so forth. The last set of studies we consider examines issues of how adolescents process songs, as opposed to what meanings they read into them. As with research comparing groups of listeners, this approach starts from the premise that what an individual brings to a song is at least as important as the manifest content the song brings to the individual.

Much of the current work on the interpretation of song lyrics derives from what is called "schema theory." *Schemas*, also known as scripts or knowledge structures, can be thought of as primitively encoded, basic mental representations of complex events stored in memory in simplified form (see Fiske & Taylor, 1991; Schank & Abelson, 1977; Taylor & Crocker, 1981). For example, most of us have primitive schemas or scripts outlining how we might behave when we enter a restaurant (wait for the waiter to seat us, peruse the menu, place an order, etc.) or providing a framework for understanding common events—anything from a political convention to a child's birthday party.

These cognitive representations play particularly important roles when detailed interpretation of specific events or messages becomes difficult. Under ideal circumstances, when an individual encounters an "event"—whether it is something that happens across the room, a letter from a friend, or a song lyric—that person will engage in cognitive "deep processing." By this we mean that the person will attend to and judge most of the elements of the event or message fully and carefully, paying attention to each particular attribute, assessing and interpreting each event as a unique case.

Sometimes, however, circumstances interfere with deep processing, making it difficult for an individual to attend and think about all the
elements in a message. Such circumstances are said to increase "cognitive
load." This, in turn, increases the influence of preexisting knowledge
structures—schemas—in the interpretation process. Increased cognitive
load may result from factors in the message (e.g., ambiguity), in the environment (noise, distractions), or in the individual (distractability, lack of
relevant knowledge). Consider, for example, an adolescent hearing a new
song at a rock concert. A variety of factors may contribute to increased
cognitive load in this environment. The words may be rendered inaudible
or unintelligible by the competing "noise" of the screaming fans or the
screeching instruments. The lyrics themselves may be ambiguous, relying
on metaphor or double entendre, or unclear because of sloppy enunciation. The listener may be tired or distracted or aroused. Any of these conditions might make it more difficult for an individual to engage in "deep
processing."

According to schema theory, when cognitive load is increased,
people turn to any available cues to make sense of incoming stimuli. If
something about the incoming information can be associated with a
knowledge structure or schema already stored in an individual's memory,
then the existing knowledge structure guides how new information is
understood. For example, even though a listener might not understand all
the details of a certain song lyric, she might still ascertain that it concerns,
for example, a father–daughter conflict about a boy–girl relationship. The
cue might come from the title, from an image in the video, from the
knowledge that a particular vocalist typically sings about love relationships, or from any number of other clues. Whatever provides the cue, once
the association is made the listener accesses his or her own schema for
father–daughter and/or boy–girl relationships. From this existing schema,
then, our hypothetical listener invents from the lyrics a scenario about
fathers, daughters, boyfriends, and so on, that may bear little resemblance
to what others might see in the song. In short, under high cognitive load—
when conditions make it more difficult for an individual to process a song
fully and deeply—preexisting knowledge structures shape the meaning as
much as the lyrics themselves.

Christine Hansen and Ranald Hansen (1991b), of Oakland
University in Rochester, Minnesota, have argued that heavy metal music
offers an excellent opportunity to examine how schemas influence comprehension of lyrics. Heavy metal music, they contend, typically creates
conditions conducive to increased cognitive load. First, the music is dis-

tracting in that its high volume levels and frequently garbled lyrics confront listeners with a difficult message to decipher. Moreover, heavy metal music has been shown to be physiologically arousing (Hansen & Hansen, 1990b), and high physiological arousal appears to decrease cognitive capacity (Kim & Barron, 1988). The Hansens argue that in heavy metal music these conditions combine to create a situation in which listeners, almost by definition, are forced to process lyrics under conditions of high cognitive load. In short, they say, heavy metal inhibits deep processing of lyrics and motivates listeners to employ their existing knowledge structures to make sense of the song.

The Hansens (1991b) tested their schema theory of heavy metal music processing in two ways. First, they had groups of college students listen to heavy metal songs dealing with one or more of these themes: sex, suicide, violence, or the occult. Several songs were used to represent each thematic category. Half the students heard the songs as normally experienced—with high volume, garbled lyrics, arousing beat, and so forth. In other words, the songs were heard under conditions of high cognitive load. For the remaining students, cognitive load was decreased by providing a written copy of each lyric for the students to read as they listened. Presumably, the written script would make it easier to process the lyrics "deeply," to focus on various elements of the message.

Comprehension was assessed in several different ways, including:

- asking students to recall and list as many key words from the songs as they could
- multiple-choice recognition questions (e.g., " (?) is slow with liquor." a. Getting high; b. Forgetting; c. Suicide; d. Happiness) (p. 382)
- phrase comprehension measures (e.g., "Evil thoughts and evil doings/Cold, alone you hang in ruins"—What does "hang in ruins" mean?) (p. 387)
- open-ended questions (asking students to retell the song's story in their own words).

As with most of the studies described earlier in this chapter, students who listened to the songs under normal circumstances—that is, under "high cognitive load"—demonstrated only low to moderate levels of comprehension. However, those given the opportunity to process the songs under "low cognitive load," with a written copy of the lyrics, performed relatively well. These results support the idea that high cognitive load interferes with deep processing, thus reducing comprehension of specific lyric content. They also suggest that decreasing cognitive load facilitates deeper processing and improves comprehension (at least insofar as one is willing to assume that some interpretations are more "correct" than others).

The Hansens next addressed the aspect of schema theory positing that under conditions of high cognitive load individuals use relevant knowledge structures to guide their interpretation of a message. They reasoned that even though students listening under high cognitive load would have difficulty answering questions about *specific* aspects of lyric content, their existing heavy metal music schemas would help them arrive at the *general* themes present in the music they heard. If so, then there should be no difference in students' ability to identify the general themes of heavy metal songs based on whether they listened with or without a written script. To test this prediction, Hansen and Hansen (1991b) had listeners judge whether each of 36 different themes occurred in the songs. Immediately after hearing each song, students rated the degree to which each particular theme (e.g., war, rape, drugs, depression, love, Satan, voodoo, aggression, God, death, suicide) was suggested. They provided ratings on 5-point scales ranging from "not at all suggested" (0) to "strongly suggested" (4).

Using factor analysis, the Hansens first demonstrated that different types of content clustered together in meaningful ways. For example, students tended to make highly similar judgments about such terms as *pornography, lust, rape, prostitution,* and *greed* (a group of terms the Hansens label "bad sex"). Not only did such terms go together, but they did not reveal strong relationships with terms that went together in other groupings. Thus, *devil, Satan, evil,* and *hell* formed a "devil" cluster; *suicide, depression, going home,* and *mental pain* formed a "suicide" cluster; and so forth.

Most listeners clearly distinguished between the songs on the basis of four general themes: "bad sex," "suicide," "violence," and "Satanism" (the latter was comprised of the devil cluster and a separate "occult" cluster). In other words, they discerned particular themes that were present in the different songs and did not impute themes that were not present. Thus, the "bad sex" songs received high scores on the cluster of "bad sex" items but relatively low scores on other content categories. Similarly, the suicide songs drew high scores on the "suicide" cluster, but not on the others; the violence songs received high scores on the "violence" cluster, but not on the others; and so on. Other content themes were also identified, but they did not differentiate among the songs. For example, all four songs contained content manifestly related to "deceit," and students rated all four as sharing the "deceit" cluster. In addition, none of the songs received high ratings on content irrelevant to the lyrics of all the songs (e.g., "God" and "closeness"). Apparently, then, cues in the songs were strong enough to implicate schemas in the relevant categories *and only* in the relevant categories.

Finally, and most important for the schematic processing hypothesis, the content ratings given by students who listened without a written script did not differ from those who listened with a written script. Both groups of students identified the same general themes. Thus, although listeners under high cognitive load may have failed to understand a specific lyric element (e.g., "suicide is slow with liquor"), they were no less likely than those under low cognitive load to see "suicide" as the song's central theme. Even when noise and arousal interfere with deep processing, then, listeners' existing schemas enable them to sort out overall themes on the basis of a few sketchy cues in the lyrics.

There may seem to be contradictions here. Earlier we pointed out that under conditions of high cognitive load, listeners depend on their own knowledge structures to interpret a song. We commented that this might well increase variability in the interpretations that different individuals give to a song. This is because we assume that different individuals bring different knowledge structures to the interpretation situation. The Hansens, however, found that college students gave highly similar thematic interpretations to songs, even under conditions of high cognitive load that one might expect to increase variability in interpretations. The contradiction is more apparent than real, however, because it involves interpretations at two different levels of generality. The Hansens were measuring awareness of general themes. The issue in their study was whether, in spite of the fact that conditions largely precluded deep processing of the specifics of a particular heavy metal song, there were enough cues to let listeners correctly infer the general topic of the songs. Thus, the Hansens were asking if students could understand that a particular song dealt with suicide even though they might have been confused about the specific means, motives, and outcomes described in the lyrics. It should not be surprising that there are commonalities in response at this level of generality. After all, just as most of us have roughly similar schemas for what to do when we enter a restaurant, we probably have roughly similar general schemas for suicide, bad sex, and violence. Students from the same culture should give similar *general* responses. The differences should occur primarily on more particularized interpretations: Although there may well

be agreement among adolescents about the general dimensions of violence or bad sex, there are likely to be dramatic differences when we
examine specifics. What constitutes "bad sex" or "good sex" in *specific*
terms might be quite different from one person to another. The next study
illustrates the point.

Margaret Thompson and her colleagues took a slightly different
approach in their study of music video interpretation (Thompson, Walsh-
Childers, & Brown, 1993; see also Thompson, Pingree, Hawkins, &
Draves, 1991). They conceived of two different kinds of mental knowledge
structures: "content-specific structures" and "generic structures."
Content-specific structures are quite similar to the Hansens' schemas.
They are defined as "mental structures" composed of each individual's
personal "knowledge about and experiences with the particular subject
that is the focus of media content" (p. 253). Thompson et al. (1993) argued
that such content-specific structures come into play when individuals
associate something in media content with the content of an existing
schema. For example, the general awareness that Madonna frequently
sings about sex might cue a listener/viewer to access his or her "sexual
relationship" schema on hearing Madonna, hence, lead to the interpretation of all Madonna songs in sexual terms.

Generic mental structures operate at a much more general level,
shaping or filtering media messages regardless of specific content. Generic
structures are similar to cognitive styles or information processing styles.
They refer to ways in which different individuals usually deal with new
information, regardless of what that information is about. For example,
some people typically absorb new information uncritically, whereas others
tend to test, evaluate, and elaborate on it; some individuals tend to focus on
message sources, whereas others focus on message content; and so on. In
other words, generic structures guide how different individuals tend to
process information irrespective of content or situational factors.

Thompson and her colleagues (1993) tested the idea that content-
specific and generic structures affect kids' interpretations by questioning
186 9th- to 12th-grade students before and after they watched a Madonna
video. Two weeks before seeing the video, students completed a questionnaire (which they believed to be unrelated to the video) about their ideas
concerning teen pregnancy in general as well as their own particular sexual and pregnancy experiences. The researchers used this information to
classify the teenagers as having more or less complex "content-specific
sex/pregnancy schemas." This pre-video questionnaire also obtained
information that could be used to assess generic knowledge structures. For

this, the kids were asked about the underlying structure of the "communication environment" within each of their families, specifically, the degree to which their family's communication environment typically emphasized the maintenance of social harmony in interpersonal relations (e.g., "You shouldn't argue with adults") and the degree to which the communication environment emphasized the exploration of controversy and testing of new ideas (e.g., "You should look at all sides of an issues before making up your mind"). Responses to questions of this type were used to classify students as coming from one of four types of family communication environment: (a) one that primarily emphasized "socio-orientation," placing maintenance of interpersonal harmony above all other considerations; (b) one that primarily emphasized "content orientation," placing the exploration and challenging of ideas above all other considerations; (c) one that emphasized both; and (d) one that emphasized neither. Thompson and her colleagues reasoned that family communication environment establishes a kind of generic structure or filter that is applied to the interpretation of all information, implying that kids from different environments would interpret a music video differently (for a more complete discussion of family communication environment, see Chaffee & McLeod, 1972; Chaffee, McLeod, & Atkin, 1971; Ritchie, 1991).

Two weeks after completing the background questionnaire, the students watched Madonna's "Papa Don't Preach" video, then answered a series of questions designed to measure the nature, complexity, and depth of their interpretations. On 5-point scales ranging from "Not at all" to "A lot," they indicated how much the video made them think about content specific to the video (e.g., "During the video, how much were you thinking about what will happen to the girl in the future?"; ". . . about why the girl got pregnant?"; ". . . about what the father wants to do about the girl's pregnancy?"). They were also asked about content stimulated by, but not directly concerned with, the storyline of the video ("What would you feel like if you were the girl/boy?"; ". . . if someone you know who got pregnant as a teenager?"; ". . . how would your father react if you were in the girl's/boy's place?"). The number of times each student indicated thinking about content specific to the video was taken as a measure of "complexity of inference" and the reported intensity of those thoughts provided a measure of effort. The number of times students reported making connections to their own lives served as a measure of "complexity of connections," and the reported intensity of those thoughts provided a parallel measure of effort.

The teenagers clearly paid attention both to content specific to the video (for instance, what would happen to the pregnant girl) and to how the video's themes connected to their own lives. More important to the central concern of the study, both content-specific and generic structures influenced responses to the video. The effects of these knowledge structures, however, depended on the students' gender. Boys and girls processed the video quite differently depending on their family communication environment. Boys from concept-oriented family environments—that is, from families that emphasized testing new ideas—drew more inferences about the video, expended more effort making those inferences, and made more connections between the video and their own lives than did boys from families that put no stress on concept orientation. The degree to which families emphasized maintenance of interpersonal harmony (their socio-orientation) had little effect on boys' responses to the video. The results were essentially the reverse for girls. Girls from families that emphasized the maintenance of social harmony drew more inferences about the video and expended more effort both on drawing inferences and on making connections between the video and their own lives than did girls from families characterized by little emphasis on social harmony. In other words, it appears that the father–daughter conflict portrayed in the "Papa Don't Preach" video was particularly likely to trigger personal responses among girls from socio-oriented families—families that stressed the importance of avoiding disagreements, particularly with parents, whereas fewer personal connections were stimulated in girls from families in which such conflict was acceptable. No relationship emerged between concept orientation and girls' responses.

Gender also related to the influence of content-specific schemas. Girls with more complex teen pregnancy schemas and girls with more sexual and pregnancy experience responded to the video more personally, making more connections between the video and their own lives and exerting more effort making those connections than girls with less complex teen pregnancy schemas or sexual and pregnancy experience. Among boys, no relationship emerged between content-specific schemas and responses to the video.

Thompson et al. (1993) used much the same approach to reanalyze the data Brown and Schulze (1990) collected in their comparison of African-American and White students' perceptions of Madonna videos. The reanalysis confirmed that both generic and content-specific cognitive structures influence adolescents' involvement with and interpretations of music videos.

MARES EAT OATS—ON THE GREEN . . . SOMETIMES

Studies of the influence of knowledge structures on interpretation help explain the general finding that different individuals often interpret songs and music videos in dramatically different ways. As we have noted, however, although interpretations may be divergent, they are not random. Young listeners with similar knowledge and experience, similar backgrounds, similar needs or concerns tend to respond to song lyrics in similar ways. Moreover, even though some lyrics, under some conditions, and among some youth elicit a wide range of interpretation and misinterpretation, many songs produce quite general agreement, at least among older adolescents.

The level of agreement on the meaning of a song (or music video) depends on a number of factors, including the characteristics of the song itself, the manner in which it is performed, the conditions under which it is heard, and, of course, the nature of the kids doing the listening. The more literal and concrete the lyrics, the more agreement; the more ambiguous or metaphorical, the greater the variance. The clearer the enunciation, the more agreement; the more words are shrieked or drowned out by instruments, the more open their interpretation. Not surprisingly, hearing a recording or watching a video in a quiet, private setting may generate quite different interpretations than hearing the same song in a noisy, chaotic, public milieu such as a rock concert.

Which brings us back to "Mondegreens." After reviewing the different research traditions that examine how kids make sense of popular songs, Mondegreens do not seem so silly. At times, in fact, they may be quite functional. Young children, especially, often produce what strike us as hilarious misinterpretations because they lack the experience and knowledge needed to deal with the message on the adult level. Given the concerns about the content of many popular songs, this is probably a good thing. Temporarily, at least, their ignorance helps preserve their innocence. Whether variant readings are functional or not, they are much more prevalent than most critics and observers of contemporary popular music assume. If we were to cull one principle from the research, it would be this: When it comes to interpreting popular music, it is not so much a case of "you are what you hear" as "you hear what you are."

7

DID THE DEVIL, THE DRUMMER, OR THE "DOO-WOP" MAKE 'EM DO IT:
THE EFFECTS OF EXPOSURE TO MUSIC MEDIA

This pornographic smut being sold to our children coerces, influences, encourages and motivates our youth to commit violent behavior, use drugs and abuse women through demeaning sex acts.
—Dr. C. Delores Tucker, Chair, National Political Congress of Black Women (1994)

Some have suggested. . .that the music contributes to a preponderance of violence and misogyny in our communities. Of course, that suggestion ignores both history and reason.
—David Harleston, President, Def Jam Recordings/Rush Associated Labels (1994)

Webster's New Collegiate Dictionary (1980) defines *effect* as "something that inevitably follows an antecedent (as a cause or agent)." Our concern in this chapter is the degree to which popular songs or music videos serve as such an antecedent. Do adolescents change the way they think or act as a result of listening to popular music or watching MTV? As with so many questions raised in this book, the answer is not a simple yes or no.

181

A few years ago, Ellen Goodman (1986), the syndicated *Boston Globe* columnist, described Madonna"s "Papa Don't Preach" as "a commercial for teenage pregnancy" (p. A-23). As her advertising metaphor indicates, Goodman worried that the song would sell adolescent girls on a life of irresponsible sexual indulgence. Her column made the same assumption that most of us make—that messages influence the way we think and behave—which of course they do. We encounter message effects all the time. We ask a friend to pass the sugar or share a section of the newspaper, and we are given what we ask for. We encounter a stop sign at an intersection, and we stop—or slow down, anyway. We view a political ad urging us to vote for Candidate X, and some of us do. Occasionally, we may also hear that a heavy metal lyric extolling suicide has caused a teenager to take his own life, or that pop music's message that true lovers are not planners contributes to our horrendous teen pregnancy problem. In each instance, the connection seems clear: The message is the antecedent that causes or contributes to the outcome—except, of course, when it does not.

Most teenage girls did not get pregnant after hearing "Papa Don't Preach"; sometimes, people do not stop for stop signs; and political ads seldom change the votes of more than a relatively small proportion of the electorate. How many times have you asked a friend to pass the sugar, only to sit there with bitter coffee growing cold . . . or for that matter, having been handed the salt or a section of the newspaper? Clearly, messages do not inevitably lead to predictable effects. Sometimes they do and sometimes they do not, depending on the circumstances and conditions. And sometimes the "effect" may not be at all what we expected.

POPULAR VERSUS SCIENTIFIC CONCEPTIONS OF MEDIA EFFECTS

The rather temperate, "conditional" point of view suggested in the preceding paragraph runs counter to the approach that predominates in popular discourse. Typically, when media critics or the popular media discuss media impact, effects tend to be characterized as obvious, direct, large, and usually negative. Consider, for example, *Rising to the Challenge*, a video produced by the Parents' Music Resource Center (Vision Videos, 1988) to warn parents about the dangers posed to adolescents by music videos. It opens with scenes from *Sesame Street*. Images of muppets and preschoolers dance across the screen as a narrator proclaims that *Sesame Street* has "proven" that music, words, and images are powerful teachers of children.

The narrator then intones the question that frames the rest of the video: "At what age does a child cease to learn from music, words, and images?" Attention then switches to scenes from heavy metal music videos— images of sex, rape, violence, and drug use juxtaposed with shots of glassy-eyed teenagers straining maniacally to touch their equally maniacal heavy metal idols—and shots of leather-and-lace-clad, prepubescent Madonna wannabees mugging for the camera. The question repeats: "At what age does a child cease to learn from music, words, and images?" The question, of course, is a rhetorical device. We all know the answer is "never"—that learning from music, words, and images continues throughout life. The survival of our species probably depends on it. However, the approach taken in *Rising to the Challenge* is particularly instructive here because it incorporates two assumptions common in popular treatments of media influence: (a) that exposure to "negative" media images leads inevitably to negative effects; and (b) that children and adolescents are most at risk.

In his book, *Evil Influences*, Stephen Starker (1989) chronicled a long history of adult concern and agonizing over the harm wreaked by media on youth. The banishing of storytellers from Plato's Republic, the bowdlerizing of Grimm's fairy tales, the debate over labeling record albums, and the recent congressional decision to mandate a "V-chip" in new television sets—all were motivated by the conviction that media messages do things, typically bad things, to kids. Although the current, most popular culprit tends to be television (Postman, 1985; Winn, 1985), concern about the impact of music and recordings, films, videogames, and the Internet is also quite common. Most of us have encountered headlines that read something like: "What is Rock 'n' Roll Doing to Our Kids?"

Basically, this "powerful effects" approach assumes that because mass media reach many people, they engender massive effects; that is, they affect masses of people in a uniform way (see Roberts & Maccoby, 1985). Receivers are viewed as passive, at least as far as message interpretation is concerned. Contrary to the studies reviewed in our discussion of how people make sense of lyrics (Chapter 6), little attention is given to variations in how different people interpret messages at different times or under different conditions. The critical event in the process is simple exposure. Given the wide acceptance of such assumptions, it is not surprising that policy debate often ignores the many sources of individual variation in outcome and focuses primarily on various means of message control—changing messages, labeling messages, censoring messages.

Empirical research on media effects paints a different picture from the one found in the popular literature (for reviews, see Comstock et al., 1978; Comstock & Paik, 1991; McGuire, 1986; Roberts, 1993; Roberts & Maccoby, 1985). If "massive effect" is construed to mean that media messages influence large numbers of people to change how they think or act, then even the earliest empirical examinations of the effects of mass communication failed to demonstrate much of an impact. Relatively few people changed their votes as a result of mass mediated election campaigns (Berelson, Lazarsfeld, & McPhee, 1954; see also Chaffee & Hochheimer, 1982), or fled the Martian invaders that Orson Welles brought to earth with his broadcast of "The War Of the Worlds" (Cantril, 1947), or behaved in new or different ways after watching television (Klapper, 1960). William McGuire (1986) reviewed the empirical research findings related to the impact of several different kinds of media content, including the impact of product advertising, political campaigns, violent and stereotyped television portrayals, and television news. McGuire's title summarized his conclusions: "The Myth of Massive Media Effects." He found few if any instances of changes in the behavior of large numbers of readers, listeners, or viewers as a result of media exposure.

As in earlier chapters of this book, we again face a bipolar choice between opposing models of social behavior. One not very well-documented approach assumes massive message effects; another, based on at least some research, argues for minimal or even no message effects. As we have said before, when explanations of human social behavior are articulated in such starkly contrasting terms, the reality probably lies somewhere in between. McGuire himself was careful not to deny completely the existence of media effects. "Limited effects," which usually means effects on smaller numbers of people, occurred in many of the studies McGuire reviewed.

IMPORTANT, LIMITED, CONDITIONAL EFFECTS

Perhaps it is not productive to search for "massive" media effects at all. First, a focus on massive effects confuses "massive" with "important." Obviously it can be important when messages directly influence many people to change in the same way, but it also can be trivial. More to the point, it can also be extremely important when a message influences the thoughts or behavior of relatively few people, depending, of course, on who they are and the nature of the influence. For instance, political advertisements may change relatively few votes, but in some elections a few vote changes can make all the difference. Adding rap or heavy metal to a radio playlist might attract (or repel) only a few additional listeners to a station, but for many pop music stations, a slight increase or decrease in audience can mean the difference between survival and extinction. Most kids probably ignore songs extolling Satanism, but the parent whose child turns up wearing a chain dangling a silver "666" is quite likely to think the song's influence was extremely important. Clearly, categorizing a change as "important" requires a subjective judgment. However, just as clearly, we make such judgments all the time, and frequently they have little or nothing to do with the sheer number of individuals affected by a given message.

A massive effects approach also glosses over critical differences among members of any given population. We have seen that different subgroups interpret music lyrics in different ways. There is no more reason to expect all young listeners to react the same way to a particular song than there is to expect them to respond in unison to a given teacher, educational curriculum, or for that matter, "Keep Off the Grass" sign. Indeed, nothing in the social world elicits identical, or even highly similar, responses from all members of the population. Current mass communication research recognizes that populations are comprised of myriad sub-groups, that people belong to multiple groups, and that the importance of these groups for the individual at any given time depends on a variety of conditions. Moreover, individuals within subgroups also differ, and the role of such individual differences varies depending on conditions. This "conditional approach" (see Chaffee, 1977; McLeod & Reeves, 1980) also assumes that a variety of conditions influence different subsets of people to respond to mass-mediated messages in many different ways, depending on what they bring to the message—their prior attitudes, values, beliefs, knowledge, experience, and so on. This substantially precludes the possibility of demonstrating "massive, uniform effects."

Steven Chaffee (1977) describes conditional research as a trend away from studies that find effects on 10% of a full population—studies that seek but fail to find massive effects—toward studies approaching something like a 100% effect on a specifiable subgroup that may comprise only 10% of the population. The trick, of course, is to identify that 10% ahead of time, that is, to specify the conditions in the receiver, the environment, and the message that predict message effects. For example, if one is concerned with the potential influence of the sexual content of rock lyrics, a conditional approach might argue that a more relevant audience than all adolescents would be those teenagers for whom issues of sexual relationships are currently central, and that critical times to reach them might be just before the prom or just after they have learned that one of their classmates is pregnant (see also McLeod & Reeves, 1980; Roberts & Maccoby, 1985).

Two additional distinctions are necessary before we conclude this general discussion of effects. First, there is a difference between the effect of a medium and the effect of message content. The overwhelming tendency in both popular and scholarly discussion of mass media is to focus on what the message says, on content construed in largely cognitive terms. Few critics want to burn all books, ban all television, or label all music—rather, they want to burn certain books, censor certain TV shows, and label certain albums based on what they say. However, media can have important consequences independent of content. They consume large amounts of time, displace other activities, give pleasure, change moods, provide important social linkages, and so on. These effects are every bit as important as content-linked effects. This point is fundamental when considering music. As we noted in our discussion of themes and portrayals in popular music (Chapter 5), the beat and melody play central roles in the experience of popular music, and these are not "content" in the usual sense.

Second, we need to distinguish between intended and unintended effects. Much of the empirical research that calls the power of the media into question has focused on the degree to which intended effects are achieved—whether the ad leads to a purchase, the political appeal alters a vote, the health appeal prevents smoking, and so on. However, media content also produces incidental learning and unintended consequences. The willowy MTV songstress intends to entertain, attract a large following, and sell recordings; she probably does not intend to make a statement about what constitutes an appropriate body image. Nevertheless, a video featuring our hypothetical songstress (or more likely, many videos featuring a number of different slim and sexy singers) may well influence some viewers' concept of beauty, and perhaps even lead them to try to lose weight. This, of course, is the same logic that underlies much of the research on the effects of media violence. Police action drama does not *set out* to teach children how or when to perform aggressive behaviors, but there is little question that at least some children learn these lessons very well (American Psychological Association, 1993; Comstock & Paik, 1991). In other words, regardless of whether the message is intended to teach or whether a desire to learn motivates listening or viewing, kids do learn from media content—both from words and images. The rapid diffusion of a hair or clothing style following their appearance in a music video and the adoption of a new verbal expression after its use in a hit song attest to such "incidental" learning.

Indeed, a major reason kids learn so much from "entertainment" content is precisely because such learning *is* incidental. Entertainment fare is not perceived as an attempt to teach or persuade, and so audiences are less likely to examine critically or actively resist the information contained therein (cf. Blosser & Roberts, 1985). Wilbur Schramm (1971) introduced the idea that communication occurs within the context of an implicit cultural contract. He argued that people have different expectations, hence, interpret messages in different ways, depending on whether they think the primary reason for a message is to teach, inform, persuade, or entertain. For example, our culture teaches us to examine and test the truth value of didactic or persuasive communication. The credibility of such messages and their congruence with our personal belief and value systems are always at issue. "Disinterested" messages, however—those with no perceived axe to grind—are less likely to be questioned, tested, and resisted. Most entertainment messages are not perceived as exercises in axe grinding. To the contrary, an important expectation in most entertainment situations is that the audience will suspend disbelief. (This is a major reason why the people who produce commercials work so hard to make them "entertainment.") Kids are highly unlikely to think about entertainment content in terms of its credibility or congruence with existing belief systems; they simply "go with the flow," including the flow of incidental information. This uncritical posture, of course, underlies much adult concern with the potential impact of entertainment content on youth, particularly content that kids find attractive and that adults find troublesome—for example, popular music lyrics and music videos.

Our approach to media effects, then, presumes that important effects need not and probably do not extend to a large proportion of the total audience. Rather, young listeners respond in terms of various social, psychological, and physical conditions that influence how they use music, how they interpret messages, and whether, when, and how they act on what they have learned. In a sense, this calls for a redefinition of what constitutes a "relevant" audience, forcing us to consider the various conditions that identify specific groups and individuals who may be particularly susceptible to the influence of music media messages. As we discuss in the following pages, such conditions as "fandom," family background, gender, and race influence whether and how popular music affects young listeners.

SURVEYS VERSUS EXPERIMENTS

Not only do we have to worry about our conceptualization of effects, we need to be concerned with the methods used to study them. The most common empirical methods in scientific mass media research are surveys and experiments. Typically, a survey employs a questionnaire about kids' media exposure—how much they listen and to what kinds of music—and about their beliefs, attitudes, and behaviors related to whatever outcomes are of interest: sexual behavior, academic performance, belief in Satanism, and so on. Assuming responses are truthful and accurate (for taboo issues such as sex, this is always a question), the relationship between music listening and other variables can be assessed. We can see, in other words, whether more listening correlates with more of a certain attitude, value, or behavior.

Finding such a relationship is a first step in determining the effects of exposure to popular music, but only a first step. If no association is found between amount of listening and, for example, grade point average, then it is relatively safe to conclude that popular music does not influence teenagers' academic performance. However, even if a relationship exists—for example, even if we find that the more kids listen to heavy metal, the lower school grades they report—we still cannot make a causal inference because our hypothetical survey would not enable us to determine whether: (a) listening to heavy metal caused grades to decline, (b) getting poor grades influenced kids to turn to heavy metal; or (c) whether some third variable influenced both things (e.g., perhaps parental problems caused teenagers in our sample both to listen to more heavy metal music and to ignore their school work). This is the basis for a social science "bromide": "Correlation does not prove causation."

In order to decide whether something is a cause or an effect, it is necessary to know with certainty which is the antecedent variable (the cause) and which is the consequent variable (the outcome). It is also necessary to eliminate the influence of extraneous variables on the relationship. Experiments are conducted in order to address these issues. In a nutshell, a hypothetical experiment on the effects of music videos on sexual attitudes might begin by randomly assigning kids to one of two different treatment groups, thereby creating identical groups of teenagers. The researcher might then administer different "treatments" to the two groups, taking care to hold all other factors constant (the type of television set, the room in which they view, the time of day, etc.). For example, kids in one group might be shown several concept music videos containing a number of highly suggestive sexual images, whereas those in the other group might see performance videos portraying musical groups playing their songs on stage. On all other dimensions, the two groups' experiences would be the same. After viewing, the students might answer questions about their attitudes toward premarital sex. Because the two groups were identical before viewing, and because the only difference in their experience was the video content they saw, we can assume any postviewing differences in their attitudes about premarital sex must have come from exposure to the different video treatments. More specifically, if those who saw the concept videos show more acceptance of premarital sexual activity than the kids who saw the performance videos, we can legitimately say that watching music videos containing sexual imagery "caused" viewers to express more liberal sexual attitudes.

It is tempting to conclude that researchers should always use experiments to investigate message effects. Both the experimental and survey approaches, however, have strengths and weakness. Although surveys do not usually give us the information needed to make causal inferences, they can provide us with information from samples of people who are reasonably representative of the larger population. If a survey is designed properly, we can be relatively confident that the results apply to the larger population of people outside the study sample. Social scientists refer to this as "external validity." Experiments are typically much lower than surveys in external validity. Experiments are usually conducted with fewer participants than surveys are, and there is little or no attempt to make sure the participants are representative of any larger population. Rather, the primary concern is that participants are divided into identical groups that are treated in the same ways except for the "treatment" variable—in our example, exposure to different sorts of music videos. This control often tends to make experiments somewhat artificial. In day-to-day life, students do not usually listen to a selection of three songs in a university professor's laboratory expecting to answer some questions for the purpose of earning extra class credit; in experiments they sometimes do. Finally, measures of outcomes in experiments often differ substantially from what really interests the researcher, particularly in areas of such taboo behaviors as sex or violence. For example, in surveys, researchers can relate kids' reports of past exposure to violent videos to their reports of how often they "really have" used a weapon in a fight (see, e.g., Belson, 1978). To the extent we are willing to accept their responses as accurate (that is, assume that the kids remember accurately and report truthfully), a case can be made that the measure assesses "real" aggression. It is more difficult, however, to measure "real" aggression in an experiment in which the outcome of interest must follow exposure to the violent videos. Although a measure of whether the video really caused subsequent aggressive behavior might be obtained by something like handing the kids knives and counting how often they used them in subsequent school-ground altercations, no ethical researcher would ever do such a thing. Rather, experiments must develop surrogate indicators of aggressive-ness—for instance, have kids "evaluate" someone else's behavior under the assumption that more hostile evaluations indicate more aggressive-ness, or have them indicate how some third party ought to behave in a frustrating situation. Because surrogate measures are not the real-life behavior of concern, they are often criticized for lacking validity. Given these tradeoffs, the most effective way to examine the effects of popular music is to pay attention to the results of both methodological approaches (with perhaps the addition of an occasional case study). Accordingly, we discuss both survey and experimental evidence.

DOMAINS OF EFFECT

Most popular discussions of kids and music focus on how song lyrics or music video images influence adolescents' beliefs, attitudes, or behaviors. The fundamental concern is whether song lyrics or music video images provide models on which kids base their own thoughts and actions. The most accurate label for such outcomes is "content-related social effects"—that is, effects on social attitudes and behavior that follow directly from the particular content of the song (see McLeod & Reeves, 1980; Roberts & Maccoby, 1985). However, these are not the only consequences that may follow from exposure to popular music. "Popular music" is a highly com-plex stimulus with many different dimensions, any of which may "cause" some outcome. For example, simply devoting time to listening can be con-ceived as an effect both in and of itself ("Good grief! You listened to the stereo for eight hours?") and in terms of other activities that music listen-ing might displace ("What do you mean you watched music videos instead of doing your homework?"). Consequences also flow from the sound of music: Both melody and beat can affect listeners' moods and emotional states, volume or loudness may affect kids' ability to hear, and so forth. Music is also claimed to influence other domains such as social interac-tions and academic performance. These latter outcomes, of course, may or may not be independent of content. For example, not only might devoting excessive amounts of time to music listening affect school performance, so too might the lyrics of a song about school. In other words, depending on what aspect of music one wishes to consider, popular music might influence young listeners in a variety of ways and through a variety of processes or mechanisms. In the balance of this chapter we examine: first, the research related to such domains as academic performance, hearing, social interaction, and mood and emotional state; and second, research more clearly focused on the issue of content-related social effects—that is, on how exposure to specific kinds of popular music content influences adolescents' social beliefs, attitudes, and behavior.

ACADEMIC PERFORMANCE

Several correlational studies suggest that as popular music use increases, various indicators of academic performance decrease. Over 30 years ago, Burke and Grinder (1966) found an inverse relationship between the amount of time 13- to 17-year-olds spent listening to "youth culture music" and their grade point averages, hours of study per week, and academic aspirations. The more these kids listened, the less they studied, the lower their aspirations, and the lower their grades. Larson and Kubey (1983) also reported that teenagers who listened more often spent less time in class and had lower levels of academic performance. Sun and Lull (1986) found that the more time their sample of California high school students spent watching MTV during the week, the less happy they reported being at school. Interestingly, there was no relationship between amount of viewing MTV on weekends and attitude toward school (see also Chapter 4 on the relationship between popular music and school achievement). Interesting as these correlational findings may be, they do not prove that exposure to popular music causes changes in school performance or school attitudes. Indeed, before we even consider the possibility of influence, it is necessary to specify a mechanism through which such an influence might occur. Two frequently cited mechanisms are time displacement and interference.

TIME DISPLACEMENT

Our earlier discussion of amount of listening (Chapter 3) illustrates that adolescents devote significant chunks of their waking hours to music. Sometimes the music is in the foreground and sometimes it is in the background, but seldom is it absent. Whether this time expenditure is a concern largely depends on whether it might have displaced other, more highly valued activities. Most people would probably impute a negative effect if music media use reduced time devoted to schoolwork. If it displaced time spent hanging around on street corners, one might infer a positive effect. Obviously, whether there is a problem depends almost entirely on somebody's judgment of the relative value of alternative activities.

We have found no studies directly examining the displacement effect of music media. However, recent work on children's and adolescents' use of television provides little support for the theory that television takes significant amounts of time away from schoolwork or valued non-media-related activities such as sports, clubs, hobbies and so on. TV viewing does affect functionally similar entertainment activities such as movie attendance and radio listening (see Mutz, Roberts, & van Vuuren, 1993; Ritchie, Price, & Roberts, 1987; Roberts, Henriksen, Voelker, & van Vuuren, 1993). Because music listening functions more easily as a background or secondary activity than television does, there is even less reason to suspect that music listening displaces time spent on valued, non-media-related activities. Music listening is considerably more likely to *accompany* homework, household chores, or talking with friends than to replace them. Evidence for this conclusion comes from unpublished data gathered in the study reported by Roberts and Henriksen (1990); only 6% of the 7th, 9th, and 11th graders in their sample said they ever listened to music without also doing something else.

INTERFERENCE

It is unlikely, then, that music actually displaces time spent on schoolwork. More likely, it detracts from the effectiveness of studying by reducing concentration or comprehension. There is little question that adolescents use music as a backdrop to their homework. Over 58% of the California teenagers surveyed by Roberts and Henriksen (1993) said they "often" or "always" listened to music while they did homework, a finding that replicates results obtained with elementary, junior high, and high school students elsewhere in the United States (Patton, Stinard, & Routh, 1983) and in the Netherlands (Beentjes, Koolstra, & van der Voort, 1995). Older kids are slightly more likely than younger ones to listen while they study, but gender and academic ability seem to make no difference. Most adolescents report studying with music a good part of the time.

There has long been speculation that media "distractors" may negatively affect learning and performance, and teachers and parents frequently advise kids to avoid radios and televisions when they study (Keith, 1986). Many kids themselves sense the potential for distraction. Even first graders claim they can do a better job of studying when the radio or television is turned off (Miller & Bigi, 1979), and adolescents say that they would change from "nonquiet" to "quiet" conditions for "best" performance (Patton et al., 1983). Adolescents also report that whether they choose to study in quiet or with music or television in the background depends on the task; they are more likely to choose a quiet room for reading than for writing or solving mathematical problems (Patton et al., 1983; Cool, Yarbrough, Patton, Runde, & Keith, 1994). Interestingly, despite their awareness that background music may not be a good idea generally, many adolescents nevertheless also argue that music sometimes *benefits* studying (Patton et al., 1983).

Neither these attitudes about the possibility of distraction effects nor the various correlational studies cited earlier provide an adequate basis for inferring that music exposure causes decrements in academic performance. Perhaps unhappiness with school motivated the kids in Sun and Lull's (1986) survey to ignore homework in favor of such non-school-related activities as watching music videos. Or perhaps, as with any simple correlation, some third factor influenced both listening and academic performance. A teenager's peer group, for instance, might exert pressure to watch videos more and study less (see Roe, 1987). Experiments attempting to address this question have produced mixed results. Schreiber (1988) compared the grades of college students from two different psychology classes, one of which experienced popular rock music (e.g., Billy Joel) as background for the first 20 minutes of each class throughout a semester, and the other of which served as a "no music" control group. Students from the class with music earned significantly *higher* grades. Schreiber stated that the basis for the difference is unclear, and we agree. The differences between the groups may have had more to do with flaws in the study design than with the music per se. Indeed, the study was not a true experiment. There is a major problem inherent in comparing intact classes, a problem compounded when the treatment takes place over time, in this case across the course of an academic semester. Students are seldom assigned to classes randomly, and different classes always have different experiences: they meet at different times of day, in different locations, possibly with different instructors, and so on. Any teacher can testify that over the course of a 12-week semester, different classes develop quite different interpersonal dynamics. For a number of reasons, then, one suspects the two groups were not identical at the beginning of the study, and that they were treated differently in ways other than their exposure to the background music. In the absence of any compelling theory explaining why listening to popular music might produce higher grades, it seems reasonable to attribute the obtained difference to some extraneous factor related to the inequality of the experimental groups.

In a better designed experiment, Tucker and Bushman (1991) assigned college undergraduates randomly to music or no music groups. For 45 minutes, 76 students in the "music group" listened to selections from such performers as Billy Idol, Dire Straits, and Motley Crue as they worked on mathematical, verbal, and reading problems taken from the American College Test. The 75 students in the "no music" group worked on the same problems in silence. For both mathematical and verbal problems, students who worked while the music played performed significantly worse than those who worked in silence (there was no difference on reading problems). Tucker and Bushman speculate that the lyric content of the music somehow distracted students from the task, interfering with their ability to engage in the kinds of problem solving required. Their findings also suggest that the prevailing adolescent attitude that quiet is more important when reading than when doing math (Patton et al., 1983) may be misguided.

Studies conducted with younger students have produced conflicting findings. Valerie Cool and her associates (1994) report several experiments in which 11- to 13-year-olds worked on either mathematics or reading assignments in silence, with a radio playing music, or with television broadcasting in the background. Measures of academic performance included total time spent studying, total problems attempted, percentage of correct answers, and reading rate. Although television seemed to interfere with some kinds of performance, especially mathematics, the differences were not statistically significant. More pertinent to a concern with music, however, differences between studying in silence and with the radio were trivial.

LaVoie and Collins (1975) worked with over 350 9th through 12th graders from several Nebraska high schools to test the proposition that "youth culture orientation adversely affects school performance." Rock music served as their proxy for "exposure to youth culture." Groups of students were randomly assigned to spend 30 minutes studying one of four topics: literature, mathematics, physical science, or social science. For each topic, a third of the students studied with a background tape playing rock selections from Top 40 records, a third studied with classical music, and a third studied in silence. A third of the students from each subgroup completed a multiple choice test immediately, another third took the test a day later, and the final third took it three days later. Regardless of topic or when they took the test, kids who studied with rock music did significantly worse than those who studied with classical music or in silence. There was no difference in test scores between the classical music and silence groups. In this research, then, studying with rock music did interfere with learning. LaVoie and Collins suggest that because rock is an integral part of youth culture and provides adolescents with valuable, rewarding information, students in the rock condition were less motivated to or less able to block out the music and focus on the academic content than were students in the classical music condition.

As we noted in our earlier discussion of the relationship between adolescents' music preferences and academic performance (Chapter 4), there have been suggestions that the anti-establishment content characteristic of some popular music genres adversely affects kids' school achievement by encouraging them to devalue or defy traditional academic values and behavior. However, the only study that enables causal inferences about such content effects on academic performance, Roe's (1984) longitudinal examination of Swedish youth, found no such influence. Rather, early school achievement led to later music choices, generally undermining the argument that defiant content caused students to underperform.

Caution is clearly in order before generalizing the results of these studies. In any one of them, the novelty of encountering rock music in a group or in a classroom setting may have affected attention to the task. Attention may have also been influenced by expectations of being tested. Moreover, in the three "true" experiments—those with random assignment to experimental conditions—exposure time was brief. In any case, there are enough differences in performance across different kinds of study topics and types of music to suggest that background music does not always affect concentration in the same way. LaVoie and Collins' (1975) finding that rock music harmed performance but that classical music did not fits with both Wolfe (1983), who reported that instrumental music made no difference on college students' performance on mathematical problems, and Salame and Baddeley (1989), who found background instrumental music to be less disruptive of visual memory than background speech. These results indicate that the effects of background music may depend on whether it has lyrics. It may be easier to ignore instrumental music than songs with words. Most popular music, of course, has words. It also seems reasonable to ask whether such things as the music's beat, its current popularity, who performs it, and so forth, make a difference. Even with such qualifications in mind, however, the research still points to the very real possibility that adolescents' attempts to study with rock or pop music may lead to information overload, attention decrements, or other types of interference, any of which may reduce academic performance. Given the remarkably high proportion of adolescents who report that they study with music, this area clearly requires further investigation.

HEARING

One obvious characteristic of much of today's popular music is that both musicians and fans like it loud, and for many years parents have pleaded with their kids to "turn it down." Until relatively recently, such requests usually had more to do with the adults' own comfort than with that of their children. Typically, "Turn it down!" meant "You're driving me nuts!" Today, however, "turn it down" has added meaning—and for some, added urgency. The phrase is no longer just a plea for the speaker's own comfort (we accept this as an intergenerational constant), but a legitimate and serious health warning.

The last several decades have witnessed remarkable advances in audio technology, advances that have given the listening audience access to more music and to better sound reproduction than ever before. Yet there are some potential negatives to these advances. At the same time that such things as amplified musical instruments and sound systems, high-powered speakers (on stage, in homes, and in cars), and personal stereo systems deliver music fidelity at a level once never imagined (some argue even beyond what can be experienced at a live concert), they also deliver to musicians and fans alike decibel levels well in excess of what the medical profession considers safe. Herein lies one of the best documented non-content-related effects of popular music—the risk of significant physiological damage to at least some listeners' hearing.

Most of the research leading to the establishment of noise-level standards for U.S. industry has focused on the impact of "noise" (loud machinery, constant gunfire, etc.) on industrial workers and military personnel (Consensus National Conference, 1990; U.S. Dept. of Labor, 1983). The important issue, however, is not whether someone chooses to label a particular sound "noise," but simply whether it exceeds a given decibel level. In decibel terms, a quietly humming engine is no more a threat to hearing than a ballad strummed on an acoustic guitar, and an extended electric guitar riff played on powerful speakers can be just as problematic as a screaming turbine. High decibel levels affect hearing in two ways (Clark, 1992). First, acoustic trauma occurs as a result of the instantaneous peak sound pressure level from an explosive burst of sound in excess of 140 decibels. Such instantaneous sound bursts, typically produced by a fire-cracker or gunshot, can stretch inner ear tissues beyond their limits, tear-ing them apart and producing immediate and usually permanent hearing loss. Rarely, if ever, does music pose this kind of threat.

Music is of concern, however, with the second kind of hearing loss, that resulting from *extended exposure* to sound levels in the 90 to 140 decibel range. Excessive exposure over time to sound in this range leads to the death of sensory cells in the cochlea, which are ultimately replaced by scar tissue. The resulting hearing loss is slow, cumulative, and insidious. Initially it does not affect one's ability to discriminate low frequency "pure tones" (those most important to speech discrimination), but it can relatively soon impair the ability to discriminate in frequencies outside the normal speech range (those in the 4 kHz range). Moreover, decades of exposure may impair hearing even in the lower frequencies (Clark, 1992). The potential for this kind of damage and hearing loss depends on the level and duration of exposure, as well as such individual differences as the health and lifestyle of the listener (Drake-Lee, 1992).

In technical terms, the generally accepted standard for a maxi-mum safe level of exposure to high sound levels is expressed as "90-dB TWA for 8 hours, with a 5dB trading ratio"—that is, "90 decibels for a time-weighted average of eight hours, with a five decibel trading range" (Clark, 1992; Consensus National Conference, 1990; U.S. Dept. of Labor, 1983). In less technical language, this means that eight continuous hours is the maximum length of time one should be exposed to sound levels that average 90 decibels. The time-weighted average adjusts for variations in ongoing levels of sound; more weight is given to decibel levels in excess of 90 dB and less to levels below 90 dB. So, for example, if the sound level creeps above 90 decibels for a few minutes, safe exposure requires either an offsetting few minutes below 90 decibels or a reduction in total expo-sure time. The five decibel "trading ratio" means that volume operates something like a logarithmic scale; that is, for average increases or decreases of five decibels, the safe period of exposure is either halved (in the cases of increases) or doubled (in the case of decreases). In other words, if the time-weighted average sound level is 95 dB, then exposure time should not exceed four hours (half the time allowed for 90dB); if it reaches 100 dB, exposure should be further reduced to two hours; and so on. Thus, if the Occupational Safety and Health Administration is doing its job, workers should be limited to a maximum of four hours in the presence of industrial machinery producing an average of 95 dB of noise—as might be the case, for example, with a continuously running power saw.

However, what if the "workers" are not what we would typically call industrial workers and the sound, by many at least, is not considered to be noise? What if we focus on musicians and young fans at rock concerts, in clubs, or listening to boom boxes or personal stereos with the volume cranked to the maximum? Several studies have investigated maximum volume levels attainable at live rock concerts. Concern about amplified rock music was voiced at least 25 years ago, when amplifiers operated in the 20,000 to 30,000 watt range (see, e.g., Rintelmann & Borus, 1968), and has continued to grow along with the size and power of amplified public address systems, which now come equipped with 100,000- to 500,000-watt amplifiers (Clark, 1991). Peak sound levels in excess of 130 dB were reported in the 1960s (Rupp & Koch, 1969), and at least one recent study measured a peak of 139.5 dB at a Canadian rock concert (Yassi, Pollock, Tran, & Cheang, 1993).

As we have seen, however, the level of continuous sound is more important than brief peaks in volume, and a number of researchers have assessed sound levels throughout various concerts. Danenberg, Loos-Cosgrove, and LoVerde (1987), for example, measured sound levels at a high school cafeteria dance in New London, Connecticut. Volume level was recorded throughout the three and a half hour concert using sound-level meters placed at distances of 35, 18, 9, and 4 feet from the speakers; sound levels averaged 99 dB, 105.5 dB, 108 dB, and 112 dB, respectively. Clark (1992) monitored a New Kids on the Block concert in St. Louis's Bush Memorial Stadium in fall 1990. He placed a dosimeter (an instrument which continuously measures sound pressure levels) on the shoulder of an attendee who was seated in the *second deck* of the open stadium. Figure 7.1, which graphs each five-minute interval throughout the four and a half hour concert, demonstrates clearly that the bulk of the concert was conducted at sound levels well in excess of the 90 dB safe standard. The overall level for the entire concert was 99 dB, with much of the last two hours of the concert in excess of 100 dB. Clark (1991) also analyzed all the published sound-level data from rock concerts that he could locate in the research literature and found a mean in excess of 103 dB. It seems

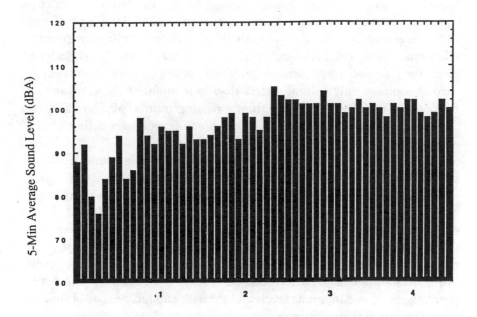

Figure 7.1. Sound levels recorded at a New Kids on the Block Concert held at Busch Memorial Stadium, St. Louis, MO, in Fall 1990. Measures are made with a dosimeter (Quest M-27) placed on an attendee seated in the second deck. Plotted are the 5-minute equivalent levels; overall level for the entire concert was 99 dBA.
Reprinted by permission from "Hearing: The effects of noise," by W.W. Clark, 1992, *Otolaryngology: Head and Neck Surgery, 106*(6), p. 674. © 1992.

fair to say that attendees at live rock concerts, discothèques, and even many school dances are routinely exposed to continuous sound levels in excess of 100 dB for significant periods of time, well in excess of generally accepted safe levels. Indeed, Canadian researchers using procedures similar to Clark's report that those attending a two-and-a-half-hour rock concert that they monitored received at least double the acceptable daily dose of high sound. Some received over four times the suggested standard (Yassi et al., 1993).

The potential for exposure to high sound levels via stereo systems is equally disturbing. Data on the maximum sound levels produced by various recreational, household, hobby, and transportation devices (Clark,

1992) show that the typical maximum volume on most home stereo systems ranges from 90 dB to about 107 dB and on personal stereo systems from 95 dB to 115 dB (some range as high as 128 dB). Output from customized automobile sound systems, sometimes called "boom cars," can produce sound in excess of 125 dB (House Select Subcommittee on Children, Youth, and Families, 1991), many times the safe level. Indeed, given the 5 decibel trading range described earlier, safe continuous exposure to sound at this volume is less than four minutes! For comparative purposes, sound pressure levels from a passing train at 50 feet can produce ranges from 82 dB to 103 dB, and home power saws deliver maximum sound pressures levels between 95 and 113 dB.

More important than these maximum attainable sound levels, of course, is the question of how loud and for how long kids actually play music. Although data on use of personal stereo equipment and earphones use is scarce, a study conducted in Hong Kong (Wong, Van Hassell, Tang, & Yui, 1990) and an informal survey reported by Clark (1992) indicate that roughly 80% of adolescents use personal stereo systems at least occasionally. Clark (1991) estimates that most listeners select listening levels lower than 90 decibels. Nevertheless, 5% to 10% of the kids who listen regularly do so at dangerous levels and for long enough periods of time to pose a hazard to their hearing.

Evidence mounts that exposure to loud music is taking a toll. Reports of hearing loss among rock musicians are becoming more and more common, as evidenced by the following statement by Snow, a member of Metallica: "Me and Lars have both got our ear problems. What they call tinnitus. . . . A cure? Blast something to drown it out. Alcohol makes it worse, and going to sleep at night I always have the TV on to drown it out. It won't go away and if you keep jamming loud, it'll get worse" (Drake-Lee, 1992, p. 617). The problem has become significant enough to lead to the founding of an organization called Hearing Education and Awareness for Rockers (HEAR) with the expressed goal of educating and encouraging musicians and concert-goers to protect their hearing ("Rock stars say it's time," 1991). Since its founding in 1988, HEAR has produced a number of public service announcements and a film in which 50 major performers, including Pete Townshend, Huey Lewis, and Ray Charles, warn about the dangers of high volume music.

Research tends to support these musicians' sense that prolonged exposure to loud music puts hearing at risk. Although one early examination of young rock musicians who had played less than three years with a rock group found little evidence of hearing loss (Rintelmann & Borus,

1968), a study of classical musicians, whose much longer careers as per-formers imply long-term exposure, found hearing loss in over 40% (Axelsson & Lindgren, 1981). Classical music, of course, is played at much lower volume levels than rock music, making these results seem ominous indeed for rockers with extended careers.

Several experiments have examined music's impact on hearing by measuring temporary threshold shifts following exposure to loud music. A *threshold* defines the quietest sound that can be heard, and a *temporary threshold shift* refers to a temporary increase in that level following expo-sure to a loud noise. Although thresholds usually return to preexposure levels after periods ranging from a few minutes to a few days, temporary shifts are now believed to be a predictor of more permanent threshold shifts, that is, of permanent hearing impairment (Yassi et al., 1993). Drake-Lee (1992) found that immediately following a 90-minute concert, all but one of the members of the British heavy metal band ManOWar—billed as the loudest rock band in the world—manifested significant temporary hearing loss (i.e., temporary elevation in auditory thresholds). The lead singer, who wore ear protection in his right ear throughout the perfor-mance, was unaffected. Similar temporary threshold shifts have also been demonstrated among concert fans. Of 22 young men and women scattered throughout the arena at the Canadian concert cited earlier (Yassi et al., 1993), over 80% showed temporary threshold shifts of 10 dB or more up to 25 minutes after exposure, and over 75% showed continued shifts at 40 to 60 minutes. Finally, Danenberg and her colleagues (Danenberg et al., 1987) reported that of 20 students and 7 adult chaperones attending the New London high school dance mentioned earlier, all but 1 student and 1 adult experienced at least a 5dB threshold shift. The shift remained with 4 of 6 students three days later. In addition, 15 of the students and all of the adults reported experiencing tinnitus, the sense of fullness or ringing in the ears mentioned earlier by a member of Metallica.

To sum up, there is no question that music equipment can and does produce dangerous volume levels. The danger is somewhat offset by the fact that most kids do not expose themselves to high levels for extend-ed periods of time. However, many do. Even if the figure is only 5% to 10%, this is still a large number. For these kids, the increasing volume lev-els and the high daily listening figures suggest serious problems when they become young adults. Widespread hearing impairment may, indeed, be one of rock's hidden legacies.

SOCIAL INTERACTION

Popular music exerts much of its impact in social settings. Indeed, each of the social uses we discussed in Chapter 3 corresponds to an effect of music. If music consistently is used to provide a party atmosphere, it presumably has that effect. If music is used for dancing, it obviously "causes" (or at least facilitates) dancing. If music allegiance is used to define subgroups within the school culture, it probably functions that way—otherwise, something else would be used. To repeat an earlier point, we recommend a simple social experiment to anybody who doubts the power of music to influence social behavior: Unplug the stereo at a party and watch what happens.

Effects such as these are generally viewed as neutral or even positive outcomes, making life better for adolescents. Yet we have hinted at some areas in which the impact of music in social settings and social groups might be viewed as problematic. Certain religious denominations do frown on dancing; for them, dance music is not a positive thing. Some adults may disapprove of certain subgroups within a school that define themselves in terms of music genres; for them, the music is a problem. Certain types of music do stand for rebellion and alienation and represent antisocial philosophies. There is legitimate concern about the possibility that the messages and sound of some kinds of music may solidify certain disaffected subgroups in adolescent culture and articulate values and feelings for their members that the larger society may condemn.

We say certain subgroups because most teens who listen to rap or heavy metal (the main culprits according to critics) are not seriously alienated or "at risk." As we discussed in Chapter 2, most kids fit reasonably well into their families, schools, and communities. For them, heavy metal is a taste, perhaps offensive to parents, but otherwise not much to worry about. For others, though, a preference for heavy metal may be more than just a "taste." It is an identity, a source of group cohesion, a life philosophy. For these listeners, many of whom fall into high-risk groups (Arnett, 1991a, 1991b; King, 1988; Klein et al., 1993), there exists a strong possibility that a certain type of music, once adopted by their group, may begin to act as a source of information, values, even behavior.

Unfortunately, we have found no direct evidence on whether this sort of process occurs. Music use and preference are usually seen as the results of other social processes, not the causes. The single strongest piece of evidence that music can act as an independent cause of adolescent peer group processes comes from Roe's (1984) longitudinal study of Swedish youth. Roe found that early adopters of pop music, those strongly interested in it at age 11, were more oriented toward peers and less oriented toward parents later in adolescence than were kids who were not interested in pop at an early age. His statistical analyses indicated that it was probably the differences in popular music involvement at an early age that caused the later differences in peer orientation. Although Roe's study is somewhat removed from our earlier speculation, it suggests that music can have deep, long-term, structural effects on social relationships in adolescence.

MOOD AND AFFECT

MOOD CONTROL

As we have discussed at some length, popular music helps kids both to express and to change mood states—to relax, to relieve tension, to escape worries, to seek excitement, or to gain solace when they are sad, lonely, or bored. Previously unpublished data on California youth gathered in the study reported by Roberts and Henriksen (1990) confirm this. When asked whether the statement "I listen to music to change my mood" applied to them, over 50% of the 7th and 9th graders and almost 70% of the 11th graders replied "somewhat" or "a lot." It seems reasonable to infer from the survey data, then, that both mood maintenance and mood change are legitimate, direct, and probably immediate effects of listening to popular music.

There is, however, a lack of direct experimental evidence on the point. A few clinical studies have indicated that some kinds of music may have positive emotional effects on disturbed listeners (Cripe, 1986; Reardon & Bell, 1970), and other clinicians (Heimlich, 1983; Mark, 1986, 1988) have reported cases in which rock lyrics seemed to stimulate alienated and disturbed adolescents to communicate more openly about their feelings and problems. Mark (1988) suggested that issues too difficult for adolescents to discuss personally can be addressed by conversation about how typical adolescent issues and problems are portrayed in rock lyrics. According to Mark, not only does rock music provide a conversational entree, but even more important, talking about rock and rock performers enables adolescents to deal with important personal experiences while "distancing themselves safely from conflicts they may themselves feel but are unprepared to address" (p. 314).

We have found no experimental studies that directly assess the affective consequences of rock, rap, or any other kind of popular music among normal populations of youth. Larson and Kubey (1983) found an association between pop music listening (i.e., radio use) and elevated mood states among young adolescent boys, but their research method did not allow them to say whether listening served as a cause or an effect. Still, both survey research on uses and gratifications as well as casual observation confirm that rock and pop can animate and delight teenagers, which strikes us as an extremely important effect. Indeed, pop music creators (writers, performers, producers) say it is one of the most important effects. After all, to a large extent that is what they aim for when they make the songs in the first place.

Suicide

Of course, if popular music has the power to elevate, it may also have the power to depress, or at least to exacerbate, negative emotional states. This assumption underlies several recent anecdotal reports of teen suicides reputedly associated with listening to heavy metal music (Litman & Farberow, 1994; "Rock on trial," 1988; "Suicides blamed," 1988). Because, with few exceptions, heavy metal music carries the most suicidal themes, the most logical place to search for direct effects would be in the heavy metal audience. Aside from occasional speculation by lawyers, psychiatrists, and clinical psychologists, evidence of heavy metal's implication in adolescent suicidal behavior must be extrapolated from surveys and interviews with "at-risk" kids. As discussed earlier, this research shows that devoted heavy metal listeners do indeed differ from the larger population of adolescents. Heavy metal attracts a coterie of highly involved, highly absorbed fans, primarily (but not exclusively) White males in the middle adolescent years. These youth are more likely than others to be at odds with parents, school, and "authority," and tend to be risk takers.

Most important to the issue of music and suicide, there exists within the larger heavy metal audience a significant subgroup of fans who are troubled or "at risk." Several correlational studies have documented that troubled teenagers are highly attracted to heavy metal. Poor academic performance and alienation from mainstream school life is associated with a preference for heavy metal (Christenson & van Nouhuys, 1995; Hakanen & Wells, 1993; Hansen & Hansen, 1991a; Tanner, 1981). Similarly, adolescent drug users (Arnett, 1991b; Eagle et al., 1989; King, 1988; Martin et al., 1993) and kids who report engaging in delinquent behavior (Epstein et al., 1990; Martin et al., 1993; Tanner, 1981; Wass et al., 1991) tend to be metal fans, as do kids with troubled family relationships (Arnett, 1991b; Christenson & van Nouhuys, 1995; Martin et al., 1993; Wass et al., 1988–1989). Clearly, heavy metal music attracts just the sort of youth most likely to be at risk of suicide and presents them with a combination of lyric content and heavy sound that might conceivably reinforce their depression and despair. Regardless of why these kids turn to heavy metal music in the first place, a certain number of them may be vulnerable to its mood and message.

Martin and his colleagues (1993) reported one of two studies we have located that directly address the suicide issue (see also Chapter 4). They questioned over 200 Australian high school students and established not only that heavy metal fans strongly manifested most of the attributes of "troubled youth" just discussed, but also that a preference for heavy metal music was directly and strongly associated with suicidal thoughts and behaviors. Among metal fans, over 20% of the males and 60% of the females reported that they had actually tried to hurt or kill themselves in the preceding six months, compared to fewer than 8% of male and 14% of female pop fans. Stack, Gundlach, and Reeves (1994) took a different approach to the question of the relationship between heavy metal and suicide. They attempted to find out if high rates of adolescent suicide tended to correlate with high heavy metal exposure. Because no national measures of heavy metal listening exist, national exposure could not be directly assessed. Reasoning, however, that teenage subscribers to heavy metal magazines were "likely to be immersed in and committed to the symbols and messages communicated through the subculture" (p. 19), they used Audit Bureau of Circulation data on teenagers' subscriptions (adjusted for the size of the 15- to 24-year-old population) to *Metal Edge* magazine for each of the 50 states in 1988. This magazine was felt to be a valid indicator of involvement in the heavy metal subculture because it focuses exclusively on metal music and personalities. National Center for Health Statistics information on suicide rates among 15-to 24-year-olds for each state in 1988 were then related to the subscription rates for each state. The results revealed a strong, positive relationship between heavy metal subscriptions and adolescent suicide; that is, the greater the strength of the heavy metal subculture in a given state, the higher the suicide rate. Moreover, the relationship remained strong and statistically significant even after such factors as divorce rate and race, both of which are associated with suicide, were taken into account (see also Stack & Gundlach, 1992, on adult suicide rates and exposure to country music).

For obvious ethical considerations, direct experimental evidence on this issue is unavailable. Nevertheless, we believe there is enough in the research to suggest the possibility that a deep involvement in heavy metal music may play a contributory role in the behavior of the minority of adolescents for whom suicide has become a possibility. Descriptions of adolescent suicide incidents indicate that this most drastic of acts is typically associated with a combination of depression, substance abuse, and "conduct disorder" (Berman & Jobes, 1991; Levy & Deykin, 1989). Litman and Farberow (1994) contend that such "addictive and antisocial behaviors" are often initially adopted as defenses against or alternatives to suicide. It is only when they fail as alternatives and conditions worsen that they may function as contributory causes of suicide. Similarly, if a preoccupation with heavy metal music is carried to an extreme, it too may become an addictive, antisocial behavior—to use Roe's (1995) term, a form of "media delinquency"—and ultimately a contributor to the problem. Indeed, heavy metal listening seems a poor strategy for coping with depression and despair. Litman and Farberow (1994) wrote that for those who become obsessed with heavy metal—for whatever reason—it encouraged "further turning away from normal pursuits into escapist fantasies, often aggressive, destructive, and nihilistic" (p. 498). This possibility becomes even more worrisome in view of Arnett's (1991a) finding that metal fans often use metal music when they are angry or in a bad mood, even going so far as using it to *accentuate* a bad mood. For this small minority of kids who become "addicted" to heavy metal and who are already alienated and disturbed, the music may introduce one more problem, one more risk factor for suicide.

CONTENT-RELATED SOCIAL EFFECTS

To what extent do music media contribute to adolescents' developing map of their universe? Do the images and themes in popular music and music videos influence young listeners' beliefs, attitudes, values, or social behavior? Do kids turn to music media for help in thinking and acting in their world? These are the kinds of broad questions that have been raised about what we have referred to as the content-related social effects of popular music. Given the human inclination to pay more attention to deviant or unusual messages than to normative information, and the well-documented tendency of some music lyrics and videos to celebrate deviant and nonnormative behavior (e.g., premarital sex, drug use, violence, and suicide), most public attention to the content-related effects of popular music has reflected a concern with negative effects. (Imagine the day when a *Newsweek* headline reads "Heavy Metal Hit Encourages Altruism!"). It is not surprising, then, that the preponderance of empirical work reflects the same bias.

As will become apparent, sex and violence provide the focus for much of the empirical research on the effects of popular music, almost all of which has been conducted since 1980. Public concern about music effects began to escalate with the introduction of MTV in the early 1980s, when the adult world began to "see" lyric content that they had previously been either able to escape or unable to hear. Leaving aside for the moment the question of whether most music videos feature sex or violence (see Chapter 5), clearly enough do to have ignited considerable public outcry. As is often the case, these public concerns were soon followed by empirical tests of whether violent or sexually suggestive lyrics and videos do, in fact, influence adolescent behavior. The balance of this chapter discusses the results of the research on the impact of music lyrics and music video imagery.

It is worth noting at the outset that adolescents themselves believe music lyrics can have negative effects. For example, over 70% of Leming's (1987) sample of academically talented teens claimed they had rejected song messages that seemed to condone casual or free sex. Of course, "talented" kids are just the kind of adolescent subgroup one might expect to reject counter-normative messages. But what about others? According to Wass and her colleagues (Wass et al., 1988–1989), "normal" adolescents think "problem kids" might be influenced. They interviewed 694 middle and high school students from central Florida and found that about half believed that depressed or troubled teenagers should not listen to rock music about murder, suicide, and Satanism because the lyrics might influence subsequent behavior.

Correlational studies demonstrate relationships between music listening and various measures of sex and violence, particularly among "at-risk" kids. We cited in Chapter 3 the work of Strouse and his colleagues (1995), which revealed that among girls from "unsatisfactory" family environments—environments that provided them little support or satisfaction—more music video viewing was associated with increasingly permissive attitudes about premarital sex. As noted earlier, several other studies have identified heavy metal music as a particular favorite of at-risk and delinquent kids. At the peril of sounding like a cracked record (older readers, at least, will resonate with this simile), we repeat that correlational data such as these usually cannot tell us much about what causes what. It is as likely that permissive sexual attitudes lead to a preference for MTV or that social alienation leads to a taste for heavy metal music, as it is that MTV and music influence sexual attitudes and social integration. Indeed, Roe's (1984) longitudinal study of Swedish youth indicated that alienation from the school culture precedes, rather than follows, the development of oppositional music preferences. Roe, however, did not address the issue of the relationship of oppositional music preferences to other problematic behaviors or among other populations. In our view it would be a mistake to ignore the fact that many troubled kids prefer music with themes that might, at least in theory, contribute to their problems. Students who are alienated from the majority culture may be particularly responsive to the kinds of rebellious, anti-establishment lyrics typical of much heavy metal music. As we suggested in our discussion of suicide, regardless of why they develop an allegiance to heavy metal in the first place, the music seems well designed to further legitimize their dissatisfaction and disaffection. For such youth, music may reinforce and even intensify an existing negative philosophy.

We have located two experiments in which participants responded to audio recordings of songs rather than to music videos. The first, reported by Wanamaker and Reznikoff (1989), found no differences in listeners' levels of hostility as a result of hearing "aggressive rock music." In this study, identical groups of college students wrote "stories" about each of five ambiguous pictures as they listened to a recording of: (a) aggressive music and aggressive lyrics (e.g., "Louder than Hell" by Motley Crue), (b) aggressive music and nonaggressive lyrics (e.g., "The Way" by Stryper, a heavy metal Christian band), or (c) nonaggressive music and nonaggressive lyrics (e.g., "In My World" by the Moody Blues). The songs repeated continuously for 20 minutes while the students wrote their stories. They then completed the Buss–Durkee hostility scale. Counter to expectation, no differences emerged among the three groups in the amount of hostility expressed in the stories or in scores on the hostility scale. There was some evidence that the students either did not listen to or did not understand the lyrics of the songs. On this basis Wanamaker and Reznikoff concluded that "teenagers do not attend to rock music lyrics" (p. 367), implying that effects cannot occur unless differences in content are perceived.

The second audio-only study found an effect of listening to heavy metal music, but not the effect expected. St. Lawrence and Joyner (1991) set out to test whether listening to sexually violent heavy metal would increase acceptance of gender-role stereotypes and sexually violent behavior. Groups of undergraduate males heard either sexually violent heavy metal rock, Christian heavy metal rock, or easy-listening classical music. A month before and immediately after listening, the students answered a questionnaire measuring gender-role stereotyping, adversarial sexual beliefs, acceptance of interpersonal violence, rape myth acceptance (the idea that women invite and/or enjoy rape), and self-reported sexual arousal. The somewhat surprising result was that it did not matter whether participants heard sexually violent heavy metal or Christian heavy metal. Relative to classical music, exposure to either type of music produced more negative attitudes toward women. In other words, the lyrics did not make a difference, but the heavy metal musical form did. Here again there is reason to wonder whether the students really "heard" the lyrics. St. Lawrence and Joyner interpret the finding that the young men in their study correctly identified the basic genres of the music they heard (rock, country, classical, etc.) as evidence of some minimal level of attention to the songs. There was, however, no measure of lyric comprehension; correct identification consisted simply of labeling either sexually violent or Christian heavy metal as "rock," something easily achieved on the basis of the sound alone. The fact that both types of heavy metal produced the same effect implies that the students were responding to the sound only, and that the sound elicited a stereotyped response such as: "That's heavy metal, and if it's heavy metal, then it must be sexual and violent." In any case, the results suggest that "content-related" effects can occur even without conscious awareness of the lyrics' meaning.

In some ways, music videos are easier to decode than straight audio recordings. Words may be garbled, masked by a screaming guitar, or otherwise unintelligible. However, even if the "story" in a video is inscrutable, it is difficult when watching a video to miss such visual standbys as threatening displays of weapons, fighting, or sexually suggestive body movements. Perhaps because of the addition of this visual dimension to the audio, the experimental evidence indicates that viewing music videos can affect adolescents in quite substantial ways. We describe next the results of several of these experiments, then consider some different theoretical explanations for the effects found.

Greeson and Williams (1986) reported one of the first experimental studies on the social effects of music video exposure. The participants were 7th and 10th graders from middle-income, working-class homes. Half the students within each grade saw just over 30 minutes of videos randomly recorded off MTV, and the other half saw a "high-impact" stimulus composed of videos selected especially for their high concentration of sex, violence, and anti-establishment themes. Comparisons of measures obtained before and after viewing showed that both the random and high impact videos increased students' approval of premarital sex. In addition, the high-impact video reduced 10th graders' disapproval of violence. Greeson and Williams took this as an indication that watching videos saturated with violent images may have desensitized these older teenagers. The two groups of 7th graders did not differ in their attitudes toward violence.

Peterson and Pfost (1989) showed 144 undergraduate males one of four collections of music video content: erotic–violent (e.g., scantily clad women coupled with scenes of knives and blood), erotic–nonviolent (e.g., bare-breasted women dancing), nonerotic–violent (e.g., a singer fighting Soviets and using a bomb to destroy them), and nonerotic–nonviolent (performance videos with no erotic or violent images). Immediately after viewing, the students responded to a "Student Sexual Attitudes Scale" (Malmuth, 1983) that measured rape myth acceptance, acceptance of interpersonal violence, adversarial sexual beliefs, and gender-role stereotypes. They also filled out scales assessing mood states and sexual arousal. Of the four types of content, only violent images had much effect, and this only when there were no erotic images present. That is, young men who saw the nonerotic–violent videos scored significantly higher than men in the three other groups on measures of negative affect (e.g., anger, anxiety, frustration) and on the adversarial sexual belief scale. There were no differences between any of the other groups. Peterson and Pfost speculated that the erotic–violent videos may have failed to increase negativity and adversarial sexual beliefs because the pleasurable reactions elicited by the erotic images offset or countered the aggressive responses elicited by the violent images. They concluded that "certain types of rock videos can foster a calloused and antagonistic orientation toward women" (p. 321). We think a more appropriate characterization of the results should read: "Certain types of *violent videos* can foster a calloused and antagonistic orientation toward *others*." After all, the evidence points only to violent videos, not to erotic videos, and the measures tested antagonism only toward women. Had men been included as targets in the measures, they too might have drawn increased antagonism. It is also worth noting that this kind of experimental design can be highly reactive. That is, it is difficult to believe that the men participating in the study did not suspect a connection between the videos and the questions they answered. Studies in which participants may have developed an idea, correct or not, of what the experiment is testing are difficult to interpret and generalize. That is why so many researchers go to great lengths to disguise their intent.

Johnson, Jackson, and Gatto's (1995) recent study of the effect of rap music videos typifies several more complex and better disguised studies. Their experimental design required convincing participants that they were involved in two different, unrelated experiments, which were, of course, not unrelated at all. Three identical groups of 11- through 16-year-old, lower income, African-American youth watched either eight violent rap videos, eight nonviolent rap videos, or served as a control group that saw no videos. The violent videos (e.g., "Roughneck" by M.C. Lyte; "Hazy Shade of Criminal" by Public Enemy) contained images of weapons and violent acts (guns, knives, shootings, and assaults), as well as lyrics that condoned or glorified violence. The nonviolent videos (e.g., "Everyday People" by Arrested Development; "I Get Around" by Tupac Shakur) focused on dancing and partying, portraying young rappers being admired by scantily clad dancers and other onlookers .

The students were led to believe they would participate in two experiments. The first, which was presented as a test of their ability to recall the content of music videos, served as a disguise of the study's real concern. After participants viewed the videos and completed a brief "memory test," the second study was introduced in the guise of an unrelated examination of "decision-making skills" in which the boys, including those in the nonvideo control group, would answer questions about two brief stories. Their answers provided the primary information on which the researchers based inferences about the effects of watching the videos. The first "decision-making story" introduced a dating couple (John and Susan) and an old friend of Susan's (Jerry). It told how Susan went out one night and happened to see her friend who gave her "a big hug and a small kiss on the lips." The boyfriend, John, hearing about this, went to Susan, "grabbed and pushed her" and told her never to kiss another boy. He then found Jerry, "hit him and knocked him to the ground," and told him to "leave my girlfriend alone."

After reading this passage, the boys in all three experimental groups were asked about their attitudes toward the use of violence (e.g., "Should John have hit Jerry?") and the probability that they would engage in similar violent behavior ("Would you have pushed your girlfriend if she had kissed another boy?"). They gave their answers on 9-point scales ranging from "definitely no" to "definitely yes." In the second story, which followed immediately, a young man named Bobby, who had chosen to go to college and pursue a law degree, comes home on break and goes to meet his friend Keion, who has opted not to attend college. Keion arrives in a "new BMW," wearing "nice clothes and nice jewelry," and soon picks up four girls who admire and comment on his car and clothes. Keion declines to explain how he can afford such nice things, but tells Bobby that he "did not need college" to get them. Following this passage, the teenagers answered two questions intended to assess academic perceptions: "Which boy would you rather be like?" and "Do you think Bobby will ever become a lawyer?"

The students in the three different groups answered the various questions quite differently. First, those who saw the violent video were more likely to condone the violence against Jerry (the girl's old friend in the first story) and more likely to indicate that they would have done the same thing than were kids in either of the other two treatment groups. Second, boys in the violent video group revealed more positive attitudes toward the use of violence and were more likely to say that they would engage in violence toward the girl themselves than were boys in the control group. The nonviolent video group fell in between, but their scores did not differ significantly from the other two groups. There were also differences between the control group and the two video groups in response to the story about Bobby and Keion. Boys who watched either type of video were considerably less likely than those in the control group to want to be like Bobby (i.e., to go to college) or to believe that he would ever finish school.

In short, assuming that control group scores provide a reasonable baseline, Johnson et al. (1995) showed that exposure to approximately 24 minutes of violent rap videos could significantly increase boys' acceptance of violence. Equally disturbing, perhaps, exposure to either kind of rap videos, violent or nonviolent, significantly reduced academic aspirations. Concerning this latter finding, Johnson and his colleagues speculated that exposure to the rap videos increased the accessibility of images related to "the culture of poverty"—images with implications of inferiority, marginality, and helplessness—which might have led these lower income, African-American males to think about academic failure as they responded to the questions. We return to this explanation later.

Hansen and Hansen (1990b) also used a two-part experimental design to test the theory that viewing "antisocial" rock videos would increase viewers' acceptance of antisocial behavior. An elaborate cover story gave university students the impression that they were to evaluate two applicants for a job hosting a TV show about rock music. While waiting for the job interview to begin, groups of students killed time by watching either three antisocial or three neutral videos. The antisocial videos portrayed such things as trashing a home in the course of a raucous party, car theft, joy-riding, and defiance of authorities. The neutral videos were unrelated to antisocial behavior. Next, the students "accidentally observed" what they (incorrectly) believed to be a real event in which one job applicant, while telling a joke to the other, was brusquely warned to "settle down" by an authority figure, who then left the room. Half the students in the violent video condition and half in the neutral condition then saw the rebuked "job applicant" make an obscene gesture toward the retreating authority figure; the other half saw him merely adjust his clothing. This procedure resulted in four different treatment groups: antisocial video/obscene gesture, antisocial video/no gesture, neutral video/ obscene gesture, and neutral video/no gesture. Subsequently, all students saw a taped interview—which they thought was live—of the two job applicants, then completed a questionnaire indicating the degree to which each applicant was someone they would like personally, and expressing their evaluation of each applicant on various pairs of bipolar adjectives (honest–dishonest, positive–negative, polite–impolite, etc.).

The analysis focused on the differences between students who did or did not see the job candidate make the obscene gesture, and the results were rather straightforward. Students who saw the neutral videos liked the job applicant less and ascribed less positive traits to him if they had seen him make an obscene gesture as opposed to simply adjusting his clothing. For those who watched the antisocial videos, however, evaluations of the job applicant were the same regardless of whether he had made the gesture; that is, the students liked him no less when he made the gesture than when he did not. In other words, a relatively brief exposure to antisocial videos essentially canceled out the natural tendency to dislike those who exhibit rude, defiant behavior.

The Hansens have conducted several studies using similar experimental designs (e.g., Hansen, 1989; Hansen & Hansen, 1988; Hansen & Krygowski, 1994). They have consistently found that music video content alters viewers' assessments of other people. For example, Hansen (1989) found that viewing videos portraying men and women behaving in highly gender-role-stereotypic ways influenced how college students judged the behavior of a young couple engaged in similar behavior. Hansen and Hansen (1988) also reported that videos containing gender-role-stereotyped behaviors had a sizable influence on students' judgments of male–female interactants. Compared to students who saw a neutral (nonstereotypic) video, those who saw a video depicting a woman reciprocate a man's advance in highly stereotypic ways later perceived another "real" woman acting in a similar way as more submissive, less threatening, more sensitive, more sexual, and more competent. Similar results were found for judgments of male behavior. The underlying point is that students' evaluations of a second interaction, one that they believed was independent of the video content, were strongly influenced in a number of ways by music video content.

These findings are consistent with the principles of schema theory introduced in our earlier discussion of interpretation processes. Recall that schema theory argues that when cues in a new message are related to an existing knowledge structure, that knowledge structure or schema strongly influences the "meaning" one finds in the new message. According to schema theory, the rock videos in the first phase of the studies just reviewed may have served to elicit or activate preexisting knowledge structures, which then guided interpretation of subsequent messages containing elements similar to those in the schema. In other words, watching a music video portraying gender-role-stereotyped interactions "primed" students' gender-role-stereotyped knowledge structures. These primed schemas, in turn, shaped interpretations of subsequently observed interactions.

Hansen and Krygowsky (1994) extended these findings by showing that music videos can alter interpretations of observed behavior even when the behavior does not contain cues clearly linking it to the schemas activated by the videos. They selected four music videos containing distinct, identifiable "sex-object" schemas. Two of the videos featured opposing portrayals of male "sexiness," one portraying a lead as possessing many sexy qualities, the other stressing the lead's lack of such qualities. Both female videos featured "sex for sale" themes, one about phone sex, the other about prostitution. In order to be certain that the videos did, in fact, portray or activate different and identifiable schemas, Hansen and Krygowsky showed the videos to a group of college students who rated them on a variety of attributes (e.g., aggressive, attractive, boring, sexy, amusing, arousing, disgusting). The students showed a high level of agreement in their ratings of the four videos, which were seen as being quite distinct in their portrayals of the targeted attributes. The "sexy guy" video was rated as more pleasant, more amusing, sexier, and less aggressive than "the unsexy" guy video. The phone sex video was seen as sexier, more humorous, less disgusting, and less aggressive than the prostitute video. These evaluations provided the necessary assurance that appropriate stimuli had been selected to test the hypothesis that schemas activated by music videos would influence evaluations of subsequently observed, neutral portrayals of men and women—portrayals, that is, with few cues relating specifically to the previously activated knowledge structures.

In the main phase of the study, different groups of undergraduates viewed one of the four videos immediately followed by a 30-second commercial featuring either a man or a woman engaging in behavior that one would not likely interpret as "sex object" related. Participants in this phase of the study were asked to rate the commercials, not the videos. Those who watched either of the male character videos saw a commercial in which an attractive male demonstrated exercise equipment. Students who watched the female videos saw an attractive female promoting a soft drink. Hansen and Krygowsky also added another element to the study by having half the students in each condition engage in mild exercise while viewing (this was the "low physiological arousal" group) and having the other half exercise vigorously ("high physiological arousal"). Recall that in Chapter 6 we noted that schemas are said to exert a greater influence on the interpretation of new information under conditions of high cognitive load, and that high physiological arousal increases cognitive load. The critical question in terms of this element of the theory, then, was whether engaging in vigorous exercise (that is, watching under conditions of high cognitive load) would result in greater reliance on activated schema.

The results of this experiment demonstrated again the power of video-primed schemas to influence perceptions of subsequently observed behavior. The ratings of the actors in the commercials almost exactly recreated the ratings previously given to the actors in the four music videos. Students who watched the "sexy guy" video rated the neutral male commercial to be more pleasant, more amusing, sexier, and less aggressive than students who watched the "unsexy guy" video. Those who had seen the phone sex video rated the neutral female commercial as sexier, more humorous, less disgusting, and less aggressive than students who watched the prostitute video. Moreover, in accord with schema theory, the "priming" effect of the different videos was exaggerated among participants who exercised vigorously, that is, who responded under conditions of high arousal.

Finally, Dolf Zillmann and his colleagues (1995) at the University of Alabama used a two-stage experimental design to bring empirical evidence to the debate about the impact of radical rap music. Their primary purpose was to test whether, as some critics have suggested, radical political rap promotes ethnic divisiveness and polarization. They were also interested in the effects of different genres of music video on academic self-esteem. In the first stage of the study, groups of White and African-American high school students were shown one of three sets of music videos: four popular rock videos (e.g., "Live and Let Die" by Guns-n-

Roses), four nonpolitical rap videos (e.g., "Don't Pass Me By," by Hammer), or four radical political rap videos (e.g., "Fight the Power," by Public Enemy). Immediately after viewing, students answered questions about their self-esteem and about how much they liked the set of videos they had seen.

Next, the students took part in what they thought was an unrelated, second study of student politics. In this second stage they heard speeches by one of six ostensible candidates for student office at a local university. Three of the candidates were White and three were African-American. Within each race the candidates advocated one of three different political platforms: racially liberal, neutral, or racially radical. That is, one African-American and one White candidate advocated liberal policies designed to promote racial harmony on campus; one African-American and one White gave racially neutral speeches, calling for various improvements in school facilities; and one African-American and one White candidate ran on radical race-based platforms, accentuating racial differences and advocating conditions favoring each candidate's own race. Specifically, the radical African-American candidate called for quotas to ensure enrollment of more Black students, and the radical White called for the abolition of minority scholarships and social privileges based on race or ethnicity. To summarize, this procedure exposed Black and White high school students to either popular rock, nonpolitical rap, or political rap music, then had them rate six different candidates for student government—African-Americans and Whites who espoused racially liberal, neutral, or racially radical platforms. Immediately following each speech, students evaluated their assigned candidate's political platform and leadership potential and answered questions related to their own academic self-esteem. The research question was whether exposure to the different types of music videos, particularly to the radical political rap video, would influence either the academic self-esteem or political opinions of the Black and White students.

As it turned out, the music video conditions did not affect African-American kids' political evaluations and self-esteem. Video conditions did, however, influence the White students. White students exposed to the popular rock videos produced significantly lower scores on an academic self-esteem subscale than those exposed to the rap videos. The most interesting finding—in fact, Zillmann et al. used the term "astounding"—was that exposure to radical rap dramatically influenced the opinions and candidate choices of the White teenagers. Indeed, contrary to the critics' claim that radical rap makes White kids more ethnically defensive, White kids in this study actually became more tolerant following exposure to radical rap. In other words, compared to White kids who watched either popular rock or nonpolitical rap videos, those exposed to radical rap were more supportive of a liberal African-American candidate advocating racial betterment by nonconfrontational means and less supportive of a conservative White candidate arguing against affirmative action. Support for the radical African-American candidate was not affected. In short, not only did exposure to radical rap fail to produce the expected increase in White adolescents' support for a White radical platform, it increased their sympathy for a message of racial harmony advocated by a black candidate.

Experimental research thus shows unequivocally that exposure to music videos affects how teenagers and college undergraduates perceive, interpret, evaluate, and respond to a variety of social stimuli. To summarize some of the key studies:

- Videos laced with many violent images made viewers more antagonistic in their orientation toward women and more likely to condone violence in themselves and others (Johnson et al., 1995; Peterson & Pfost, 1989)
- Antisocial videos increased acceptance of subsequently observed antisocial behavior (Johnson et al., 1995; Hansen & Hansen, 1990b)
- Highly gender-stereotyped videos increased acceptance of gender-stereotyped behavior (Hansen, 1989; Hansen & Hansen, 1988)
- Sexually charged videos led viewers to perceive subsequently observed ambiguous behavior as sexier (Hansen & Krygowski, 1994) and to be more accepting of premarital sex (Greeson & Williams, 1986)
- Rap videos in general reduced academic aspirations among African-American teens (Johnson et al., 1995)
- Politically radical rap videos caused White teenagers to become more racially tolerant and less likely to sympathize with reactionary racial political positions (Zillmann et al., 1995).

In addition, there is at least tentative evidence from experiments conducted with audio-only stimuli that exposure to the *sound* of popular music, even when that sound may not accompany accurate perception of lyrics, also affects listeners' subsequent responses. Here we refer to St. Lawrence and Joyner's (1991) finding that heavy metal music, regardless of whether its lyrics were violent or Christian, caused undergraduate males to express somewhat more negative attitudes toward women.

THE PROCESS OF EFFECTS

Important as it is to demonstrate the existence of such effects, it is just as important to specify how they might occur. How is it that listening to a popular song or watching a music video can lead adolescents to change their beliefs, perceptions, or behaviors? What are the processes underlying the effects we have just described? To answer these questions we need to extend our earlier consideration of schema theory and introduce some discussion of cultivation theory and observational learning.

Much of the recent research on music effects is based on the schema theory introduced in Chapter 6. Recall that according to schema theories humans store in their memory mental representations of complex events which, depending on conditions, provide a framework for processing new information. As noted earlier, research indicates that people are most likely to rely on schemas when conditions make it either unnecessary or difficult to interpret and evaluate incoming information. Hansen and Hansen (1991b), for instance, showed how the "noise" in some heavy metal music can interfere with listeners' ability to understand particular song lyrics, hence influencing them to interpret the lyrics in terms of preexisting schemas cued by the song's general sound or type. This process also provides a reasonable explanation for St. Lawrence and Joyner's (1991) finding that sexually violent heavy metal and Christian heavy metal both produced negative attitudes toward women. Quite likely, the young men in the study either ignored or were unable to decipher the lyrics of the songs, but still recognized the sound as heavy metal. This association then evoked their heavy metal schema—sound = heavy metal = sexism and violence—leading them to interpret the music in terms of the schema rather than the actual messages embedded in the songs they heard.

Schemas operate even when it is not particularly difficult to process new information. Indeed, to some extent, how people make sense of new information always depends on what they already know; that is, on their existing schemas. The question is, when and why are some mental representations more likely to be accessed than others? Two important conditions that govern the use of schemas are recency and frequency—that is, the likelihood that an individual will use a given schema to interpret new information depends on how recently that particular schema has been primed and on how frequently it has been used. These factors, in turn, depend on people's backgrounds, interests, and needs. To put it another way, the mental representations we construct, their complexity, and the ease with which they are accessed largely depend on who we are, how we live, what we are interested in, and what we do. For example, most U.S. teenagers have at least a rough schema for something like "football game," but most Korean or Finnish or Chilean teenagers probably do not ("American" football, that is). Among U.S. kids, the football schema is probably more complex and more easily accessed by male athletes than by most girls or nonathletic boys. Finally, regardless of how complex or frequently accessed a football game schema might be for any particular teenager, kids who have just watched a football game are more likely to interpret roughly similar subsequent information using a football game schema than those who have just attended a rock concert. In schema theory terms, watching the game "primes" the football game schema, and primed schema are near at hand and easy to access (Wyer & Srull, 1981).

The frequency with which particular schemas are accessed also makes an important difference in the likelihood that they will be invoked again. The "activation frequency hypothesis" (Bargh, Bond, Lombardi, & Tota, 1986; Hansen, 1989) within schema theory holds that the more we use a particular mental representation, the more accessible it becomes, thus the more likely we are to use it in the future. Returning to our example of the football game schema, football fans probably have a relatively more complex and more accessible football game schema than do other kids because they watch/play/think about the game frequently and use the schema more often. As a result, fans not only perceive football games differently than nonfans, but they also are more likely to perceive other subsequent events in football terms, particularly when these events are ambiguous. Unless conditions demand otherwise, it is simply easier to continue to use a frequently used schema to interpret whatever comes next than to deal with new information solely on its own terms.

To put this idea into the context of popular music, adolescents who spend a great deal of time listening to popular music or watching music videos presumably access typical music media schemas more often than kids who pay little or no attention to popular music or MTV. To the extent these schemas are relatively consistent in what they portray, then an adolescent's own schema structure may come to resemble the representations embedded in the music and the videos to which they are exposed. The process is facilitated to the extent that the expectations inherent in such schema are reinforced, rather than disconfirmed, by information from other sources. If we assume that the boy-meets-girl schemas in TV dramas, advertising, or gossip columns correlate with the boy-meets-girl schemas encountered in music and videos, then exposure to those sources reinforces popular music schemas. The implication is that kids who spend a great deal of time with pop music are more likely to base their interpretation of incoming information on pop music schemas than are those who spend less time with music media.

The general idea that media images, whether in words or pictures, somehow help construct, "cultivate," or influence people's mental representations is by no means new. Cultivation theory, as articulated by George Gerbner and his colleagues (Gerbner, 1970; Gerbner & Gross, 1976; Gerbner, Gross, Morgan, & Signorelli, 1994), offers one possible explanation of how media images shape people's schemas even as those schemas influence interpretation of media images. According to Gerbner et al.'s cultivation theory: (a) our mass media system (especially TV drama) presents a highly uniform picture of the world; (b) this picture is presented in a quasi-realistic manner that tends to conceal from the audience the highly biased and selective nature of message production; and (c) media messages tend to be universally and nonselectively consumed by most people—that is, people "just watch" television, rather than certain types of television. Given these assumptions, cultivation theory has argued that the more one uses a given medium, the more one's view of social reality will reflect that medium's version. Indeed, cultivation theory has spawned a great deal of research showing that heavy TV viewers are more likely than those who watch little television to hold a "TV view of the world."

Cultivation theory has sparked a good deal of debate about its assumptions and the degree to which the mostly correlational methods employed by Gerbner support the kinds of causal inferences that are often made. That debate extends well beyond the scope of this book (see Roberts & Maccoby, 1985), but one criticism is particularly relevant to adolescents and popular music. Several scholars have questioned the assumption of audience nonselectivity. These critics say that many viewers are quite selective in their media choices: They watch primarily news, or primarily situation comedies, or primarily sports, and so on. It follows that overall amount of television use (we relate this to music use later) is a poor indicator of exposure to any specific dimension of television's view of social reality (Christenson & Roberts, 1983; Hawkins & Pingree, 1982). It is difficult to see, for instance, how people who watch mostly situation comedies would develop the "mean and scary" view of the world that

Gerbner and his colleagues argue characterizes the television world (Gerbner & Gross, 1980; Gerbner et al. 1994). If different people watch different kinds of TV programs, and if these different genres present different views of the world, then it is reasonable to suspect that different sorts of world views—or schemas—will be cultivated in them. The world of the situation comedy, for example, strikes us more as silly and sex-obsessed than mean and scary. Accordingly, Hawkins and Pingree (1982) have argued that, because global measures of total viewing neglect variations between different kinds of content, narrower, more focused measures of exposure would increase the probability of discovering a cultivation effect. For example, if we are interested in the likelihood that media images of suicide influence the way adolescents think, then it makes sense to focus on kids who are most exposed to those images. Turning to music, recall our earlier points that different music genres contain different sorts of messages—which, of course, runs counter to cultivation theory's assumption of message uniformity—and that most kids are attracted to particular genres rather than popular music generally. This suggests that we are more likely to find cultivation of rebellious attitudes among kids who prefer heavy metal music than among the audience for mainstream pop. Conversely, a more romantic view of love should be cultivated within the audience for mainstream pop than among heavy metal or rap fans.

   Another problem with cultivation theory is that it does little to explain how media images shape mental representations. It pays scant attention to the learning process, thus fails to explain why some images or schemas might be learned with but a single exposure and others not learned even after hundreds of exposures. To understand this process, we turn briefly to Albert Bandura's (1977, 1986, 1994) social cognitive theory of learning—variously called social learning, observational learning, or modeling theory. According to social cognitive theory, when people pay attention to and think about new information, they acquire new ideas (mental representations, schemas) or modify existing ideas internally in symbolic form before performing an observed behavior or expressing an observed belief. Bandura uses the term *observational learning* to refer to this internal process. Think, for example, of the very first time a person tried a new dance step. In order to take even a first step he or she had to have some idea of how to move, of what to do and what not to do. Very likely that idea was developed by watching someone else perform the dance—or, in the terms of the theory, by observing a model. Models transmit information by displaying, describing, or otherwise depicting beliefs, attitudes, and/or behaviors. Modeling displays can take various forms, such as physical demonstrations (e.g., a father showing his daughter how to dance), pictorial representations (e.g., a video in which someone dances), or verbal descriptions (e.g., a spoken or written description of how to dance).

Whether elements of the display are learned and what particular parts are learned depends on a number of factors, including the form of the display (e.g., words vs. pictures), characteristics of the modeled display (e.g., a live vs. animated film), characteristics of the model (e.g., male or female), characteristics of the observer (e.g., physically coordinated vs. less coordinated learners), the circumstances under which the model is observed (in a quiet room or in a crowded dance hall), and so forth. However, although many different factors influence the process, a few seem particularly relevant to how adolescents may be influenced by popular music. Kids are particularly likely, for example, to respond to the consequences of modeled behavior (Bandura, 1986). If an act leads to positive consequences for the model, it is much more likely to be learned and performed later than if it is punished or fails. Kids also pay more attention to models they admire or find attractive and to models who are similar to themselves, especially if those models are just a few years older—a powerful model for a typical 12-year-old is a typical 14- or 15-year-old. Naturally enough, they pay more attention to information they perceive as immediately relevant to their lives. Finally, the more often they see a particular display or type of display, the more likely they are to learn it and perform it. Each of these principles connects directly to what popular music and music videos provide to adolescents.

As we have noted, most popular music is of, by, and for adolescents. Typically, it is performed by adolescent icons (albeit sometimes graying adolescent wannabees). Many, perhaps most, pop lyrics and music videos deal with central adolescent issues—love, sexuality, independence, family and school relationships, concepts of beauty, friendship, and so on. Moreover, popular music addresses these issues frequently. The same themes—indeed, the same songs—are heard again and again. The consequences of behavior—even antisocial behavior—in pop music are often positive. Sex is usually safe, rudeness is cool, threats toward police or other authorities are rarely punished, and tatoos are never for life. Obviously, given the principles of observational learning, each of these characteristics increases the probability that kids will attend to and be influenced by lyric and video content.

Much of this information, moreover, stands relatively uncontested. Typically media messages must compete with information from other, more powerful sources. Parents, teachers, churches, and so forth are often important influences in the ongoing discourse about many of the issues with which adolescents struggle. At the same time, however, it must be recognized that a disturbing number of adolescents have either weak or antagonistic relationships with these traditional sources of socialization. Even those who have positive relationships with the competing influences may rely largely on the media for information about some domains of social behavior. A good case in point is the area of sexual and romantic relationships. Although parents and teachers occasionally discuss some of the biological and health dimensions of sex, they appear to play a relatively minor role when it comes to informing their teenagers about such important adolescent concerns as petting, masturbation, prostitution, intercourse, premarital sex, and so forth. Topics such as these apparently are too difficult or too dangerous for many parents and teachers to address. And because they tend to avoid taboo topics, their influence wanes. Not surprisingly, given the ubiquity and the nature of the mass media, the influence of media messages grows (Roberts, 1993). Several researchers have found that adolescents now obtain much of their information about sex and sexuality from sources other than parents and teachers—particularly peers and mass media (Fabes & Strouse, 1984, 1987; Thornburg, 1981). In absence of competing information, then, the media—and this certainly includes music media—fill a void that adolescents are quite eager to fill, and can become an important voice in sexual socialization.

To the extent, then, that popular music serves as a dominant, often uncontested, source of information for an adolescent, the likelihood that it will influence his or her beliefs and behavior increases dramatically. This applies to issues other than sex and romantic relationships. When it comes to issues of style, fashion, body image, language, and the nature of friendship—indeed, even suicide and violence—adolescents more often turn to music and MTV than to parents or teachers. In our view, many of the characteristics of popular music are uniquely suited to influence adolescents' values, ideas, and images of reality. Whether they will act on what they learn depends on a multitude of factors. However, learning from the music media, in one form or another, will occur. As Bandura (1977) put it, "after the capacity for observational learning has fully developed, one cannot keep people from learning what they have seen" (p. 32)—or, we would add, what they have heard.

8

POP POLICY:
WHAT SHOULD WE DO
ABOUT POPULAR MUSIC?

I know it's only rock and roll, but I like it.
—Rolling Stones, 1974

In 1994, Dr. Milton Chen, Director of the Center for Education and Lifelong Learning at KQED-TV in San Francisco, published *The Smart Parent's Guide to Kids' TV*. The book is predicated on these assumptions: (a) that television influences children, (b) that some of this influence is good and some bad, (c) that people can do something to shape and control the influence, and (d) that the influence is big enough to warrant the effort to do so. Can these assumptions be extended to popular music? With regard to the first three, the answer is clearly yes. The music media influence the lives of adolescents in a number of ways. Some of the effects of music use are positive or beneficial (e.g., the relief of loneliness) and some negative or harmful (deafness seems an obvious case in point). Furthermore, whatever the influences may be, people—be they government, industry, parents, teachers, or adolescents—have considerable power to control or channel them.

     Whether the influence of music is big enough to warrant intervention is somewhat more difficult to answer. We believe, however, that given the importance of music to adolescents, the nature of the messages in the music, the way music is used, the existing evidence on music media effects, and logical extrapolation from the extensive research on the effects of television, it appears certain that popular music is a highly influential agent of socialization for many American youth. The problem is that the balance between existing evidence and logical extrapolation is far more tilted toward the latter than one would like. In other words, the question of effect size is more speculative with music than it is with television. The admonition appears at the end of just about every student paper and an amazing number of published articles, but we repeat it here once again: More research is needed, especially of the kind that allows a sorting out of the cause–effect relationships between music use and exposure, on the one hand, and adolescent behavior, values, and attitudes, on the other.

Of course, more research is always needed, and, whether for good or ill, public and private policy often proceed without much regard for it anyway. Accordingly, in this chapter we discuss and comment on some of the things being done about music and some of the things that might be done with it, considering in this order: government censorship and regulation; industry self-regulation, including record labeling; and parental intervention.

GOVERNMENT CENSORSHIP AND REGULATION

When culture offends people or when they think it threatens their children, they often turn to government regulation as a remedy. Rightly or wrongly, constitutionally or otherwise, governments at all levels frequently respond to such concerns with restrictive action. In the 1940s, state and local governments routinely banned blues records containing sexual lyrics. Ultimately, blues artists circumvented the censors to some extent by the use of indirect, figurative language (including the very term "rock and roll"), but the suppression was there. In the 1950s, although most of the censorship was exercised by squeamish record companies and broadcasters, government also got into the act with repeated record bans. In Houston, for instance, the Juvenile Delinquency and Crime Commission banned 50 records in just one week—not because their lyrics were particularly racy, but simply because they were rock 'n' roll (McDonald, 1988). The music of the 1960s and early 1970s stimulated even more hysteria, censorship, and harassment of reputedly offensive music and musicians. For example, Country Joe McDonald (of Country Joe and the Fish) was fined $500 in Massachusetts for "lewd, lascivious and wanton" behavior, and the Jefferson Airplane was assessed the same amount for saying "that's a bunch of shit" at a concert. These are only a few incidents in the long and perhaps not-so-proud tradition of government action against music and musicians (McDonald, 1988).

Much of the current debate in this area—on both sides in the culture war—is little more than politics and posturing. Those who advocate censorship often know well ahead of time that their proposed laws will never withstand judicial review, just as those in the industry who label any government action as unconstitutional know that the Supreme Court has never taken an absolutist position on the First Amendment. Yet there are still a number of ways government either is involved in regulating popular music or probably could be if it so chose.

Because most critics focus on sexual words and images, the application of obscenity laws is a reasonable place to begin the discussion of state action concerning popular music. For years the Supreme Court has held that obscene speech has no protection under the First Amendment, and laws prohibiting obscenity exist at both the federal and state levels. At first blush, then, the application of obscenity laws would appear to be an effective weapon for those who would restrict sexually explicit lyrics. In all likelihood, however, although the blush may remain, the attempts at restriction seem likely to fail, at least through this avenue. The problem for those who would use government censorship to restrict sexually explicit music lies in the extreme difficulty of establishing a given text— whether a book, a movie, or music lyrics—as legally obscene. The basic standard for defining legal obscenity comes from the landmark Supreme Court decision in the case of *Miller v. California* (1973). In that case, as in many others, the Court made it quite clear that in most instances when there is an interest, perhaps even a majority interest, in suppressing explicit sexual material, the benefit of the doubt goes toward free expression. Specifically, the Court laid out a three-pronged test in the *Miller* case. A work could be legally obscene only if:

1. The average person, applying contemporary community standards, would find that the work, taken as a whole, appeals to the prurient interest
2. The work depicts or describes in a patently offensive way, sexual conduct specifically defined by the applicable state law
3. The work, taken as a whole, lacks serious literary, artistic, political or scientific value.

Only a minuscule portion of popular music lyrics would "fail" all three tests and thus qualify as legally obscene. First, very few songs, and even fewer albums, *as a whole* appeal to the "prurient" (sexual) interest (Block, 1990). Usually only a few words in a given song or a song or two on the album contain the offending language. Second, even the most offensive sexual lyrics seldom constitute the kind of graphic description of hard core sexual activity the Court seems to require under the second part of the test. The third prong of the test, though, is the trump card. Even if a musical work qualifies as obscene under the first two prongs of the *Miller* test, it can be held legally obscene only if, taken as a whole, it lacks literary, artistic, or political value (somehow scientific seems irrelevant here). Considering its very broad and forgiving application of this standard, it is clear that the Supreme Court would find some degree of literary, political, or artistic value in even the most explicit and degrading music lyrics. In any case, even though local police and judges have made arrests for rock obscenity (e.g., the 1989 Florida arrest of the rap group 2 Live Crew), it is extremely difficult to obtain a conviction on such charges. Moreover, if convictions are obtained in lower courts, higher courts, which tend to give First Amendment issues more weight than do local authorities, usually reverse on appeal.

Most of the concern expressed about sexual lyrics focuses on their potential to influence children and adolescents, and indeed the Supreme Court allows state and local governments somewhat more latitude when it comes to protecting minors. Works can be ruled obscene or harmful to minors even though they may not be obscene for adult audiences, and access to minors can be restricted so long as the applicable law is neither too vague nor overbroad: The law must be clear on what is being banned and on what basis, it must not extend to forms of expression outside the scope of its original intent, and it must not restrict unreasonably the rights of adults (Block, 1990; Holt, 1990; Reimer, 1987). In other words, the obscenity standard may vary somewhat depending on the age of the target audience, but, in the words of former Supreme Court Justice Frankfurter, a state cannot "burn the house to roast the pig" (quoted in Overbeck & Pullen, 1995, p. 310). Another major check on would-be government censors lies in the requirement that laws be drafted narrowly enough so that only minors are denied access. Holt (1990) argues reasonably that music bans originally aimed at children may have the inevitable result of making the music unavailable even to adults because stores would simply stop stocking albums with a limited potential youth market. Moreover, he points out that children retain considerable First Amendment rights of their own. In other words, music may not be placed off limits to minors simply because a squeamish legislative body thinks the language is too mature for them.

Of course, the difficulty of meeting Supreme Court obscenity standards has not prevented states from experimenting with new approaches to the regulation of sexually oriented music lyrics. Since 1985, when Tipper Gore's Parents' Music Resource Center (PMRC) aired the "porn rock" problem in front of the Senate Commerce Committee and, through the national press, to the nation as a whole, at least 35 states have taken legislative steps to address the "threat" of explicit lyrics (RIAA, 1992). In many instances the action consists simply of adding the phrase "sound recordings" to existing obscenity laws, an approach that is not opposed by the music industry and that will certainly withstand judicial review (even though, as we have noted, very few popular music works would be covered).

However, laws have been proposed—and even passed—which lie in far murkier First Amendment waters. Some of the proposed legislation would: make it a crime to sell to minors albums with the industry's parental advisory label (Missouri, Pennsylvania, Louisiana); punish minors who buy labeled albums (a Pennsylvania bill, for instance, would sentence offending minors to 25 hours of community service at a rape crisis center); allow each township in a state to replace the state's general obscenity or "harmful to minors'" definitions with its own local standards (Ohio); ban completely the sale of all labeled albums (city of Leominster, MA); allow local prosecutors and judges to ban the sale of "erotic" music to minors (Washington); and make mandatory a system of labeling sexually explicit or offensive lyrics (Missouri and other states) (RIAA 1994, 1995). A proposed 1990 Missouri House bill would have instituted a state-run labeling system requiring offending albums to be identified by a yellow fluorescent label with the words:

> "WARNING": May contain explicit lyrics descriptive of or advocating one or more of the following: nudity, satanism, suicide, sodomy, incest, beastiality (sic); sadomasochism; adultery; murder, morbid violence, or any deviate sexual conduct in a violent context, or the use of illegal use of drugs or alcohol.
> "PARENTAL ADVISORY" (House Bill 1406, p. 2)

The music industry and free speech advocates such as the American Civil Liberties Union (ACLU) have generally managed to thwart the enactment or enforcement of such laws. In some cases proposals are simply dropped at the idea stage when it becomes clear they are unconstitutional—the Leominster, Massachusetts, proposal to ban all labeled music, for instance, would have failed the "overbreadth" test because it would have affected adults as well as children. In other instances, industry and ACLU lobbying has led to a significant narrowing of the scope of the legislation. Finally, as we have said, many of the proposals that are enacted into law are likely to be overturned when they confront the Supreme Court's definition of obscenity and the very strong "preferred position" given to First Amendment rights over competing interests.

There may be some close legal calls among the proposals, though, particularly in the area of mandatory music labeling. In a report to the Congressional Research Service, Reimer (1987) argues that mandatory labeling laws do not constitute censorship, at least under the logic of the Supreme Court in *Meese v. Keene* (1987). In that case the Court upheld the constitutionality of a Justice Department decision, pursuant to the Foreign Agents Registration Act of 1938, to place "Foreign Propaganda" labels on copies of three Canadian documentary films. The Court held that the label was not official censorship because the films could still be distributed without alteration and because the distributor was free to add whatever information it wanted to the "Political Propaganda" label (see Holt, 1990, for a contrary view on the legality of mandatory labeling laws). Whatever the ultimate fate of the various legal proposals, the fact remains that they stimulate the same sort of debate and media coverage as Congressional hearings on "porn rock" and "gangsta rap." Even if, as seems likely, most of these bills are dropped or ruled unconstitutional, the government is seen to have criticized the music industry and threatened it with regulation. The governmental eyebrow is raised and public opinion is fomented. This alone may be enough to influence record industry policies—especially the policies of local music stores—concerning explicit lyrics, thus producing a "chilling effect" on the range of free expression in music lyrics.

Two other areas of governmental and judicial action deserve mention here: the issue of civil liability for harm done by music, and the role of the federal government in regulating "indecent" broadcasting. With regard to the first area, the question is this: Are there circumstances under which musicians or record companies should be held responsible for damages their music causes to listeners? The two most celebrated cases in this area are *McCollum v. CBS* (1988) and the case involving the hard rock band Judas Priest (*Vance v. Judas Priest*, 1990). *McCollum* involved the suicide of a 19-year-old who shot himself after listening obsessively for hours to Ozzy Osbourne music, including a song entitled "Suicide Solution." The boy was found dead from a self-inflicted gunshot wound with his stereo headphones still around his head and the record still spin-ning. In the Judas Priest case, two Nevada youths shot themselves, one fatally, after an afternoon of beer drinking, pot smoking and listening to Judas Priest's album *Stained Class*. As we noted in Chapter 5, the claim in this case was that subliminal messages, including the words "Do it," had been embedded in the music, thus inciting the double suicide attempt. In both of the lawsuits, the boys involved had a history of serious emotional and behavioral problems.

Although the facts of the two cases differ somewhat, the essential claim was similar: that something in the music had incited the boys to their suicides, and that the musicians and their recording companies were therefore responsible. Ultimately, decisions in both cases were rendered for the defense, and there is every reason to believe similar suits will fail in the future, not only on First Amendment grounds, but because of the difficulty of establishing the specific intent on the part of the artists and the immediate cause-effect relationship the courts require to establish incitement. These cases are little more than legal curiosities in our view, and are no more likely to meet with success than other cases claiming so-called "negligent" broadcasting and publishing (Hoffman, 1985).

Thus, under existing law, neither the government censorship nor the civil liability avenues seem to present any serious threat to artistic freedom—or, to frame it from the other side, provide much remedy to those who perceive lyrics as a threat—at least as long as the offending material is not broadcast over the public airwaves. Indeed, would-be regu-lators are allowed considerably more leeway to control broadcast commu-nication than they have concerning nonbroadcast material. The Federal Communications Act of 1934 empowers the Federal Communications Commission (FCC) to ban from the airwaves speech that is "indecent," even though it may not be legally obscene and therefore cannot be banned from other media. The landmark Supreme Court opinion regarding regu-lation of indecent speech came in the Pacifica case (*FCC v. Pacifica Foundation*, 1978). In 1973, several of the noncommercial radio stations licensed by the Pacifica Foundation aired a monologue by comedian George Carlin in which Carlin lampooned societal taboos about vulgar language. During the monologue he repeatedly uttered "the original seven words" that could never be said on television—"shit, piss, fuck, cunt, cocksucker, motherfucker and tits" (Overbeck & Pullen, 1995). The FCC issued an official reprimand against Pacifica station WBAI in New York City after a complaint from a father who had inadvertently tuned in while driving with his son. The Supreme Court upheld the legitimacy of the FCC's action, citing broadcasting's unique ability to intrude into the privacy of the home audience as well as the well-established governmental responsibility to protect the welfare of minors. The Court's definition of "indecent speech" is still current: "language that describes, in terms patently offensive as measured by community standards for the broadcast medium, sexual or excretory activities or organs" (Overbeck & Pullen, 1995, p. 364). In the years since *Pacifica*, the FCC has taken a decidedly active role against indecent broadcasting. Especially hard hit have been stations carrying "shock jock" Howard Stern's radio show. For years Stern's broadcast has been known primarily for its outrageous humor and offensive language, much of it falling squarely under the *Pacifica* definition of indecency. In 1992, the FCC levied the stiffest fine in broadcasting history—$600,000—against a group of stations in the Northeast. As of 1994, stations carrying the show had been hit with almost $1.7 million in fines (Overbeck & Pullen, 1995).

Issues surrounding the FCC's power to regulate indecency remain unresolved. For instance, should there be a late-night "safe harbor" for indecent materials during which few children would be in the audience? At one point the FCC adopted an around-the-clock ban, reasoning that a certain number of children are in the audience even after midnight. The courts have since ruled that this policy poses an unreasonable infringement on the rights of adults, and the FCC now recognizes a safe harbor from 10:00 p.m. to 6:00 a.m. The definition of *child* has also varied. Originally, the FCC defined a child as anybody 12 or younger, but more recently it has expanded "protection" to anybody under the age of 18. Whatever the age or safe harbor boundaries, the FCC has made clear its intent to act on complaints about indecent broadcast language, including music lyrics. In response, stations have begun to scrutinize and screen their music more carefully (Overbeck & Pullen, 1995).

In any event, of the various approaches discussed in this section, the FCC's indecency power seems the most effective regulatory tool. Whether it is appropriate, of course, is another question. Legal scholar Alan Lazarus (1987) has criticized not only the key "media differences" arguments of the *Pacifica* decision, such as the notion that the broadcast audience is somehow more captive and less able to control its environment than the audiences for other media, but also the assumption of harm to minors. Indeed, even though there may be harm, neither the research we have reviewed in this book nor the literature on the effects of sexual portrayals in television and movies provides convincing evidence of a major negative influence on moral values or sexual behavior. A similar position was taken by Donnerstein and his colleagues in a 1992 review article in the *Journal of Broadcasting and Electronic Media* (Donnerstein, Wilson, & Linz, 1992). Like Lazarus, Donnerstein and his colleagues opposed a crackdown on indecent broadcasting. They argued that children under 12, the group about which the most concern is expressed, are essentially "sexual illiterates," lacking both an interest in and an understanding of sex and sexual innuendo. In one study they cited, for instance, not a single child in a sample of 9-year-olds could provide a reasonable definition of the word *uterus*. By the time kids have the interest and the knowledge, they claim, moral values are in place that insulate against negative effects. Most important, they say, research on the impact of the sort of material that would be deemed indecent by the FCC fails to show any significant influence other than the learning of some new language and terminology.

We might cavil a bit here. First, although a 9- or 10-year-old might not understand sexual innuendo or recognize clinical terms such as *uterus*, we suspect few would have much trouble understanding the much more direct depictions of sex in many popular songs or recognizing George Carlin's seven words you can't say on television. Second, we would point out that effects on language, after all, are *effects*. Indeed, one could easily argue that the increasing incivility that characterizes contemporary conversation—among young and old alike—marks a serious degradation of the quality of life. This said, Lazarus (1987) was probably close to the mark when he wrote:

> In the absence of any convincing evidence that offensive language is actually harmful to minors, it is evident that any curb on offensive speech visits its most prominent benefits on adult, rather than youthful, psyches. To imagine that children are offended or scarred by words or pictures they do not understand is just that—imagination. . . . As for older children, they are far more likely to be titillated or amused than injured or offended. . . . It is thus apparent that it is adults and their notions of decency being protected, in derogation of the First Amendment rights of other adults and the minors themselves. (pp. 496–497)

INDUSTRY SELF-REGULATION

Whatever the limited potential of government to dictate the content of popular music, it is the process of music industry decision making that largely determines which bands get signed and promoted, which songs are played on the radio, which art work makes its way onto an album cover, and which videos are produced and aired. Naturally enough, the profit motive drives most of these decisions, and the essential issue for record companies, radio stations, and cable broadcasters is to decide what will sell to the youth market. However, the industry occasionally responds to other concerns as well. Public controversy and criticism, the individual tastes and prejudices of radio station deejays and record company executives, the threat of government censorship, and, yes, even a sense of responsibility to the public or the audience, all figure in the process to a certain extent. At various points in the history of U.S. popular music, all of these factors have resulted in various forms of industry censorship and self-regulation.

In the turbulent early days of rock and roll, radio stations and deejays routinely banned music of certain types, by certain artists or with certain lyrics and themes. In the early 1950s, for instance, many White-owned radio stations often refused to play R&B records by Black musicians, an action that was usually justified on the basis of the immorality of Black R&B, but which was assuredly in many cases pure racism (McDonald, 1988). Operating under a broadcast code of ethics that forbade the airing of songs that were profane or contributed to juvenile delinquency, both radio stations and television networks exercised restraints on early rock and roll. In the mid-1950s, KWK in St. Louis not only banned all rock and roll from its playlist, but its employees collected all the rock and roll records in their library and ceremoniously smashed them to bits. Responding in 1956 to the negative coverage in the press of Elvis's provocative pelvis, radio station WKMH in Boston banned all Elvis Presley records. Television host Ed Sullivan reluctantly invited Elvis on his show, but directed the cameramen to shoot him only from the waist up, and a few years later on the same show the Rolling Stones were forced to alter the words "Let's spend the night together" to "Let's spend *some time* together." Several radio stations banned Lou Christy's mid-1960s hit "Rhapsody in the Rain" because of the lines, "On our first date we fell in love in the car/ And in this car our love went much too far" (Ward, Stokes, & Tucker, 1986, p. 323).

Sex was the main reason for banning music, but it was not the only one. In the 1950s, songs with violent or morbid themes were frequently axed from playlists. For instance, the controversy over the Shangri-Las' hit "Leader of the Pack," which describes (with sound effects) a despondent lover's fatal motorcycle crash, drove the song off several stations, and a similar fate was met in 1959 by Link Wray's *instrumental* song "Rumble" because its title suggested gang violence (Bronson, 1994). In the 1960s, even the hint that a song might be about drug use could get it pulled off the air, as, for instance, the Byrds' "8 Miles High." Record companies, too, occasionally responded to public controversy with restrictions on their artists. In our chapter on music content we mentioned the brouhaha over the Beatles' "Yesterday and Today" album. The cover art, itself a protest of Capitol Records' butchering of the group's work, showed the Beatles in bloodied meatcutters' aprons surrounded by chunks of meat and dismembered baby dolls. Capitol responded to the ensuing public outcry by pulling 750,000 records from stores and reissuing them with new covers. By the end of the 1960s, "censorship was everywhere" (Ward et al., 1986, p. 325)—and it was not government censorship.

The furor over the popular music of the late 1980s and 1990s has led to similar sorts of actions, and for many of the same reasons. Before these are described, however, a few points should be made about industry "censorship." First, although censorship may be "everywhere" in the sense that numerous examples can be pointed out, most decisions by the industry are marketing decisions. For every controversial album or artist that is toned down or kept off the air, hundreds and perhaps thousands with essentially the same sort of content are produced and distributed without regard to public sensibilities or controversy. Second, an important distinction must be made between government censorship, which in our view is not only quite dangerous but usually unconstitutional, and industry control. The people who produce, sell, and broadcast music and music videos have a perfect legal right to exert behind-the-scenes control over the content and distribution of their products. To put it another way, musicians possess no First Amendment right to a record contract. Indeed, when it comes to industry action, one person's censorship is another's social responsibility and good taste. As Jonathan Alter (1993) put it in a *Newsweek* editorial: "If a record company executive or an art-gallery owner or a book publisher declines to disseminate something, that's not censorship, it's judgment. It might be cowardly judgment or irresponsible judgment, but it's what they're paid to do" (p. 67). Alter also notes that when private citizens like former Secretary of Education William Bennett or organizations such as the National Political Congress of Black Women call for corporate restraint, they are simply suggesting that a sense of social responsibility should enter into the mix when the inevitable business judgments are made.

Whether one sides with those who say the music industry should temper its business decisions with a concern for social impact or with the typical industry stance that its only responsibilities are to provide an unfettered "marketplace of ideas" and a reasonable return for its stock-holders, industry organizations at various levels are beginning to respond to public criticism of popular music. Some of the most assertive action has come from Black-owned and Black-oriented radio stations. In response to the growing concern among African-American community and religious leaders about the effects of gangsta rap—both in terms of its influence on African-American youth and its potential to perpetuate negative stereo-types of African-Americans among Whites—several stations have banned songs with particularly offensive lyrics. KACE-FM in Los Angeles has stopped airing all songs it considers "negative or offensive," including depictions of violence as a means of resolving disputes, drug use, violence against homosexuals, and the sexual exploitation or abuse of women. The stations of Inner City Broadcasting, a chain of Black-owned stations including WBLS in New York, will no longer play "music containing derogatory, profane or misogynist lyrics, or lyrics which advocate vio-lence" ("Gangsta rap under the gun," 1993, p. 1). WPGC-FM, Washington, DC's top-rated station, applies a similar policy. In the words of WPGC deejay Albie Dee: "I don't care *how* big the record is, if I cannot edit it and take out words like 'gat' and 'gun,' and if the message is violent, I'm not going to carry it" (quoted in R. Harrington, 1993, p. G6; emphasis in original). Music videos are often scrutinized for many of the same con-cerns. In 1993, the Black Entertainment Television Network (BET) announced an intent to go completely "gun-free"—that is, it would sim-ply not show videos that displayed guns. MTV, whose audience is primar-ily White, frequently "fuzzes" out guns and gang symbols and "bleeps" out offensive language in rap videos.

Self-regulatory action occurs at other levels within the music industry as well. Although record store policies vary considerably, many independent stores and even some national chains have adopted restric-tions on the purchase of albums bearing the industry's parental advisory labels to children over a certain age—usually 18 (Christenson, 1992a; "Popular music under siege," 1994). At the highest level of the industry, Time-Warner announced in September 1995 a decision to sell its rap sub-sidiary, Interscope Records, shortly after several prominent critics, includ-ing Bob Dole, William Bennett and C. Delores Tucker of the National Political Congress of Black Women, had singled out Time-Warner for its particularly egregious rap offerings. Time-Warner said the move was purely a business decision, but the timing seemed too perfect to be mere coincidence.

RECORD LABELING

Probably the most widely familiar and most broadly applied form of industry self-regulation is the system of parental advisory labeling. The current labeling system can be traced back to 1985, when a group of concerned parents headed by two prominent "Washington wives," Tipper Gore and Susan Baker (wife of then-Secretary of State James Baker) organized under the name Parents' Music Resource Center (PMRC) and succeeded in focusing national attention on the perceived threat of sexually explicit, violent, and otherwise offensive music lyrics. The efforts of the PMRC culminated in two events that summer and fall: a series of hearings on the porn rock issue in the Senate Commerce Committee; and the announcement by Stanley Gortikov, head of the Recording Industry Association of America (RIAA), of an industry agreement to identify blatantly explicit lyrics with a parental warning label (Zucchino, 1985).

From 1985 through 1989, most major music recording companies participated in some form of record labeling, albeit haphazardly and at times with tongue firmly in cheek. In 1989, though, the labeling issue assumed a new sense of urgency. Partly because of complaints over the inconsistency with which labeling was being conducted (about half the offensive content was getting through unscathed, the PMRC said), and partly because of the furor over certain new releases (e.g., 2 Live Crew's *As Nasty as They Wanna Be*), several state legislatures began to consider some form of mandatory, state-monitored music labeling scheme. In response to the renewed criticism and the threat of governmental intervention, the RIAA announced early in 1990 a beefed-up voluntary record labeling plan, one they promised would be more widely and consistently applied (Holland, 1990). Record companies were still to be in charge of their own screening process, but a standard message—PARENTAL ADVISORY: EXPLICIT LYRICS—was to be used, and its placement on records, CDs, and tapes was to be standardized (see Figure 8.1). (The occasional tongue-in-cheek mockery of labeling did not stop, however. An album released in 1991 by the hard rock band Guns N Roses featured two warning labels, the standard one and another that read: "Warning: This album contains language which some listeners may find objectionable. They can F?!* off and buy something from the New Age section.")

Whether one views record labeling as helpful "consumer information" for involved parents or as a thinly disguised attempt to restrict and stigmatize non-mainstream cultural values (Goldberg, 1990), the standard advisory label—or variations of it such as one that substitutes the word "content" for "lyrics"—is in wide use. In 1994, one of our students

Figure 8.1. Parental advisory sticker applied to cassette and CD boxes

Note: The precise wording of the advisory may vary. One version, for instance, substitutes "content" for "lyrics."

conducted a systematic random sampling of over 1,000 albums from three record stores in the Portland, Oregon area: Tower Records, Sam Goody and a large independent store. The following are the percentages of labeled records by music type:

Rap	59%
Heavy metal	13%
Alternative	8%
Pop/rock	1%
All Combined	8%

The question is, what impact does the advisory label have on music preferences and purchases? This is a complex question with no simple answer. For one thing, the answer depends on who uses the information. Is it primarily parents, as the system's proponents hope, or mostly the youth themselves? Recently we asked a sample of 500 3rd-through 12th-grade students if their parents had a policy of forbidding them to have albums with a "parental advisory" sticker. The percentage who said "yes" was, by age group: 37% of the 3rd through 5th graders, 30% of the 6th through 8th graders, and 23% of the 9th through 12th graders (Christenson, 1996). Clearly, many parents do use the advisory label to supervise their children's music listening. Nevertheless, many—probably *most*—do not. In another study, Christenson (1992a) found that only 13% of a sample of middle school students said their parents had ever taken an album away from them because they disapproved of it, and the same small percentage said that a parent had ever inspected their music collection for objectionable material. Taken together, these findings suggest that although many parents may *pronounce* a disapproval of explicit or violent music, most take little active interest in or action concerning their children's music purchases or music listening behavior. Most of the time, then, parental advisory labels are "consumer information" not for parents but for the real consumers—the kids who actually listen to the music. Given this, the appropriate question is, how do kids themselves react to the presence of parental advisory labels on music albums?

Christenson (1992a) has proposed two competing theories on the effects of labeling: the "forbidden-fruit" theory, which predicts that the presence of an advisory label will produce a reactive effect, thus enhancing the attractiveness of music; and the "tainted-fruit" theory, which argues that labels will serve to warn kids of material they may find unacceptable or disturbing, thus decreasing the music's appeal. Of the two, the forbidden fruit theory receives much more intuitive support from lay observers. In our discussions with friends and acquaintances, for instance, the overwhelming reaction is that the advisories will make kids want the music more, not less. In fact, even though few kids say labels have much impact, those who do think labels make a difference are more likely to predict an increase than a decrease in the music's attraction. Our recent survey of 3rd through 12th graders bears this out: 71% said labels would make no difference to the kids they know, 23% said it would make them want the music more, and only 6% said it would make them want it less (Christenson, 1996; Christenson, 1992a, presents similar results).

The argument for a forbidden-fruit effect is grounded in psychological theory as well as lay intuition. It springs logically from the venerable "storm and stress" and rebellion models of adolescence discussed earlier in this book, and it receives additional support from research showing increasing peer orientation and decreasing parent orientation during the years of adolescence. As we have noted in earlier chapters, some writers have portrayed the role of music in parent–child relationships as dramatically conflictual. To Lull (1987), popular music's essential meaning lies in its utility in the battle between youth and parents, and Grossberg (1987) suggests that the basic "work of music" is to provide a mechanism for separating the "Us" (youth) from the "Them" (adults). To the extent that kids use music to express their alienation from the adult world, it seems logical to expect indications of parental disapproval may enhance, rather than decrease, the appeal of labeled music.

Perhaps the strongest theoretical argument for a forbidden-fruit effect comes from Brehm's (1972) theory of "psychological reactance." Reactance theory argues that when an individual is threatened with the loss of free choice, he or she is motivated to restore that freedom, usually with the result of wanting the proscribed choice even more. As Simmons (1992) has noted, the process of psychological reactance operates in a variety of situations and with a variety of groups, including adolescents. He cites, for instance, a study showing a positive relationship between teens' desire and love for an opposite-sex friend and the extent of parental intervention against the relationship—the so-called "Romeo and Juliet effect" (Driscoll, Davis, & Lipetz, 1972). The implications of these various theoretical views to record labeling are direct: Because adolescents are by nature rebellious against adult authority, because one of the key modes for their expression of this rebellion is through their music behavior, and because the threat of restriction produces a motivation to "react," then the presence of a label ought to make kids want the music more.

Reasonable as this theory may be, however, there are also reasons to expect a tainted fruit effect among many youth. As noted in Chapter 2, most current empirical research in the field of adolescent development describes this period of life in reasonably temperate terms, popular characterizations and classical theorizing notwithstanding. Especially in childhood or early adolescence, when there is still a high level of parent orientation, kids may interpret advisory labels as a sign that certain material might not be suitable or comfortable for them. Indeed, many early adolescents express discomfort with explicit sexual imagery in music (Christenson, 1992b). In fact, the very process of peer orientation cited earlier in support of the forbidden fruit model may work in support of a tainted fruit effect. If, as seems to be the practice, advisory labels are applied to only the most objectionable music, one effect of labeling may be to place that music outside of the adolescent mainstream, thus invoking the powerful conformist tendency among most adolescents. The presence of a label might indicate the boundaries between the fringe and the mainstream, thus motivating those who seek the mainstream to avoid labeled music.

To date, only one study has directly examined the impact of music advisory labels. Christenson (1992a) randomly assigned a group of 145 11- to 14-year-olds to one of two experimental conditions: For one group, the album cover of the music the kids evaluated bore the standard "PARENTAL ADVISORY: EXPLICIT LYRICS" label; for the other group, a control condition, students heard and evaluated the same music but did not see an advisory label. Two different target albums were employed in the study: a hard rock album by a regional Pacific Northwest band, and a nationally released pop/urban contemporary dance album. Neither album was previously familiar to the students. The students rated on 5-point scales how much they liked the albums and how much they would like to own them. In general, the presence of the parental advisory label produced a small (about .3 of a point on the 5-point scale) but statistically significant effect in the tainted-fruit direction. That is, those who heard the album while being shown a labeled cover gave lower ratings than those in the no-label control group.

There are several obvious limitations to this study, and it is by no means the last word on the issue. First, the subjects were young; as we discuss later, there is reason to believe older students might respond differently. Second, given that rap is the most likely type of music to be labeled, the issue needs to be explored using rap music as well as rock and pop. Furthermore, the study provided no data on individual or subgroup differences. Even in a relatively homogeneous suburban sample such as the one used in this study, wide ranges still exist in important factors such as music taste and parent–child conflict. Quite possibly these sorts of factors mediate the impact of the advisory label. Most important, the study was limited by its removal from the physical settings and social context where music decisions are actually made. Qualifications aside, however, the common view that labels will act as an incentive received no support from this study. Perhaps the safest conclusion is that the mere presence or absence of a parental advisory label matters much less to kids than most people think. Advisory labels are a statement about lyrics, and although lyrics matter to kids in some ways, they are not as important in making music choices as is the "sound." As we have seen, most kids are aware of this, even if adults are not.

As we have suggested, the forbidden-fruit effect may operate in some circumstances and with certain segments of the youth music audience. A study by Simmons (1992) on the effects of censorship on college students' music preferences is particularly relevant in this regard. Arguing directly from reactance theory, Simmons predicted that the threat of government censorship would enhance the attractiveness of music. College students were given the task of ranking the appeal of nine music albums. Eight of the albums were "legitimate," and one—the target album for the study—was fictitious. A week later, under the ruse that the original results had been misplaced, the students were asked to rerank the albums. In this phase of the study, half the students were given a bit of supplementary information concerning the target album, specifically that it was "the only album to have been declared legally obscene in Great Britain." The other half reranked the albums without this new information on the target album.

Among those who received the obscenity information, the average attractiveness ranking of the fictitious album rose from 6th on the first measure to 4th on the second. The album's average rank was essentially unchanged within the control group. Here, then, one finds at least some support for a forbidden-fruit or reactance effect. Of course, it was impossible to tell in this study whether the improved ranking was due to the implied threat of government censorship or a simple curiosity about what kinds of lyrics might so deeply offend the British authorities. (The same question can be raised about the current music labeling system: Do kids pay attention to the "Parental advisory" or the "explicit lyrics?") Moreover, the censoring agency here was the government, not parents. Still, to the extent that this study can be compared with Christenson's work on labeling effects, the sensible conclusion is that age is an important factor in deciding whether forbidden-fruit or tainted-fruit processes will dominate.

Recent research on the effects of advisories for movies and television programs strengthens the argument that age probably plays a role in the process, adds gender into the equation, and also points to the importance of how advisories are worded (Cantor & Harrison, 1996; Cantor, Harrison, & Nathanson, 1997; Morkes, Chen, & Roberts, 1997). Cantor and her colleagues conducted several experiments in which students ranging from 5 to 15 years old voted on which "programs" they would like to see on the basis of a brief written description presented in mock TV programming schedules. Each program description was associated with variations of different rating or advisory system labels. For example, the following program description was associated with either no rating or one of the standard Motion Picture Association of America (MPAA) advisories: "*Highly Dangerous.* A newspaper reporter travels with a scientist on a secret mission." Twenty percent of the students saw this description with a "G" label, 20% with a "PG" label, 20% with a "PG-13" label, 20% with an "R" label, and 20% with no label. Similarly, other program descriptions were associated with other types of labels, including "Viewer discretion advised," "Parental discretion advised," and various additional forms ranging from the informational icons and descriptions used by the Recreational Software Advisory Council (RSAC) for computer games to the descriptive statements currently used by the Canadian Broadcasting System (see Cantor et al., 1997; Federman, 1996).

When the MPAA ratings were used, the appeal of the target film varied according to rating, age, and gender. Cantor and Harrison (1996) found that for boys, 20% of the 5- to 9-year-olds picked the target film when it was rated "G" versus none of the 10- to 14-year-olds. At the other end of the MPAA rating scale, only 5% of the younger group voted for the film under an "R" rating, compared to half the older boys. The age trend was similar for girls—that is, more votes for the PG-13 or R-rated film among the older group than among the younger—but girls in general were less likely to vote for a PG-13 or R movie than boys of the same age. For instance, only 11% of the older girls voted to view the target film when it was rated R, a much lower percentage than for boys. Cantor, Harrison, and Nathanson (1997) obtained very similar results with more ethnically, racially, and socio-economically diverse students from an urban Wisconsin setting, as did Morkes, Chen, and Roberts (1997) with a group of relatively affluent middle-school students from northern California.

Both Cantor studies also looked at different types of "discretion advised" labels, and their findings in this area carry particular relevance to the impact of the current music advisory. In general, when they compared the attractiveness of TV shows with and without the words "Parental discretion advised," an advisory had no impact on girl's preferences but produced a "boomerang" or forbidden-fruit effect on boys. That is, boys were significantly more attracted to the show when it came with the advisory. However, when the wording was changed to "viewer discretion advised," boys were unaffected either way, and girls responded in the intended tainted-fruit direction. Assuming the goal is to protect kids from objectionable material, Cantor and Harrison (1996) suggest that the word *parent* should be avoided because it implies that an outside agent might deny privilege, a situation conducive to psychological reactance. The use of the word *viewer*, however, puts the child or adolescent in control and eliminates the motivation to react against authority. These findings strongly support Brehm's (1972) reactance theory, and lead Cantor and her colleagues and Morkes et al. (1997) to argue for the use of informational as opposed to evaluative or proscriptive labels (see also Bushman & Stack, 1996; Federman, 1996).

Despite this suggestion, it seems unlikely that the current music label will be changed from "Parental" to "Listener advisory." The industry's cooperation in the ratings system is predicated on the assumption that parents bear the primary responsibility for dealing with the impact of music, and labeling has been sold to the public as an effective parenting aid for that (presumed) vast number of parents who have the time and inclination to accompany their kids to music stores and flip through their CD collections. The industry view on labeling is quite clear in this triumphant statement from RIAA President Hilary Rosen, made in 1994 just after the defeat of a proposed Louisiana labeling law: "This victory validates the value of the industry's dependable and proven voluntary labeling program. The beauty of the program is that it places responsibility for who or what kids listen to, where it belongs—with parents—and not with the government or special interest groups" ("Louisiana music censorship," 1994, p. 1).

Because of the lack of research directly related to music labeling, its long-term effect on music listening and purchase behavior remains uncertain. A few things, though, can be said with some assurance. First, no matter what their intended or stated purpose, explicit lyrics advisories must be understood primarily as information for young music listeners and not their parents. Second, among the mix of factors that influence music preferences and choices—gender, social class, group affiliation, parent–child relationships, social alienation, and so on—advisories probably play a minor role at most. Finally, whatever influence advisory labels may exert, the effect will vary from one youth to the next. Ironically, perhaps, if the intent is to protect children and adolescents from exposure to harmful or offensive material, labeling probably protects those who are already "safe"—younger listeners, females, those who are less inclined to rebel against mainstream values, those with especially involved (some kids might say "nosy") parents, those doing well in school, and so on. These sorts of kids would be expected to respond in a tainted fruit direction, but they are not much attracted to the "bad stuff" anyway. Whatever they listen to, they are fortunate enough to be surrounded with plenty of positive countervailing influences. However, those whose tastes run in the direction of defiant, antisocial, "troubling" music often possess the reactant, alienated personality characteristics that might lead to a forbidden-fruit effect.

Of course, the effects of music labeling depend on much more than the individual reactions of young listeners. As we have seen, music companies and their parent corporations worry about their public image as corporate citizens, and at times have taken actions—including their agreement to label music with explicit lyrics—which seem to run counter to immediate marketing concerns and can only be understood as part of a broader strategy. The unknown term in the formula is how music distributors, responding to pressure from local parents and pressure groups, handle labeled music. Many music stores, including some national chains, refuse to sell minors albums that carry the explicit lyrics advisory label ("Popular music under siege," 1994), whereas others seem to ignore the issue completely.

In an informal phone survey of Pacific Northwest record stores, we found a wide range of practices in the way record distributors, store managers, and individual clerks deal with labeled recordings. Some stores, especially chains housed in suburban shopping malls where parents might easily drop by to complain, finessed the entire issue by refusing to carry any labeled recordings at all. At the other extreme were local independents who objected on principle to labeling and who saw the labeling process as a sanctimonious intrusion into the sacred realm of rock and roll. These outlets refused to limit the access of children, however young, to labeled music. In the middle were stores who enforced an 18-to-buy rule, placed labeled recordings behind the counter, or, in one case, limited access to records to anybody who "doesn't look old enough to drive." Some national chains had definite central policies; others gave considerable leeway to individual outlets and store clerks. One distributor we encountered actually added his *own* stickers to recordings he personally found offensive, even if the recordings had escaped labeling by the music company. To repeat an earlier point, regardless of whether one interprets these practices as corporate responsiveness to public concern or, like the ACLU, as a serious restriction on free expression ("Popular music under siege," 1994), if they become sufficiently widespread, the market for labeled music will be curtailed and, inevitably, record companies will trim their range of offerings.

The fundamental problem with advisory labels, however, lies in their vagueness and inconsistency of meaning. Moviegoers are often mystified at why one movie gets an "R" and another a "PG-13" or "PG" rating because they have no way of knowing, independent of actually viewing a film, whether the MPAA ratings board based its classification on sex, violence, the type of sex or violence, or something else entirely. For that matter, the identity of the members of the ratings board is kept secret (Federman, 1996). However, at least the MPAA rating system provides a range of classifications, some suggested age guidelines, and applies an industry-wide standard, however cloaked in mystery the behind-the-scenes process may be. With music labeling it is all or nothing—either an album gets the label or not. Not only are the standards unknown to the public, but each company applies its own standards internally. Thus, neither parents nor listeners know for certain what it is in any given album that might be objectionable (Federman, 1996). It is easy to mock the sort of laundry lists of human sin and degradation that often accompany proposed state labeling legislation, but at least these lists acknowledge a range of concerns. Clearly, not all parents are equally concerned about

sex, violence, racism, homophobia, drug use, suicide, and so on. If the purpose of labeling is to provide parents with information, the industry could
improve the service by providing more of it.

Given the industry's initial reluctance to apply *any* labeling system, however, and given its position that the current system is "dependable and proven," it is likely the one we will live with for some time to
come. Whatever the limitations or complications, it is probably better
than nothing, if only because it recognizes the undeniable facts that music
has changed and that many parents and citizens are concerned about the
impact of the change. Although it is easy to be cynical about the industry's
motivations for engaging in music labeling, the practice stands as testimony that public concerns can influence corporate practice. Still, it is clear
that labeling and other modes of industry self-regulation will never override in any significant way the deeper cultural forces and market mechanisms that produce disturbing music. Disturbing music will be, and in a
free society should be, produced—and it will find an audience. In the end,
those who speak for the music industry are probably right about one
thing: If changes are needed, and if children and adolescents need to be
protected, citizens and parents must assume the pivotal role in the
process.

FAMILY POLICY: WHAT'S A PARENT TO DO?

Although we typically associate "policy" with large, relatively formal
organizations, procedures to guide behavior are inherent in any form of
social organization. They may vary in the degree of formality with which
they are articulated, but regardless of whether we talk about a state legis-
lature, a local school district, a community grocery store, or a neighbor-
hood soccer team, all organizations establish rules, guidelines, and expectations that influence members' actions. So, too, do families. Explicitly or
not, consciously or not, families develop policies about such things as
bedtimes, chores, allowances, Sunday dinners, holiday gift giving, TV
viewing, and even popular music consumption. Whether they take the
form of clearly articulated and strictly enforced parental rules ("There
will be no rock and roll in this house!"), implicit judgmental statements
(parental rolling of the eyes at the sound of an amplified guitar), or even
complete unawareness ("Heavy metal? Do my kids listen to heavy
metal?"), families do establish guidelines and expectations that shape
behavior.

Indeed, given the legal and political obstacles to government action and industry hesitancy to impinge on the bottom line, the most effective policies on adolescent use of music media are likely to be implemented at the level of the family—provided, that is, that they respect the needs and interests of the kids. As we saw in Chapter 2, the vast majority of teenagers get along reasonably well with—indeed, even like—their parents. For most kids most of the time, parental concerns and pressures probably exert significantly more influence than any exhortations from politicians or public guardians ever will. Most parents can influence their children's use of and responses to music media.

We do not mean to imply that most kids will change their music tastes in response to parental criticism or that they will unfailingly adhere to parental proscriptions and rules. Indeed, it is probably a mistake for parents to lay down "rules" about the music to which their adolescent offspring can and cannot listen. Even though rebellion is not the norm among most kids, adolescents do struggle against what they perceive to be threats to the increased freedom accorded them by virtue of their increasing age, including perceived threats imposed by parents. Because most kids think of music as "their" medium, unilateral parental attempts to impose controls are certain to be resented and resisted.

At the same time, we believe that family guidelines regarding popular music can be effective. The critical difference between unilateral controls and family guidelines lies in the recognition that adolescents are part of the family and as such should be actively involved in formulating any "policy" concerning their music media consumption. If parents wish to avoid open rebellion, they would be wise to initiate, as early as possible, an ongoing discussion with their kids about music in general and current popular music in particular, with the aim of negotiating guidelines that all can live with.

Negotiating a family policy about music media is not easy. For parents successfully to negotiate an understanding with their kids regarding music, they need to understand how their kids relate to the music. This requires a great deal of listening—to both the music and the kids. Above all, parents need to keep in mind that music is not mere leisure. A major theme throughout this book has been that music is at the very core of adolescent culture. Kids use popular music to define themselves, their peer groups, and their relationship to the rest of the world. It accompanies most of their activities; it is often at the center of their conversation and thought. Not surprisingly, they tend to view criticisms of their music as attacks on their identity. Although we are not convinced by characterizations of popular music as the ammunition for an ongoing war between youth and adults, it does seem that attacks on the music—because they are of necessity attacks on adolescent culture and adolescent identity—may well start some battles. Perhaps the best advice, then, is for parents to avoid blanket condemnations. Unfortunately, it is all too easy for parents to respond viscerally and fail to separate current popular music from other external trappings of youth culture such as body piercing, superbaggy jeans, shaved heads, and tattoos—not to mention dire headlines about adolescent drug use, violence, and teenage pregnancy rates. When these are all lumped together, the discussion frequently reverts to a lecture, a fear-motivated, critical parental monologue about the problems of adolescence rather than a dialogue about popular music.

Even if parents are able to limit the discussion to music, they are often tempted to label what their kids listen to as mere noise. As we saw in our discussion of music preferences, adolescent taste groups do this to each other all the time: Heavy metal fans sneer at alternative rock aficionados; rappers have little tolerance for fans of mainstream pop. However, when the criticism crosses generations, the problem is magnified because the parental role so strongly implies control. When parents refer to their offspring's music as noise because the beat or the instrumentation or the genre differs from what they grew up with, they risk igniting or fueling intergenerational conflict because of the implied threat against something their teenagers consider central. All too often parents and other adults lose credibility because their comments are uninformed, exaggerated, shot from the hip, or just plain *un*hip.

Parents might do well to recall exchanges they may have had with their own parents. We suspect that most readers over the age of 35 can remember a time or two when their father or mother characterized the music they prized as junk or issued dire warnings that their favorite artists—Elvis, the Beatles, the Stones, Janice Joplin, Marvin Gaye, and so on—were leading them, if not to perdition, then at least into a bleak future in which they would have trouble finding a decent job, a decent mate, even a decent meal. Yet most of us survived, went to work, got married, and clearly have eaten our share of decent meals. It will help parents put things in perspective if they keep in mind that they too survived popular music.

We also encourage parents to listen carefully not just to their kids but to some of their music. In order to hold up their end of a dialogue and engage in truly mutual negotiations, parents need to know at least something about what they want to discuss. To the extent that they confuse heavy metal with grunge, they undercut the foundation on which mutual agreement is likely to occur. Paying attention to popular music and current music culture can also provide parents with opportunities to take advantage of what educators call "the teachable moment." A teachable moment refers to times when events—whether in real life or in a mass mediated message—converge to raise a question, or to make the observer particularly ready for or sensitive to an answer. For example, an event such as a lunar eclipse can heighten curiosity and create a particularly opportune time to teach about the movement of the earth, sun, and moon—create, in other words, a teachable moment.

In the same way, events such as the suicide of rock star Kurt Cobain, public outcries over the content of some of Madonna's controversial videos, or the trial and subsequent murder of rapper Tupac Shakur, all created moments for fruitful discussions of such topics as drugs, suicide, sex, and violence. Teachable moments can also emerge from the lyrics of a particular song, an image in a music video, or simply the presence of a parental advisory label on a teenager's latest album purchase. Teachable moments like these provide kids an opportunity to articulate what they think and give parents an opportunity to express (not expound) their own views, values, and standards. The point is that parents who pay attention, who occasionally watch a music video or listen to an album with their kids, can take advantage of such opportunities. Whether we like it or not, given the ways in which our society, our schools, and our media have evolved since the end of World War II, parenting in the 1990s is unlikely to be successful if it is predicated on the top-down, authoritarian model many of us grew up with. Mutual respect is required, and negotiation must go on; in their absence, resistance, reactance, and even alienation become likely.

To advocate a negotiated family policy in which adolescent music preferences are respected, however, is not to say parents must cede authority to their adolescent offspring. Quite the contrary, we believe that it is the parents' role to be the final arbiter of the values, beliefs, and behaviors that each family ultimately defines—and is defined by. Parents can and should make it clear how they feel about popular music's messages and whether, where, and when it is appropriate or not for their offspring to hear them. Simply engaging in such discussions tells children that their parents are concerned and that they have standards that are sometimes at odds with what the music seems to represent. Even if some of the fears about the sinister impact of popular music on youth are overblown, some aspects of music culture are legitimately troublesome to parents and others concerned with contemporary values and behavior.

When parents are troubled, they need to make it clear where they stand. It is possible and necessary for parents both to acknowledge their kids' cultural choices as genuine (if not ideal) and to make clear their own value positions.

For example, it is quite appropriate for a parent to say something like: "Look, I know I cannot and should not censor your music. I cannot and should not keep you from listening to whatever songs you choose. But I want you to know that I not only disagree with but fundamentally abhor any message that degrades women or different ethnic groups, and I request that you not play them in my presence. Can we agree on that?" Most of the time, most kids will agree. Such a statement does not forbid them to hear the music, nor does it really restrict their freedom, and most will understand and probably respect their parent's honest expression of disapproval. (When they really think about it—and such parental statements will motivate them to think—most kids probably disapprove too.) Perhaps most important, the message is sent: "Here is a value I hold for my family and for my home, and I would like you to respect it."

CODA

We have not spoken of the role of schools in this context, but we would suggest that school authorities might do well to approach the issue of popular music and "problem kids" with a similar sort of balanced policy. As Roe (1995) has pointed out, teachers and administrators often stigmatize certain peer groups based on the negative values these groups and their music seem to represent. Roe argues convincingly that this process may lead to a "negative spiral of association," wherein kids who affiliate with alienated peer groups become even further alienated from the goals and norms of the school as a result of their condemnation by well-meaning school authorities. Thus, the wedge between these kids—who, after all, are often the ones who most need to be reached—and the mainstream school culture is driven even deeper. Roe's suggested remedy for this spiral is very close to what we have suggested for parents: to listen to the kids and respect the importance of their affiliations, while at the same time attempting to redirect their peer groups into more positive directions.

Indeed, we might ask all those who express concern about the nature of contemporary popular music to adopt a similar stance of respectful disagreement. The title of this book incorporates a line from a 1974 Rolling Stones song which reads: "I know it's only rock and roll, but I like it." The Stones knew this was a lie even as they sang it; then as now, it wasn't *only* rock and roll, and kids didn't just like it, they *loved* it. The music was their greatest source of pleasure, and it stood for who they were. Clearly, we should all respect and recognize the importance of music in the lives of adolescent listeners.

Finally, there is another sense in which it's not only rock and roll, and this meaning is as important as the first. A few years ago *Washington Post* columnist Charles Krauthammer wrote an op-ed piece on the obscenity charges against the rap group 2 Live Crew. He wrote: "Most people, and in particular 2 Live Crew's intellectual defenders, fervently believe in the connection between good art and the good society. . . . And yet the corollary—if good art can elevate, bad art can degrade—is a proposition they refuse to grasp" (p. A27). Krauthammer's point is simple, but irrefutable. If culture is important to people, if they take it seriously, then it has some influence on them as well. In his phrase, "culture has consequences." As we have attempted to show throughout this book, although some of its consequences are positive, some negative, and some more or less neutral, there is no question that popular music has important consequences. In this sense, just as much as the first, it's not "only" rock and roll.

REFERENCES

Adams, G., & Gullotta, T. (1989). *Adolescent life experiences* (2nd ed.). Pacific Grove, CA: Brooks/Cole.

Adoni, H. (1978). The functions of mass media in the political socialization of adolescents. *Communication Research, 6*, 84-106.

Alter, J. (1993, November 29). Let's stop crying wolf on censorship. *Newsweek*, p. 67.

American Psychological Association. (1993). *Violence and youth: Psychology's response*, Vol. I, *Summary report of the American psychological association commission on violence and youth*. Washington, DC: Author.

Arnett, J. (1991a). Adolescence and heavy metal music: From the mouths of metalheads. *Youth and Society, 23*(1), 76-98.

Arnett, J. (1991b). Heavy metal music and reckless behavior among adolescents. *Journal of Youth and Adolescence, 20*, 573-592.

Aufderheide, P. (1986). Music videos: The look of the sound. *Journal of Communication, 36*(1), 57-78.

Avery, R. (1979). Adolescents' use of the mass media. *American Behavioral Scientist, 23*(1), 53-70.

Axelsson, A., & Lindgren, F. (1981). Hearing in classical musicians. *Acta Laryngologica, Supplement* 377, 1-74.

Ayers, L.K. (1994). *Teenage girls: A parent's survival manual*. New York: Crossroad.

Bandura, A. (1964). The stormy decade: Fact or fiction? *Psychology in the Schools, 1*, 224-231.

Bandura, A. (1977). *Social learning theory.* Englewood Cliffs, NJ: Prentice-Hall.

Bandura, A. (1986). *Social foundations of thought and action: A social cognitive theory.* Englewood Cliffs, NJ: Prentice-Hall.

Bandura, A. (1994). Social cognitive theory of mass communication. In J. Bryant & D. Zillmann (Eds.), *Media effects: Advances in theory and research* (pp. 61-90). Hillsdale, NJ: Erlbaum.

Bargh, J. A., Bond, R. N., Lombardi, W. J., & Tota, M. E. (1986). The additive nature of chronic and temporary sources of construct accessibility. *Journal of Personality and Social Psychology, 50,* 869-878.

Baxter, R., De Riemer, C., Landini, A., Leslie, L., & Singletary, M. (1985). A content analysis of music videos. *Journal of Broadcasting and Electronic Media, 29,* 333-340.

Beentjes, J.W.J., Koolstra, C.M., & van der Voort, T.H.A. (1995, May). *Combining homework with background television or audio media.* Paper presented at the annual meeting of the International Communication Association, Albuquerque, NM.

Belson, W. (1978). *Television violence and the adolescent boy.* London: Saxon House.

Bengston, V. (1970). The generation gap. *Youth and Society, 2,* 7-32.

Berelson, B., Lazarsfeld, P.F., & McPhee, W. (1954). *Voting.* Chicago: University of Chicago Press.

Berlyne, D. (1965). *Structure and direction in thinking.* New York: Wiley.

Berman, A.L., & Jobes, D.A. (1991). *Adolescent suicide: Assessment and intervention.* Washington, DC: American Psychological Association.

Bleich, S., Zillmann, D., & Weaver, J. (1991). Enjoyment and consumption of rock music as a function of rebelliousness. *Journal of Broadcasting and Electronic Media, 35,* 351-366.

Block, P. (1990). Modern-day sirens: Rock lyrics and the First Amendment. *Southern California Law Review, 63,* 777-832.

Bloom, A. (1987). *The closing of the American mind.* New York: Simon and Schuster.

Blos, P. (1970). *The young adolescent: Clinical studies.* London: Collier Macmillan.

Blosser, B., & Roberts, D.F. (1985). Age differences in children's perceptions of message intent: Responses to news, commercials, educational spots and public service announcements. *Communication Research, 12,* 445-484.

Brehm, S. (1972). *Responses to loss of freedom: A theory of psychological reactance.* New York: Appleton-Century-Crofts.

Britt, B. (1992, February 1). Music's increasing tolerance for intolerance. *The News of Mexico City*, p. B-3.

Bronson, F. (1994, March 26). A selected chronology of musical controversy. *Billboard*, p. N36+.

Brooks-Gunn, J., & Reiter, E.O. (1990). The role of pubertal processes. In S. S. Feldman & G. R. Elliott (Eds.), *At the threshold: The developing adolescent* (pp. 15-53). Cambridge, MA: Harvard University Press.

Brown, B. B. (1990). Peer groups and peer cultures. In S. S. Feldman & G. R. Elliott (Eds.), *At the threshold: The developing adolescent* (pp. 171-196). Cambridge, MA: Harvard University Press.

Brown, J.D., & Campbell, K. (1986). Race and gender in music videos: The same beat but a different drummer. *Journal of Communication, 36*(1), 94-106.

Brown, J.D., Campbell, K., & Fischer, L. (1986). American adolescents and music videos: Why do they watch? *Gazette, 37*, 19-32.

Brown, J.D., Childers, K., Bauman, K., & Koch, G. (1990). The influence of new media and family structure on young adolescents' television and radio use. *Communication Research, 17*, 65-82.

Brown, J.D., & Schulze, L. (1990). The effects of race, gender and fandom on audience interpretations of Madonna's music videos. *Journal of Communication, 40*, 88-102.

Brown, J.R. (1976). Children's uses of television. In R. Brown (Ed.), *Children and television* (pp. 116-136). Beverly Hills, CA: Sage.

Brown, R., & O'Leary, M. (1971). Pop music in an English secondary school system. *American Behavioral Scientist, 14*, 401-413.

Buntman, P., & Saris, E. (1982). *How to live with your teenager: A survivor's handbook for parents.* New York: Ballentine.

Burke, R., & Grinder, R. (1966). Personality-oriented themes and listening patterns in teen-age music and their relation to certain academic and peer variables. *School Review, 74*, 196-211.

Burns, G. (1994). How music video has changed, and how it has not changed: 1991 vs. 1985. *Popular Music and Society, 18*(3), 67-79.

Bushman, B. J., & Stack, A.D. (1996). Forbidden fruit versus tainted fruit: Effects of warning labels on attraction to television violence. *Journal of Experimental Psychology: Applied, 2*, 207–226.

Butler v. Michigan, 352 U.S. 380, 383 (1957).

Cantor, J., & Harrison, K. (1996). Ratings and advisories for television programs. In *National Television Violence Study: Scientific Papers* (pp. III-1 to III-26). Studio City, CA: Mediascope, Inc.

Cantor, J., Harrison, K., & Nathanson, A. (1997). Ratings and advisories for television programming: University of Wisconsin-Madison study. In

National Television Violence Study 2 (pp. 267–322). Thousand Oaks, CA: Sage.

Cantril, H. (1947). The invasion from Mars. In E.E. Maccoby, T.M. Newcomb, & E.L. Hartley (Eds.), *Readings in social psychology* (3rd ed., pp. 291-300). New York: Holt, Rinehart and Winston.

Carey, J. (1969) Changing courtship patterns in the popular song. *American Journal of Sociology, 4,* 720-731.

Carnegie Council on Adolescent Development (1989). *Turning points: Preparing American youth for the 21st century.* Washington, DC: Author.

Carroll, J. (1992a, August 10). One-shop stopping: Mondegreens r us. *San Francisco Chronicle,* p. E-14.

Carroll, J. (1992b, August 11). Once again, mondegreens r us. *San Francisco Chronicle,* p. E-12.

Carroll, R., Silbergleid, M., Beachum, C., Perry, S., Pluscht, P., & Pescatore, M. (1993). Meanings of radio to teenagers in a niche-programming era. *Journal of Broadcasting and Electronic Media, 37*(2), 159-176.

Chaffee, S.H. (1977). Mass media effects: New research perspectives. In D. Lerner and L. Nelson (Eds.), *Communication research—a half century appraisal* (pp. 210-241). Honolulu: East-West Center Press.

Chaffee, S.H., & Hochheimer, J.L. (1982). The beginnings of political communication research in the United States: Origins of the "limited effects" model. In E.M. Rogers & F. Balle (Eds.), *The media revolution in America and Western Europe* (pp. 263-283). Norwood, NJ: Ablex.

Chaffee, S.H., & McLeod, J.M. (1972). Adolescent television use in the family context. In G.A. Comstock & E.A. Rubinstein (Eds.), *Television and social behavior: Vol. 3. Television and adolescent aggressiveness* (pp. 149-172). Washington, DC: Government Printing Office.

Chaffee, S.H., McLeod, J.M., & Atkin, C.H. (1971). Parental influences on adolescent media use. *American Behavioral Scientist, 14,* 323-340.

Chen, M. (1994). *The smart parent's guide to kids' TV.* San Francisco: KQED Books.

Christenson, P. (1992a). The effects of parental advisory labels on adolescent music preferences. *Journal of Communication, 42*(1), 106-113.

Christenson, P. (1992b). Preadolescent perceptions and interpretations of music videos. *Popular Music and Society, 16*(3), 63-73.

Christenson, P. (1994). Childhood patterns of music use and preferences. *Communication Reports, 7*(2), 136-144.

Christenson, P. (1996). *A comparison of video game, popular music and television use among children and adolescents* (Report to Beaverton School

District). Portland, OR: Department of Communication, Lewis and Clark College.

Christenson, P., & DeBenedittis, P. (1986). "Eavesdropping" on the FM band: Children's use of radio. *Journal of Communication, 36*(2), 27-38.

Christenson, P., Debenedittis, P., & Lindlof, T. (1985). Children's use of audio media. *Communication Research, 12*, 327-343.

Christenson, P., & Peterson, J. (1988). Genre and gender in the structure of music preferences. *Communication Research, 15*(3), 282-301.

Christenson, P., & Roberts, D.F. (1983). The role of television in the formation of children's social attitudes. In M.J.A. Howe (Ed.), *Learning from television: Psychological and educational research* (pp. 79-99). London: Academic Press.

Christenson, P., & Roberts, D.F. (1990). *Popular music in early adolescence.* Washington, DC: Carnegie Council on Adolescent Development.

Christenson, P., & van Nouhuys, B. (1995, May). *From the fringe to the center: A comparison of heavy metal and rap fandom.* Paper presented at the annual meeting of the International Communication Association, Albuquerque, NM.

Clarke, P. (1973). Teenagers' coorientation and information-seeking about pop music. *American Behavioral Scientist, 16*, 551-556.

Clark, W.W. (1991). Noise exposure and hearing loss from leisure-time activities: A review. *Journal of the Acoustical Society of America, 90*, 175-181.

Clark, W.W. (1992). Hearing: the effects of noise. *Otolaryngology: Head and Neck Surgery, 106*(6), 669-676.

Cocks, J. (1989, Sept. 4) New directions for the next decade. *Time*, p. 63.

Cole, R. (1971). Top songs in the sixties: A content analysis. *American Behavioral Scientist, 14*, 389-400.

Coleman, J. (1961). *The adolescent society.* London: Collier-Macmillan.

Coleman, J. (1974). *Relationships in adolescence.* London: Routledge & Kegan Paul.

Coleman, J. (1978). Current contradictions in adolescent theory. *Journal of Youth and Adolescence, 7*, 1-11.

Coleman, J. (1993). Adolescence in a changing world. In S. Jackson & H. Rodriguez-Tome (Eds.), *Adolescence and its social worlds* (pp. 251-268). Hove, UK: Erlbaum.

Coleman, J., George, R., & Holt, G. (1977). Adolescents and their parents: A study of Attitudes. *Journal of Genetic Psychology, 130*, 239-245.

Collins, W.A. (1983). Interpretation and inference in children's television viewing. In J. Bryant & D. R. Anderson (Eds.), *Children's understanding of television: Research on attention and comprehension* (pp. 125-150). New York: Academic Press.

Comstock, G., Chaffee, S., Katzman, N., McCombs, M., & Roberts, D.F. (1978). *Television and human behavior*. New York: Columbia University Press.

Comstock, G., & Cobbey, R.R. (1979). Television and the children of ethnic minorities: Perspectives from research. In G.L. Berry & C. Mitchell-Kernan (Eds.), *Television and the socialization of the minority child* (pp. 245-259). New York: Academic Press.

Comstock, G., (& Paik, H. 1991). *Television and the American child*. San Diego: Academic Press.

Conger, J., & Peterson, A. (1984). *Adolescence and youth: Psychological development in a changing world* (3rd ed.). New York: Harper & Row.

Consensus National Conference. (1990). Noise and hearing loss. *Journal of the American Medical Association, 263,* 3185-3190.

Cool, V.A., Yarbrough, D.B., Patton, J.E., Runde, R., & Keith, T.Z. (1994). Experimental effects of radio and television distractors on children's performance on mathematics and reading assignments. *Journal of Experimental Education, 62,* 181-194.

Coombs, H.S. (1995). *Teenage survival manual*. San Francisco: Halo Books.

Cooper, B.L. (1991). *Popular music perspectives: Ideas, themes and patterns in contemporary lyrics*. Bowling Green, OH: Bowling Green University Popular Press.

Cooper, V. (1985). Women in popular music: A quantitative analysis of feminine images over time. *Sex Roles, 13,* 499-506.

Coward, N. (1965). *Three plays: Private Lives; Blithe Spirit; Hay Fever*. New York: Dell.

Cripe, F. (1986). Rock music as therapy for children with attention deficit disorder: An exploratory study. *Journal of Music Therapy, 23,* 30-37.

Czikszentmihalyi, M., & Larson, R. (1984). *Being adolescent: Conflict and growth in the teenage years*. New York: Basic Books.

Danenberg, M.A., Loos-Cosgrove, M., & LoVerde, M. (1987). Temporary hearing loss and rock music. *Language, Speech and Hearing Services in Schools, 18,* 267-274.

Davidson, G. (1993). *Treasure: The trials of a teenage terror and her mom*. Oakland, CA: Zenobia Press.

Davis, D. (1984, November). *Nihilism in music television*. Paper presented at the annual meeting of the Speech Communication Association, Chicago, IL.

Deihl, E., Schneider, M., & Petress, K. (1983). Dimensions of music preference: A factor analytic study. *Popular Music and Society, 9*(3), 41-50.

Denisoff, R.S., & Levine, M.H. (1970). Generations and counterculture: A study in the ideology of music. *Youth and Society, 2*(1), 33-58.

Denisoff, R.S., & Levine, M.H. (1971). The popular protest song: The case of "Eve of Destruction." *Public Opinion Quarterly, 35,* 119-124.

Denisoff, R.S, & Levine, M.H. (1972). Youth and popular music: A test of the taste culture hypothesis. *Youth and Society, 4*(4), 237-255.

Denisoff, R. S., & Peterson, R. (1972). Theories of culture, music and society. In R. Denisoff & R. Peterson (Eds.), *The sounds of social change: Studies in popular culture* (pp. 1-11). Chicago: Rand-McNally.

Dominick, J. (1974). The portable friend: Peer group membership and radio usage. *Journal of Broadcasting, 18*(2), 164-169.

Dominick, J. (1996). *The dynamics of mass communication* (5th ed.). New York: McGraw-Hill.

Donnerstein, E., Wilson, B., & Linz, D. (1992). On the regulation of broadcast indecency to protect children. *Journal of Broadcasting and Electronic Media, 36,* 111-118.

Dortch, S. (1994, July). Why teens have less green. *American Demographics,* p. 9.

Douvan, E., & Adelson, J. (1966). *The adolescent experience.* New York: Wiley.

Drake-Lee, A. B. (1992). Beyond music: Auditory temporary threshold shift in rock musicians after a heavy metal concert. *Journal of the Royal Society of Medicine, 85,* 617-619.

Driscoll, R., Davis, K., & Lipetz, M.E. (1972). Parental influence and romantic love: The Romeo and Juliet effect. *Journal of Personality and Social Psychology, 24,* 1-10.

Dykers, C. (1992, May). *Rap and rock as adolescents' cultural capital at school.* Paper presented at the annual meeting of the International Communication Association, Miami, FL.

Eagle, C., Hawkinson, B., & Stuessy, J. (1989, July). *The relationship of music preference between chemically dependent and general high school adolescents.* Report prepared for the Parents' Music Resource Center, Arlington, VA.

Eissler, K. (1958). Notes on problems of technique in the psychoanalytic treatment of adolescents. *The Psychoanalytic Study of the Child., 13,* 223-254.

Elliott, G.R., & Feldman, S.S. (1990). Capturing the adolescent experience. In S.S. Feldman & G.R. Elliott (Eds.), *At the threshold: The developing adolescent* (pp. 1-13). Cambridge, MA: Harvard University Press.

Epperson, D. (1964). A re-assessment of indices of parental influence in "The Adolescent Society." *American Sociological Review, 29,* 93-96.

Epstein, J., Pratto, D., & Skipper, J. (1990). Teenagers, behavioral problems and preferences for heavy metal and rap music: A case study of a Southern middle school. *Deviant Behavior, 11*, 381-394.

Erikson, E.H. (1968). *Identity, youth, and crisis.* New York: W.W. Norton.

Faber, R., Brown, J., & McLeod, J. (1979). Coming of age in the global village: Television and adolescence. In E. Wartella (Ed.), *Children communicating: Media and development of thought, speech, understanding* (pp. 215-249). Beverly Hills, CA: Sage.

Fabes, R.A., & Strouse, J. (1984). Youth's perceptions of models of sexuality: Implications for sexual education. *Journal of Sex Education and Therapy, 10*, 33–37.

Fabes, R.A., & Strouse, J. (1987). Perceptions of responsible and irresponsible models of sexuality: A correlational study. *Journal of Sex Research, 23*, 70–84.

FCC vs. Pacifica Foundation, 438 U.S. 726 (1978).

Federman, J. (1996). *Media ratings: Design, use and consequences.* Studio City, CA: Mediascope.

Fedler, F., Hall, J., & Tanzi, L. (1982). Popular songs emphasize sex, de-emphasize romance. *Mass Communication Review, 9*, 10-15.

Feldman, S.S., & Elliott, G.R. (Eds.). (1990). *At the threshold: The developing adolescent.* Cambridge, MA: Harvard University Press.

Fine, G., Mortimer, J., & Roberts, D.F. (1990). Leisure, work, and the mass media. In S. S. Feldman & G.R. Elliott (Eds.), *At the threshold: The developing adolescent* (pp. 225-252). Cambridge, MA: Harvard University Press.

Fink, E., Robinson, J., & Dowden, S. (1985). The structure of music preference and attendance. *Communication Research, 12*, 301-318.

Finnas, L. (1989). A comparison between young people's privately and publicly expressed musical preferences. *Psychology of Music, 17*, 132-145.

Fiske, S.T., & Taylor, S.E. (1991). *Social cognition* (2nd ed.). New York: McGraw-Hill.

Flavell, J. H. (1977). *Cognitive development.* Englewood Cliffs, NJ: Prentice-Hall.

Fox, W., & Williams, J. (1974). Political orientation and music preferences among college students. *Public Opinion Quarterly, 38*, 352-371.

Fox, W., & Wince, M. (1975). Musical taste cultures and taste publics. *Youth and Society, 7*(2), 198-224.

Frank, S. (1994, March). *Coverage of children in television news magazines, talk shows, and local news.* Paper presented at the second annual Children

Now National Conference on Children and the Media, Stanford, CA.

Freedman, D. (1984). Psychiatric epidemiology count. *Archives of General Psychiatry, 41*, 931-933.

Freud, A. (1966). *The ego and the mechanisms of defense* (rev. ed.). New York: International Universities Press. (Original work published 1936)

Freud, A. (1958). Adolescence. *Psychoanalytic Study of the Child, 13*, 255-278.

Freudiger, P., & Almquist, E. (1978). Male and female roles in the lyrics of three genres of contemporary music. *Sex Roles, 4*, 51-65.

Frith, S. (1981). *Sound effects: Youth, leisure and the politics of rock'n'roll*. New York: Pantheon.

Frith, S. (1987). Why do songs have words? *Sociological Review Monographs, 34*, 77-106.

Fry, V., & Fry, D. (1986). MTV: The 24 hour commercial. *Journal of Communication Inquiry, 10*(1), 29-33.

Gabriel, H.P., & Wood, R. (1995). *Anticipating adolescence: How to cope with your child's emotional upheaval and forge a new relationship*. New York: Henry Holt.

Gans, H. (1967). *Popular culture and high culture: An analysis and evaluation of taste*. New York: Basic Books.

Gantz, W., Gartenberg, H., Pearson, M., & Schiller, S. (1978). Gratifications and expectations associated with popular music among adolescents. *Popular Music and Society, 6*(1), 81-89.

Geleed, E. R. (1957). Some aspects of psychoanalytic technique in adolescence. *The Psychoanalytic Study of the Child, 12*, 263-283.

Gerbner, G. (1970). Cultural indicators: The case of violence in television drama. *The Annals of the American Academy of Political and Social Science, 388*, 69–81.

Gerbner, G., & Gross, L. (1976). Living with television: The violence profile. *Journal of Communication, 26*(2), 173–199.

Gerbner, G., & Gross, L. (1980). The violent faces of television and its lessons. In E.L. Palmer & A. Dorr (Eds.), *Children and the faces of television: Teaching, violence, selling* (pp. 149-162). New York: Academic Press.

Gerbner, G., Gross, L., Morgan, M., & Signorielli, N. (1994). Growing up with television: The cultivation perspective. In J. Bryant & D. Zillmann (Eds.), *Media effects: Advances in theory and research* (pp. 17-41). Hillsdale, NJ: Erlbaum.

Gladwell, M. (1991, May 13). Rock lyrics: Parents worry but the young aren't listening. *Washington Post*, p. A3.

Goldberg, M. (1990, May 31). At a loss for words. *Rolling Stone*, pp. 29-31.

Goodman, E. (1986, September 20). Commercial for teen-age pregnancy. *Washington Post*, p. A-23.

Gordon, T., Hakanen, E., & Wells, A. (1992, May). *Music preferences and the use of music to manage emotional states: Correlates with self-concept among adolescents*. Paper presented at the annual meeting of the International Communication Association, Miami, FL.

Graham, P., & Rutter, M. (1973). Psychiatric disorder in the young adolescent: A follow-up study. *Proceedings of the Royal Society of Medicine, 66*, 58-61.

Greenberg, B. (1973). Viewing and listening parameters among British youngsters. *Journal of Broadcasting, 17*, 173-188.

Greenberg, B., Ku, L., & Li, H. (1989, June). *Young people and their orientation to the mass media: An international study, Study #2: United States*. East Lansing: College of Communication Arts, Michigan State University.

Greenberg, B., Stanley, C., Siemicki, M., Heeter, C., Soderman, A., & Linsangan, R. (1986). *Sex content on soaps and prime time television series most viewed by adolescents. Report #2 to Office of Adolescent Pregnancy Programs, U.S. Department of Health and Human Services*. East Lansing, MI: Dept. of Telecommunications, Michigan State University.

Greenfield, P.M., Bruzzone, L., Koyamatsu, K., Satuloff, W., Nixon, K., Brodie, M., & Kingsdale, D. (1987). What is rock music doing to the minds of our youth? A first experimental look at the effects of rock music lyrics and music videos. *Journal of Early Adolescence, 7*, 315-329.

Greer, R., Dorow, L., & Randall, A. (1974). Music listening preferences of elementary school children. *Journal of Research in Music Education, 21*, 284-291.

Greeson, L. (1991). Recognition and ratings of television music videos: Age, gender, and sociocultural effects. *Journal of Applied Psychology, 21*, 1908-1920.

Greeson, L., & Williams, R.A. (1986). Social implications of music videos for youth: An analysis of the content and effects of MTV. *Youth and Society, 18*, 177–189.

Grossberg, L. (1984). Another boring day in paradise: Rock and roll and the empowerment of everyday life. *Popular Music, 4*, 225-258.

Grossberg, L. (1987). Rock and roll in search of an audience. In J. Lull (Ed.), *Popular music and communication* (pp. 175-197). Beverly Hills: Sage.

Hakanen, E., & Wells, A. (1993). Music preference and taste cultures among adolescents. *Popular Music and Society, 17*(1), 55-69.

Hall, G.S. (1904). *Adolescence: Its psychology and its relations to anthropology, sex, crime, religion, and education* (2 vols.). New York, Appleton.

Hansen, C.H. (1989). Priming sex-role stereotypic event schemas with rock music videos: Effects on impression favorability, trait inferences, and recall of a subsequent male-female interaction. *Basic and Applied Social Psychology, 10,* 371-391.

Hansen, C.H., & Hansen, R.D. (1988). How rock music videos can change what is seen when boy meets girl: Priming stereotypic appraisal of social interactions. *Sex Roles, 19,* 287-316.

Hansen, C.H., & Hansen, R.D. (1990a). The influence of sex and violence on the appeal of rock music videos. *Communication Research, 17,* 212–234.

Hansen, C.H., & Hansen, R.D. (1990b). Rock music videos and antisocial behavior. *Basic and Applied Psychology, 11,* 357-369.

Hansen, C.H., & Hansen, R.D. (1991a). Constructing personality and social reality through music: Individual differences among fans of punk and heavy metal music. *Journal of Broadcasting and Electronic Media, 35,* 335-350.

Hansen, C.H., & Hansen, R.D. (1991b). Schematic information processing of heavy metal lyrics. *Communication Research, 18,* 373-411.

Hansen, C.H., & Krygowski, W. (1994). Arousal-augmented priming effects: Rock music videos and sex object schemas. *Communication Research, 21,* 24-47.

Hare, E., & Christenson, P. (1996). *Dominant themes in alternative rock lyrics.* Unpublished raw data.

Harrington, R. (1990, February 5-11). The furor over shock rock. *Washington Post National Weekly Edition,* p. 33.

Harrington, R. (1993, November 14). Shooting back at gangsta rap. *Washington Post,* pp. G1, G6-7.

Harrington, L. (1994, February 24). On Capitol Hill, a real rap session. *Chicago Tribune,* pp. 1, 10.

Hartman, J., & Tucker, R. (1987). Music-video viewing in the 18-35-year-old age group from a uses and gratifications perspective. *Popular Music and Society, 11*(4), 31-46.

Hawkins, R.P., & Pingree, S.H. (1982). TV influence on social reality and conceptions of the world. In D. Pearl, L. Bouthilet, & J. Lazar (Eds.), *Television and behavior: Ten years of scientific progress and implications for the 80's* (Vol. 2, pp. 224-247). Washington, DC: National Institute of Mental Health.

Hayakawa, S.I. (1962). *The use and misuse of language.* Greenwich, CT: Fawcett.

Hayman, S. (1986). *Adolescence: A survival guide to the teenage years.* New York: Gower.

Heimlich, E. (1983). The metaphoric use of song lyrics in paraverbal communication. *Child Psychiatry and Human Development, 14*(2), 67-75.

Henriksen, L., & Roberts, D.F. (1990). *Turn on, tune in, hang out: Music use in adolescence.* Unpublished manuscript, Stanford University, Institute for Communication Research, Stanford, CA.

Hesbacher, P., & Anderson, B. (1985). Hit singers' careers since 1940: Have women advanced? *Popular Music and Society, 7*(3), 74-85.

Hey, Baby—you're playing my song. (1992, March 15). *The Montreal Gazette,* p. XXX.

Hilburn, R. (1985, September, 27). World tour ends; Springsteen: The power of idealism. *Los Angeles Times* [Home ed.], pp. 12, 20.

Hoffman, J. (1985). From Random House to Mickey Mouse: Liability for negligent publishing and broadcasting. *Tort and Insurance Law Journal, 21*(1), 65-89.

Holland, B. (1990, May 19). Here it is in black and white: The RIAA warning sticker. *Billboard,* p. 1.

Holt, J. (1990). Protecting America's youth: Can rock music lyrics be constitutionally regulated? *Journal of Contemporary Law, 16,* 53-75.

Horatio Alger Foundation. (1996). *The mood of American youth.* Alexandria, VA: Horatio Alger Association of Distinguished Americans.

Horton, D. (1957). The dialogue of courtship in popular songs. *American Journal of Sociology, 62,* 569-578.

House Bill 1406 (Missouri), 85 General Assembly, 2nd Session (1990).

House Select Subcommittee on Children, Youth, and Families (1991, July). *Turn it down: Effects of noise on hearing loss in children and youth* (Rep. No. ISBN-0-16-037022-1). Washington, DC: U.S. Government Printing Office.

Hyden, C., & McCandless, N. (1983). Men and women as portrayed in popular music lyrics. *Popular Music and Society, 9*(2), 19-26.

Ingersoll, B.D., & Goldstein, N. (1995). *Lonely, sad and angry: A parent's guide to depression and adolescence.* New York: Doubleday.

Jacobellis v. Ohio, 378 U.S. 184 (1964).

Janowitz, T. (1987, April). Sex as a weapon. *Spin,* pp. 54-62.

Jennings, M., & Niemi, R. (1975). Continuity and change in political orientations: A longitudinal study of two generations. *American Political Science Review, 69,* 1316-1335.

Jhally, S. (Producer). (1994). *Dreamworlds II: Desire, sex, power in music video* (Film). Northampton, MA: Media Education Foundation.

Johnson, J.D., Jackson, L.A., & Gatto, L. (1995). Violent attitudes and deferred academic aspirations: Deleterious effects of exposure to rap music. *Basic and Applied Social Psychology, 16*(1&2), 27-41.

Johnsson-Smaragdi, U. (1983). *Television use and social interaction in adolescence.* Stockholm: Almquist and Wiksell.

Jones, E., & Gerard, H. (1967). *Foundations of social psychology.* New York: Wiley.

Kalis, P., & Neuendorf, K. (1989). Aggressive cue prominence and gender participation in MTV. *Journalism Quarterly, 66*(1), 148-54, 229.

Kandel, D., & Davies, M. (1982). Epidemiology of depressive mood in adolescents. *Archives of General Psychiatry, 39,* 1205-1212.

Katz, E., Gurevitch, M., & Haas, H. (1973). On the use of mass media for important things. *American Sociological Review, 38,* 164-181.

Keith, T.Z. (1986). *Homework.* West Lafayette, IN: Kappa Delta Pi.

Kim, H., & Baron, R.S. (1988). Exercise and the illusory correlation: Does arousal heighten stereotypic processing? *Journal of Experimental Social Psychology, 24,* 366-380.

Kinder, M. (1984). Music video and the spectator: Television, ideology and dream. *Film Quarterly, 38*(4), 2-15.

King, P. (1988). Heavy metal music and drug abuse in adolescents. *Postgraduate Medicine, 83*(5), 295-304.

Kirchler, E., Palmonari, A., & Pombeni, M. (1993). Developmental tasks and adolescents' relationships with their peers and their family. In S. Jackson & H. Rodriguez-Tome (Eds.), *Adolescence and its social worlds* (pp. 145-167). Hove: UK: Erlbaum.

Klapper, J.T. (1960). *The effects of mass communication.* New York: Free Press.

Klein, J.D., Brown, J.D., Walsh-Childers, K., Porter, C., Oliveri, J., & Dykers, C. (1993). Adolescents' risky behavior and mass media use. *Pediatrics, 92,* 24-31.

Klodny, R. (1984). *How to survive your adolescent's adolescence.* Boston: Little, Brown.

Kotarba, J., & Wells, L. (1987). Styles of adolescent participation in an all-ages, rock 'n' roll nightclub: An ethnographic analysis. *Youth and Society, 18*(4), 398-417.

Krauthammer, C. (1990, October 26). Culture has consequences. *The Washington Post,* p. A27.

Krupinski, J., Baikie, A., Stoller, A., Graves, J., O'Day, D., & Polke, P. (1967). A community health survey of Heyfield, Victoria. *Medical Journal of Australia, 54,* 1204-1211.

Kubey, R., & Csikszentmihalyi, M. (1990). *Television and the quality of life: How viewing shapes everyday experience.* Hillsdale, NJ: Erlbaum.

Kubey, R., & Larson, R. (1989). The use and experience of the new video media among children and young adolescents: Television viewing compared to the use of videocassettes, video games, and music videos. *Communication Research, 17,* 107-130.

Kunkel, D. (1994). How the news media "see" kids. *Media Studies Journal, 8*(4), 75-84.

Kuwahara, Y. (1992). Power to the people, y'all: Rap music, resistance, and black college students. *Humanity and Society, 16*(1), 54-73.

Lacayo, R. (1995, June 12). Violent reaction. *Time,* pp. 25-30.

Larson, R., & Kubey, R. (1983). Television and music: Contrasting media in adolescent life. *Youth and Society, 15*(1), 13-31.

Larson, R., Kubey, R., & Colletti, J. (1989). Changing channels: Early adolescent media choices and shifting investments in family and friends. *Journal of Youth and Adolescence, 18*(6), 583-599.

LaVoie, J.C., & Collins, B.R. (1975). Effect of youth culture music on high school students' academic performance. *Journal of Youth and Adolescence, 4,* 57-65.

Lazarus, A. (1987). Rock is a four-letter word: The potential for FCC regulation of (un)popular music. *Hastings Journal of Communications and Entertainment Law, 9,* 423-522.

Leming, J. (1987). Rock music and the socialization of moral values in early adolescence. *Youth and Society, 18,* 363-383.

Levy, B., & Giggans, P.O. (1995). *What parents need to know about dating violence.* Seattle, WA: Seal Press.

Levy, C.J., & Deykin, E.Y. (1989). Suicidality, depression, and substance abuse in adolescence. *American Journal of Psychiatry, 146,* 1462-1467.

Lewis, G. (1992). Who do you love?: The dimensions of musical taste. In J. Lull (Ed.), *Popular music and communication* (2nd ed., pp. 134-151). Newbury Park, CA: Sage.

Litle, P., & Zuckerman, M. (1986). Sensation seeking and music preferences. *Personality and Individual Differences, 7,* 575-577.

Litman, R.E., & Farberow, N.L. (1994). Pop-rock music as precipitating cause in youth suicide. *Journal of Forensic Sciences, 39,* 494-499.

Lott, B. (1987). *Women's lives: Themes and variations in gender learning.* Monterey, CA: Brooks Cole.

Louisiana music censorship bill defeated [news release]. (1994, June 13). Recording Industry Association of America.Washington D.C.

Lull, J. (1982). Popular music: resistance to new wave. *Journal of Communication, 32*(1), 121-131.

Lull, J. (1987). Listeners' communicative uses of popular music. In J. Lull (Ed.), *Popular music and communication* (pp. 140-174). Newbury Park, CA: Sage.

Lull, J. (1992). Popular music and communication: An introduction. In J. Lull, (Ed.), *Popular music and communication* (2nd ed., pp. 1-32). Newbury Park, CA: Sage.

Lusane, C. (1992). Rhapsodic variations: Rap, race and power politics. *The Black Scholar, 23*(2), 37-51.

Lyle, J., & Hoffman, H. (1972). Children's use of television and other media. In E. Rubinstein, G. Comstock & J. Murray (Eds.), *Television in day-to-day life: patterns of use* (pp. 129-256). Washington, DC: U.S. Government Printing Office.

Madonna, the Lee Friedlander sessions. (1985, September). *Playboy*, pp. 118-131.

Malmuth, N.M. (1983). Factors associated with rape as predictors of laboratory aggression against women. *Journal of Personality and Social Psychology, 45*, 432-442.

Margolis, D. (1992). Backyard soundings: An exploration of boundaries. *Humboldt Journal of Social Relations, 18*(2), 85-100.

Mark, A. (1986). Adolescents discuss themselves and drugs through music. *Journal of Substance Abuse Treatment, 3*, 243-249.

Mark, A. (1988). Metaphoric lyrics as a bridge to the adolescents' world. *Adolescence, 23*, 313-323.

Martin, G., Clarke, M., & Pearce, C. (1993). Adolescent suicide: Music preference as an indicator of vulnerability. *Journal of the Academy of Child and Adolescent Psychiatry, 32*(3), 530-535.

Mashkin, K., & Volgy, T. (1975). Socio-political attitudes and musical preferences. *Social Science Quarterly, 56*, 450-459.

MCA, Seagram assailed for graphic lyrics (1996, December 21). *Billboard*, p. 3.

McCollum v. CBS, 249 Cal. Rptr., 187, 189 (Cal. App. 2nd, 1988).

McDonald, J. (1988). Censoring rock lyrics: A historical analysis of the debate. *Youth and Society, 19*, 294-313.

McGuire, W. (1986). The myth of massive media impact: Savagings and salvagings. In G. Comstock (Ed.), *Public communication and behavior* (Vol. 1, pp. 173-257). Orlando, FL: Academic Press.

McIver, T. (1988). Backward masking and other backward thoughts about music. *Skeptical Inquirer, 13*, 50-63.

McLeod, J.M., & Reeves, B. (1980). On the nature of mass media effects. In S.B. Withey & R.P. Abeles (Eds.), *Television and social behavior: Beyond violence and children* (pp. 17-54). Hillsdale, NJ: Erlbaum.

McQuail, D., Blumler, J.G., & Brown, J.R. (1972). The television audience: A revised perspective. In D. McQuail (Ed.), *Sociology of mass communications* (pp. 135-165). Harmondsworth, England: Penguin.

Meade, M. (1972). The degradation of women. In R.Denisoff & R. Peterson (Eds.), *The sounds of social change: Studies in popular culture* (pp. 173–177). Chicago: Rand-McNally.

Meese v. Keene, 55 U.S.L.W. 4586 (1987).

Meissner, W. (1965). Parental interaction of the adolescent boy. *Journal of Genetic Psychology, 107,* 225-233.

Meyerson, S. (Ed.) (1975). *Adolescence: The crisis of adjustment.* London: George Allen & Unwin.

Miller, P.H., & Bigi, L. (1979). The development of children's understanding of attention. *Merrill-Palmer Quarterly, 25,* 235-250.

Miller v. California, 413 US 15 (1973).

Morkes, J., Chen, H., & Roberts, D.F. (1997, May). *Young adolescents' responses to movie, television, and computer game ratings and advisories.* Paper presented at the annual meeting of the International Communication Association, Montreal, Canada.

Murdock, G. (1989). Critical inquiry and audience activity. In B. Dervin, L. Grossberg, B.J. O'Keefe & E. Wartella (Eds.), *Rethinking communication* (Vol. 2, pp. 226-249). Newbury Park, CA: Sage.

Murdock, G., & Phelps, G. (1972). Responding to popular music: Criteria of classification and choice among English teenagers. *Popular Music and Society, 1*(3), 144–151.

Murray, J.P., & Kippax, S. (1979). From the early window to the late night show: International trends in the study of television's impact on children and adults. *Advances in Experimental and Social Psychology, 12,* 253-320.

Mutz, D.C., Roberts, D.F., & van Vuuren, D.P. (1993). Reconsidering the displacement hypothesis: Television's influence on children's time use. *Communication Research, 20,* 51-75.

Myers, P.N., & Biocca, F. A. (1992). The elastic body image: The effect of television advertising and programming on body image distortions in young women. *Journal of Communication, 42*(2), 108-133.

National Coalition on Television Violence. (1984. *NCTV Music-video Monitoring Project* (Research Rep.). Marlboro, MA: Author.

Nelsen, J., & Lott, L. (1991). *Positive discipline for teenagers: Resolving conflict with your teenage son or daughter.* Rockland, CA: Prima Publishing.

Newspaper Advertising Bureau. (1980). *America's children and the mass media*. New York: Author.

Nielsen Media Research. (1989). *Nielsen newscast*. Northbrook, IL: Author.

Offer, D. (1969). *The psychological world of the teen-ager*. New York: Basic Books.

Offer, D., & Offer, J. (1975). *From teenage to young manhood*. New York: Basic Books.

Offer, D., Ostrov, E., & Howard, K. (1981). *The adolescent: A psychological self-portrait*. New York: Basic Books.

Offer, D., Ostrov, E., Howard, K., & Atkinson, R. (1988). *The teenage world: Adolescents' self-image in ten countries*. New York: Plenum.

Olbrich, E. (1990). Coping and development. In H.A. Bosma & A.E. Jackson (Eds.), *Coping and self concept in adolescence*. Heidelberg: Springer–Verlag.

Oliver, M.B. (1990, June). *An examination of the enjoyment of negative-affect producing entertainment*. Paper presented at the annual meeting of the International Communication Association, Dublin, Ireland.

Orton, P.Z. (1996). Effects of perceived choice and narrative elements on interest in and liking of story. (Doctoral dissertation, Stanford University, 1995). *Dissertation Abstracts International, 56*, 3784A.

Overbeck, W., & Pullen, R. (1995). *Major principles of media law*. New York: Harcourt Brace.

Pareles, J. (1991, June 2). Sex, lies and the trouble with videotape. *New York Times* [Sunday ed.], p. H-31.

Parents Music Resource Center (PMRC) (1989, Spring). *The record* [Newsletter].

Patton, J.E., Stinard, T.A., & Routh, D.K. (1983). Where do children study? *Journal of Educational Research, 76*, 280-286.

Peatman, J. (1944). Radio and popular music. In P. Lazarsfeld & F. Stanton (Eds.), *Radio research 1942-43* (pp. 335-393). New York: Duell, Sloan and Pearce.

Pember, D.R. (1992). *Mass media in America* (6th ed.). New York: Macmillan.

Peterson, D.L., & Pfost, K.S. (1989). Influence of rock videos on attitudes of violence against women. *Psychological Reports, 64*, 319-322.

Peterson, R. (1972). A process model of the folk, pop, and fine art phases of jazz. In C. Nanry (Ed.), *American music: From Storyville to Woodstock* (pp. 135-151). New Brunswick, NJ: Transaction Books.

Peterson, J., & Christenson, P. (1987). Political orientation and music preference in the 1980's. *Popular Music and Society, 11*(4), 1-17.

Phelan, T.W. (1993). *Surviving your adolescents: A vital parent's guide.* Glen Ellen, IL: Child Management.

Pop songs "brainwash" youth, Agnew asserts. (1970, September 15). *Toledo Times,* p. 3.

Popular music under siege. (1994). Briefing from the Arts Censorship Project of the American Civil Liberties Union (ACLU).

Postman, N. (1985). *Amusing ourselves to death: Public discourse in the age of show business.* New York: Viking.

Powell, D. (1986). *Teenagers: When to worry, what to do.* New York: Doubleday.

Prinsky, L., & Rosenbaum, J. (1987). "Leer-ics" or lyrics?: Teenage impressions of rock 'n' roll. *Youth and Society, 18,* 384-397.

Radio Advertising Bureau. (1990). *1989-90 radio facts.* New York: Author.

Reardon, D.M., & Bell, G. (1970). Effects of sedative and stimulative music on activity levels of severely retarded boys. *American Journal of Mental Deficiency, 75,* 156–159.

Recording Industry Association of America (RIAA). (1992). *A brief overview of explicit lyrics and state legislation* [Issue brief]. Washington DC: Author.

Recording Industry Association of America (RIAA). (1994, Spring). State of the arts. *RIAA Newsletter,* p. 2.

Recording Industry Association of America (RIAA). (1995, Spring). State of the arts. *RIAA Newsletter,* pp. 2, 4.

Reid, J. (1993). The use of Christian rock music by youth group members. *Popular Music and Society, 17*(2), 33-45.

Reimer, R. (1987, June 18). *Regulating record lyrics: A constitutional analysis.* Washington, DC: Congressional Research Service, Library of Congress.

Rice, R. (1980). The content of popular recordings. *Popular Music and Society, 7*(2), 140-158.

Riera, M. (1995). *Uncommon sense for parents with teenagers.* New York: Dorling Kindersley.

Rintelmann, W., & Borus, J. (1968). Noise induced hearing loss and rock and roll music. *Archives Otolaryngology, 88,* 57-65.

Ritchie, L.D. (1991). Family communication patterns: An epistemic analysis and conceptual reinterpretation. *Communication Research, 18,* 548-565.

Ritchie, D., Price, V., & Roberts, D.F. (1987). Television, reading, and reading achievement: A reappraisal. *Communication Research, 14,* 292-315.

Roberts, D.F. (1971). The nature of communication effects. In W. Schramm & D. F. Roberts (Eds.), *The process and effects of mass communication* (2nd ed., pp. 349-387). Urbana: University of Illinois Press.

Roberts, D.F. (1973). Communication and children: A developmental approach. In I. de Sola Pool & W. Schramm (Eds.), *Handbook of communication* (pp. 174-215). Chicago: Rand-McNally.

Roberts, D.F. (1993). Adolescents and the mass media: From "Leave It to Beaver" to "Beverly Hills 90210." *Teacher's College Record, 94,* 629-643.

Roberts, D.F., & Bachen, C. (1981). Mass communication effects. *Annual Review of Psychology, 32,* 307-356.

Roberts, D.F., & Henriksen, L. (1990, June). *Music listening vs. television viewing among older adolescents.* Paper presented at the annual meetings of the International Communication Association, Dublin, Ireland.

Roberts, D.F., Henriksen, L., Voelker, D.H., & van Vuuren, D.P. (1993). Television and schooling: Displacement and distraction hypotheses. *Australian Journal of Education, 37,* 198-211.

Roberts, D.F., Kinsey, D., & Gosh, S. (1993). Themes in top 40 songs of the 1980's. Unpublished raw data.

Roberts, D.F., & Maccoby, N. (1985). Effects of mass communication. In G. Lindzey & E. Aronson (Eds.), *Handbook of social psychology* (Vol. II, 3rd ed., pp. 539-598). Reading, MA: Addison-Wesley.

Roberts, T. (1994, August). Dilemma of a womanist. *Essence,* pp. 62-64.

Robinson, J.P., & Hirsch, P.M. (1972). Teenage response to rock and roll protest songs. In R.S. Denisoff & R.A. Peterson (Eds.), *The sounds of social change: Studies in popular culture* (pp. 222-231). Chicago: Rand McNally.

Robinson, J., Pilskain, R., & Hirsch, P. (1976). Protest rock and drugs. *Journal of Communication, 26*(4), 126-136.

Rock on trial. (1988, October 15). *The Economist,* p. 38.

Rock stars say it's time to start protecting hearing. (1991, September 27). *Peninsula Times Tribune,* p. A-8.

Roe, K. (1984, August). *Youth and music in Sweden: Results from a longitudinal study of teenagers' media use.* Paper presented at the meeting of the International Association of Mass Communication Research, Prague.

Roe, K. (1985). Swedish youth and music: Listening patterns and motivations. *Communication Research, 12*(3), 353-362.

Roe, K. (1987). The school and music in adolescent socialization. In J. Lull (Ed.), *Popular music and communication* (pp. 212-230). Beverly Hills, CA: Sage.

Roe, K. (1995). Adolescents' use of socially disvalued media: Towards a theory of media delinquency. *Journal of Youth and Adolescence, 24*, 617-631.

Rosenbaum, J., & Prinsky, L. (1987). Sex, violence and rock 'n' roll: Youth's perceptions of popular music. *Popular Music and Society, 11*(2), 79-89.

Rosenbaum, J., & Prinsky, L. (1991). The presumption of influence: Recent responses to popular music subcultures. *Crime and Delinquency, 37*, 528-535.

Rouner, D. (1990). Rock music use as a socializing function. *Popular Music and Society, 14*(1), 97-107.

Rubin, A. (1994). Media uses and effects: A uses-and-gratifications perspective. In J. Bryant & D. Zillmann (Eds.), *Media effects: Advances in theory and research* (pp. 417-436). Hillsdale, NJ: Erlbaum.

Rupp, R.R., & Koch, L.J. (1969). Effects of too-loud music on human ears: But mother, rock'n roll has to be loud. *Clinical Pediatrics, 8*, 60-62.

Rutter, M., Graham, C., Chadwick, O.F.D., & Yule, W. (1976). Adolescent turmoil: Fact or fiction? *Journal of Child Psychology and Psychiatry, 17*, 35-56.

Salame, P., & Baddeley, A. (1989). Effects of background music on phonological short-term memory. *The Quarterly Journal of Experimental Psychology, 41A*, 107-122.

Samuels, D. (1991, November 11). The rap on rap. *The New Republic*, pp. 24-29.

Schank, R.C., & Abelson, R. (1977). *Scripts, plans, goals and understanding.* Hillsdale, NJ: Erlbaum.

Schramm, W. (1965). Communication in crisis. In B.S. Greenberg & E.B. Parker (Eds.), *The Kennedy assassination and the American public: Social communication in crisis* (pp. 1-25). Stanford, CA: Stanford University Press.

Schramm, W. (1971). The nature of communication between humans. In W. Schramm & D. F. Roberts (Eds.), *The process and effects of mass communication* (rev. ed., pp. 3-53). Urbana: University of Illinois Press.

Schramm, W., Lyle, J., & Parker, E.B. (1961). *Television in the lives of our children.* Stanford, CA: Stanford University Press.

Schreiber, E.H. (1988). Influence of music on college students' achievement. *Perceptual and Motor Skills, 66*, 339.

Schusterman, R. (1991). The fine art of rap. *New Literary History, 22*, 613-632.

Seidman, S. (1992). An investigation of sex-role stereotyping in music videos. *Journal of Broadcasting and Electronic Media, 36*(2), 209-216.

Sellers, P. (1989, May 8). The ABC's of marketing to kids. *Fortune*, pp. 114-116, 120.

Sherman, B., & Dominick, J. (1986). Violence and sex in music videos: TV and rock 'n' roll. *Journal of Communication, 36*(1), 79-93.

Simmons, B. (1992). The effect of censorship on attitudes toward popular music. *Popular Music and Society, 16*(4), 61-69.

Singing dirty (1990), (March 25). *The Oregonian*, pp. K1, K4.

Skipper, J. (1973) How popular is popular music? *Popular Music and Society, 2*(1), 145-154.

Smith, S. (1995, June 23). Jackson plans new lyrics for album. *New York Times*, p. B-3.

Smith, T. (1994). *Adolescence: The survival guide for parents and teenagers.* New York: Dorling Kindersley.

Smith, T. (1994). Generational differences in musical preferences. *Popular Music and Society, 18*(2), 43-59.

Sommers-Flanagan, R., Sommers-Flanagan, J., & Davis, B. (1993). What's happening on music television? A gender role content analysis. *Sex Roles, 28*, 745-753.

Stack, S., & Gundlach, J. (1992). The effect of country music on suicide. *Social Forces, 71*, 211-218.

Stack, S., Gundlach, J., & Reeves, J.L. (1994). The heavy metal subculture and suicide. *Suicide and Life-Threatening Behavior, 24*, 15-23.

Starker, S. (1989). *Evil influences: Crusades against the mass media.* New Brunswick, NJ: Transaction Publishers.

Steinberg, L. (1990). Autonomy, conflict, and harmony in the family relationship. In. S.S. Feldman & G.R. Elliott (Eds.), *At the threshold: The developing adolescent* (pp. 255-276). Cambridge, MA: Harvard University Press.

Steinberg, L., & Levine, A. (1990). *You and your adolescent: A parent's guide for ages 10-20.* New York: HarperCollins.

Stipp, H. (1985). Children's knowledge of and taste in popular music. *Popular Music and Society, 10*(2), 1-15.

Stipp, H. (1990, August) Musical demographics. *American Demographics*, pp. 48-49.

Stipp, H. (1993, August). New ways to reach children. *American Demographics*, pp. 50-56.

St. Lawrence, J.S., & Joyner, D.J. (1991). The effects of sexually violent rock music on males' acceptance of violence against women. *Psychology of Women Quarterly, 15*, 49-63.

Strouse, J., Buerkel-Rothfuss, N., & Long, E. (1995). Gender and family as moderators of the relationship between music video exposure and sexual permissiveness. *Adolescence, 30,* 505-521.

Suicides blamed on music's Satanic spell. (1988, March 15). *Christianity Today,* pp. 57-58.

Sun, S., & Lull, J. (1986). The adolescent audience for music videos and why they watch. *Journal of Communication, 36*(1), 115-125.

Swets, P.W. (1995). *The art of talking with your teenager.* Holbrook, MA: Adams Publishing.

Tanner, J. (1981). Pop music and peer groups: A study of Canadian high school students' responses to pop music. *Canadian Review of Sociology and Anthropology, 18*(2), 1-13.

Tapper, J., Thorson, E., & Black, D. (1994). Variations in music videos as a function of their musical genre. *Journal of Broadcasting and Electronic Media, 38,* 103-113.

Taylor, S.E., & Crocker, J. (1981). Schematic basis of social information processing. In E.T. Higgins, C.P. Herman, & M. Zanna (Eds.), *Social cognition: The Ontario symposium* (Vol. 1, pp. 89-134). Hillsdale, NJ: Erlbaum.

Tetzlaff, D. (1986). MTV and the politics of postmodern pop. *Journal of Communication Inquiry, 10*(1), 80-91.

The rap attitude (1990, March 19). *Newsweek,* pp. 56–59.

Thompson, M., Pingree, S., Hawkins, R.P., & Draves, C. (1991). Long-term norms and cognitive structures as shapers of television viewer activity. *Journal of Broadcasting and Electronic Media, 35,* 319-334.

Thompson, M., Walsh-Childers, K., & Brown, J.D. (1993). The influence of family communication patterns and sexual experience on processing of a music video. In B. Greenberg, J.D. Brown, & N.L. Buerkel-Rothfuss (Eds.), *Media, sex, and the adolescent* (pp. 248-262). Cresskill, NJ: Hampton Press.

Thornburg, H.D. (1981). Adolescent sources of information on sex. *Journal of School Health, 51,* 274–277.

Toney, G., & Weaver, J. (1994). Effects of gender and gender role self-perceptions on affective reactions to rock music videos. *Sex Roles, 30,* 567-583.

Trostle, L. (1986). Nihilistic adolescents, heavy metal rock music, and paranormal beliefs. *Psychological Reports, 59,* 610.

Tucker, A., & Bushman, B.J. (1991). Effects of rock and roll music on mathematical, verbal, and reading comprehension performance. *Perceptual and Motor Skills, 71,* 942.

The ultimate encyclopedia of rock. (1993). New York: Harper Collins.

U.S. Department of Labor. (1983). *Department of Labor occupational noise standard* (Code of Federal Regulations 29 DFR 1910.95). Washington DC: Author.

Utterback, E., Ljungdahl, E., Storm, N., Williams, M., & Kreutter, J. (1995). *Image and sound: A comparative content analysis of gender roles in music videos.* Unpublished manuscript, Department of Communication, Lewis and Clark College, Portland, OR.

Vance v. Judas Priest, 1990 WL 130920 (Nev. Ct. August 24, 1990).

Van Nouhuys, B. (1994). *How labeling actually works in music stores.* Unpublished manuscript, Department of Communication, Lewis and Clark College, Portland, OR.

Vare, E. A. (1984, April 14). Satanic image questions industry's metal morals. *Billboard*, p. 1.

Vincent, R. C. (1989). Clio's consciousness raised?: Portrayal of women in rock videos, re-examined. *Journalism Quarterly, 66*, 155-160.

Vincent, R. C., Davis, D. K. & Boruszkowski, L. A. (1987). Sexism on MTV: The portrayal of women in rock videos. *Journalism Quarterly, 64*, 750-755

Violato, C., & Holden, W. (1987). A confirmatory factor analysis of a four-factor model of adolescent concerns. *Journal of Youth and Adolescence, 17*, 101-113.

Vision Videos. (1988). *Rising to the challenge* [video recording]. Arlington, VA: Parents Music Resource Center.

Wadsworth, A., and Kaid, L. L. (1988). Political themes and images in music videos. In D. Nimmo, & Savage, R.L (Eds.), *Politics in familiar contexts: Projecting politics through popular media* (pp. 159-170). Norwood, NJ: Ablex.

Walker, M. (1985). Backward messages in commercially available recordings. *Popular Music and Society, 10*(1), 2-13.

Walker, J. (1987). How viewing of MTV relates to exposure to other media. *Journalism Quarterly, 64*(1), 756-762.

Wanamaker, C.E., & Reznikoff, M. (1989). Effects of aggressive and nonaggressive rock songs on projective and structured tests. *Journal of Psychology, 123*, 561-570.

Ward, E., Stokes, G., & Tucker, K. (1986). *Rock of ages: The Rolling Stone history of rock and roll.* New York: Rolling Stone Books.

Warner, C. (1984, November). *Dimensions of appeals in popular music: A new factor-analytic approach to classifying music.* Paper presented at the annual meeting of the Speech Communication Association, Chicago.

Wartella, E., Heintz, K., Aidman, A., & Mazarella, S. (1990). Television and beyond: Children's video media in one community. *Communication Research, 17*, 45-64.

Wass, H., Miller, D., & Reditt, C. (1991). Adolescents and destructive themes in rock music: A follow-up. *Omega, 23*(3), 193-206.

Wass, H., Miller, D., & Stevenson, R. (1989). Factors affecting adolescents' behavior and attitudes toward destructive rock lyrics. *Death Studies, 13*, 287-303.

Wass, H., Raup, J.L., Cerullo, K., Martel, L.G., Mingione, L.A., & Sperring, A.M. (1988–1989). Adolescents' interest in and views of destructive themes in rock music. *Omega, 19*, 177-186.

Wells, A. (1986). Women in popular music: Changing fortunes from 1955-1984. *Popular Music and Society, 10*(4), 73-85.

Wells, A. (1990). Popular music: Emotional use and management. *Journal of Popular Culture, 24*(1), 105-117.

What entertainers are doing to our kids. (1985, October 28). *U.S. News and World Report*, pp. 48-55.

Wilkinson, M. (1976, April). Romantic love: the great equalizer. *The Family Coordinator*, pp. 161-166.

Will, G. F. (1990, July 30). America's slide into the sewer. *Newsweek*, p. 64.

Wilson, Y. (1994, May 31). Death metal, gangsta rap, grunge rock have a common theme: violence. *San Francisco Chronicle*, pp. E1, E3.

Winn, M. (1985). *The plug-in-drug: Television, children, and the family* (rev. ed.). New York: Penguin.

Wober, M. (1984, November). *Teens and taste in music and radio* (Working Paper). London: IBA Research Department

Wolfe, D.E. (1983). Effects of music loudness on task performance and self report of college-aged students. *Journal of Research in Music Education, 31*, 191-201.

Wong, T.W., Van Hassell, C.A., Tang, L.S., & Yui, P.C. (1990). The use of personal cassette players among youths and its effects on hearing. *Public Health, 4*, 327-330.

Wright, S. (1954, November). The death of Lady Mondegreen. *Harper's Magazine, 209*(1254), 48-51.

Wyer, R., & Srull, R. (1981). Category accessibility: Some theoretical and empirical issues concerning the processing of social stimulus information. In E.T. Higgins, C.P. Herman, & M.P. Zanna (Eds.), *Social cognition: The Ontario Symposium* (pp. 161-198). Hillsdale, NJ: Erlbaum.

X-rated (1990, May 7). *Time*, pp. 92-98.

Yassi, A., Pollock, N.,Tran, N., & Cheang, M. (1993). Risks to hearing from a rock concert. *Canadian Family Physician, 30,* 1045-1050.

Yee, S., Britton, L., & Thompson, W. (1988, April). *The effects of rock music on adolescents' behavior.* Paper presented at the annual meeting of the Western Psychological Association, Burlingame, CA.

Yeltnikoff issues bigotry memorandum. (1990, January 11). *Variety,* p. 3.

Yoshihashi, P. (1993, February 24). Deciphering lyrics is part of the fun for the music lover. *Wall Street Journal,* p. A-1.

Youniss, J. (1988, April). *Mutuality in parent-adolescent relationships: Social capital for impending adulthood* (Prepared for Youth and America's Future: The William T. Grant Foundation Commission on Work, Family and Citizenship). Washington, DC: Institute for Educational Leadership.

Youniss, J., & Smollar, J. (1985). *Adolescent relations with mothers, fathers, and friends.* Chicago: University of Chicago Press.

Zillmann, D. (1988). Mood management: Using entertainment to full advantage. In L. Donohew, H.E. Sypher, & E.T. Higgins (Eds.), *Communication, social cognition and affect* (pp. 147-171). Hillsdale, NJ: Erlbaum.

Zillmann, D., Aust, C.F., Hoffman, K.D., Love, C.C., Ordman, V.L., Pope, J.T., Seigler, P.D., & Gibson, R.J. (1995). Radican rap: Does it further ethnic division? *Basic and Applied Social Psychology, 16,* 1-25.

Zillmann, D., & Mundorf, N. (1987). Image effects in the appreciation of video rock. *Communication Research, 14,* 316-334.

Zucchino, D. (1985, November 7). Big brother meets Twisted Sister. *Rolling Stone,* pp. 10, 12+.

Zuckerman, F. (1984, December 22). Coalition blasts violence in clips. *Billboard,* p. 1.

SONG
REFERENCES

Because most readers are likely to be familiar with the popular songs cited in this book through exposure to popular recordings, we have chosen to reference the songs on the basis of popular recordings, as well as composer and publisher. Each citation begins with the song title (as it is cited in the text). In most cases, we have listed the album on which the song first appeared by the performer who made it popular. In the case of several older songs, this has not been possible; in these cases, we have included a current performer and recording. The basic form of the citation consists of the song title, the year the recording was released (originally and/or the year of current release), the performer(s), the album title, and the recording company and album serial number. This is followed by the authors of the song (words and music), its year of publication, and the publisher.

* * * * * * * * * * * * * * *

Anything Goes (1987). Guns N Roses, *Appetite for Destruction*. Geffen Records, 24148. Words and music by Slash, S. Alder, I. Stradlin, D.R. McKagan, C.G. Weber, and A.W. Rose, 1987. Guns N Roses Music, BMG Songs Inc., Los Angeles, CA.

Born in the U.S.A. (1984). Bruce Springsteen, *Born in the U.S.A.* Columbia 38653. Words and music by B. Springsteen, 1984. Bruce Springsteen Music: Greenwich, CT.

Cop Killer (1992). Body Count, *Body Count*. Sire Records, 45139. Words and music by E.T. Cunnigan and T.L. Marrow, 1982. Polygram International Publishing, Inc., Los Angeles, CA.

Empty Bed Blues (1928, 1971). Bessie Smith, *Empty Bed Blues (Parts 1 & 2)*. Columbia, 30450. Words and music by J.C. Johnson, 1928. The Songwriters Guild, Weehauken, NJ.

Evil Dick (1992). Body Count, *Body Count*. Sire Records, 45139. Words and music by E. T. Cunnigan & T. L. Marrow, 1992. Rhythm Syndicate Music and Polygram International Publishing, Inc., Los Angeles, CA.

Eve of Destruction (1965). Barry McGuire, *Eve of Destruction*. MCA Special Products, 20340. Words and music by P.F. Sloan & S. Barri, 1965. MCA Music Publishers, Los Angeles, CA.

Head Like a Hole (1989). Nine Inch Nails, *Pretty Hate Machine*. TVT, 2610. Words and music by M.T. Reznor, 1989. Zamba Songs, New York.

I Want Action (1986). Poison, *Look What the Cat Dragged In*. Capitol/EMI Records, 46735. Words and music by B. Dall, C. DeVille, B. Michaels, and R. Rockett, 1986. Cynaide Publishing, New York.

I Want a New Drug (1983). Huey Lewis and the News, *Sports*. Chrysalis, 21412. Words and music by C. Hayes & H. Lewis, 1983. Huley Music, Universal City, CA.

I'll Stick Around (1995). The Foo Fighters, *Foo Fighters*. Roswell Records, 34027. Words and music by D. Grohl, 1995. M.J.-Twelve, Polygram International Publishing, Inc., Los Angeles, Ca.

Like a Virgin (1984). Madonna, *Like a Virgin*. Sire Records, 25157. Words and music by W.E. Steinberg & T.F. Kelly, 1984. Sony Tunes, Inc., New York.

Love Is Like an Itchin in My Heart (1966). The Supremes, *Supremes a Go Go*. Motown Records. Words and music by E. Holland, L. Dozier, & B. Holland. Stone Agate Music, Hollywood, CA.

Mairzy Doats (1943, 1992). The Pied Pipers, *Capitol Collectors Series*. Capitol/EMI Records, 95289. Words & Music by M. Drake, A. Hoffman, & J. Livingston, 1943. Miller Music Corp., New York.

Material Girl (1984). Madonna, *Like a Virgin*. Sire Records, 25257. Words and music by P. Brown and R. Rans, 1984. Candy Castle Music/Warner-Tamerlane, Los Angeles, CA.

Necrophiliac (1985). Slayer, *Hell Awaits*. Metal Blade, 14031. Words and music by J. Hanneman and K. King, 1985. Bloody Skull Music/Amgine Music, Los Angeles, CA.

No Pride (1995). Greenday, *Insomniac*. Reprise, 46046. Words and music by F.E. Wright III, M. Pritchard, and B.J. Armstrong, 1995. WB Music Corp., Los Angeles, CA.

No Vaseline (1991). Ice Cube, *Death Certificate*. Priority Records, 57155. Words and music by Ice Cube, M.S. Jordan, Jinx, and B.F. Irvin, 1991. Street Knowledge Productions, Valencia, CA.

One in a Million (1988). Guns N Roses, *Guns N' R Lies*. Geffen, 24198. Words and music by I. Stradlin, S. Adler, D.R. McKagan, Slash, and W.A. Rose, 1988. Guns N Roses Music, Los Angeles, CA.

Physical (1981). Olivia Newton-John, *Physical*. MCA Records, 31110. Words and music by T. Shaddick, S. Kipner & T.J. Shaddick, 1981. EMI/April Music, New York, NY.

S&M (1979). Thin Lizzy, *Black Rose*. Metal Blade, 45172. Words and music by B. Downey & P. Lynott. Polygram International Publishing, Inc., Los Angeles, CA.

Same Dress, New Day (1995). Tripping Daisy, *I Am an Elastic Firecracker*. Island Records, 524112. Words and music by M. Pirro, B. Wakeland, T. DeLaughter, & W. Berggren. Pink Jelly Music/Chrysalis Music, Los Angeles, CA.

Somebody Groovy (1966). The Mamas and the Papas, *If You Can Believe Your Eyes and Ears*. MCA Records, 31042. Words and music by J. Phillips.

Suicide Solution (1987). Ozzy Osbourne, *Tribute*. Epic, 67240. Words and music by R.J. Daisley, J. Osbourne, R. Rhodes, and R. Rhodes, 1987. Essex Music International, New York.

Wild Thing (1966, 1992). The Troggs. *Archeology (1967-1977)*. Polydor 512936. Words and music by C. Taylor. EMI/Blackwood Music, New York, NY.

You're All I Need (1987). Motley Crue, *Girls, Girls, Girls*. Elektra Entertainment, 60725. Words and music by N. Stix, S.T. Attebery, and T. Lee, 1987. WB Music Corp., Los Angeles, CA.

AUTHOR INDEX

SUBJECT INDEX